CONSOLATION OF MIND

CONSOLATION OF MIND

H.K.Suhas

iUniverse, Inc.
New York Lincoln Shanghai

Consolation of Mind

iUniverse, Inc.

For information address:
iUniverse, Inc.
2021 Pine Lake Road, Suite 100
Lincoln, NE 68512
www.iuniverse.com

ISBN: 0-595-30874-0

Printed in the United States of America

The irony of modern life is

We spend all our time chasing money and loosing health,
When we make enough money, we loose it to regain health!

We spend all our time imposing our ideas on others believing that we are
doing a great job,
Towards the end of our career, we yearn for a few more years of active life to
undo all the wrongs!

We spend all our time believing that every thing must be kept under control
for better performance,
Towards the end of our career, we realize how wrong we were in understanding nature!

We spend all our time believing that we are in complete control of every thing,
Towards the end of our career, we realize that we were after all not in control
of any thing!

We spend all our time believing that we are doing a great job,
Towards the end of our career we yearn for another chance to redo every thing!

We spend all our time questioning the existence or non existence of God
When we come to the end of our life, we realize that God was waiting for a
call all along!

We mourn the death of our near and dear ones
Never believing that we too would one day be mourned!

The mind rationalizes the irrational
If this not consolation of mind, what else is?

Contents

List of Tables ix

Preface xi

1. God 1

2. Education 42

3. Secularism 62

4. Nationalism 78

5. Politics 106

6. Governance 116

7. Community Living 174

8. Past Future 193

9. Glossary 231

List of Tables

Table 2.2.1   Per Capita Expenditure 43

Table 2.2.2   Indicators of Indian Economy...49

Table 2.2.3   Objectives of Five Year Plans 50

Preface

The mind has the ability to theorize, rationalize and philosophize any situation, however contradicting and irrational the situation may be. Further a study of history shows that the events that have unfolded in different geographical locations involving different cultures and religions have a startling similarity. The only difference is that these events have taken place at different times and therefore appears as a replay of events with a time difference. These events that have unfolded in different societies are essentially similar in content but different only in terms of the superimposed cultural differences. This is an indicator of the fact that the human mind works alike irrespective of the conditioning to which it is subjected. The conditioning appears to influence only the superficial layer of the human of psyche and behavior, while deep down the thoughts remain very similar and in many cases present a startling coincidence or convergence of views. This observation applies to the total/complete gamut of human development from the times of the early beginnings.

The Zach Law states that man becomes rational only after all avenues for irrational behavior comes to an end. Thus, man has never evolved in real terms as the basic thought process is as primitive as it was and the tendency has always been to dominate and subjugate others. Cooperative living has never been accepted as a way of life. The human mind has the remarkable capacity to rationalize the irrational as long as the process of rationalization is beneficial to the individual (society) who (that) is attempting to rationalize a given event. Thus history has been a witness to the process of furthering of interests of the self/society through a process of rationalization that often looks as the "Consolation of Mind".

The human mind has the remarkable capacity to rationalize the irrational as long as the process of rationalization is beneficial to the individual (society) who (that) is attempting to rationalize a given event. Thus history has been a witness to the process of furthering of interests of the self/society through a process of rationalization that often looks as the "Consolation of Mind".

There is a story that illustrates the extreme case of Consolation of Mind also known as God's Perfection. The source of this story is Internet.

"In Brooklyn, New York, Chush is a school that caters to learning disabled children. Some children remain in Chush for their entire school career, while others can be mainstreamed into conventional schools. At a Chush fund raising dinner, the father of a Chush child delivered a speech that would never be forgotten by all who attended.

After extolling the school and its dedicated staff, he cried out, "Where is the perfection in my son Shaya? Everything God does is done with perfection. But my child cannot understand things as other children do. My child cannot remember facts and figures as other children do. Where is God's perfection?"

The audience was shocked by the question, pained by the father's anguish and stilled by the piercing query. "I believe," the father answered, "that when God brings a child like this into the world, the perfection that he seeks is in the way people react to this child."

The following is the story of Shaya & his father.

One afternoon Shaya and his father walked past a park where some boys Shaya knew were playing baseball. Shaya asked, "Do you think they will let me play?"

Shaya's father knew that his son was not at all athletic and that most boys would not want him on their team. But Shaya's father understood that if his son was chosen to play it would give him a comfortable sense of belonging. Shaya's father approached one of the boys in the field and inquired if Shaya could play. The boy looked around for guidance from his teammates. Getting none, he took matters into his own hands and said "We are losing by six runs and the game is in the eighth inning. I guess he can be on our team and we'll try to put him up to bat in the ninth inning."

Shaya's father was ecstatic as Shaya smiled broadly. Shaya was told to put on a glove and go out to play short center field. In the bottom of the eighth inning, Shaya's team scored a few runs but was still behind by three. In the bottom of the ninth inning, Shaya's team scored again and now with two outs and the bases loaded with the potential winning run on base, Shaya was scheduled to be up. Would the team actually let Shaya bat at this juncture and give away their chance to win the game? Surprisingly, Shaya was given the bat. Everyone knew that it was all but impossible because Shaya didn't even know how to hold the bat properly, let alone hit with it. However as Shaya stepped up to the plate, the pitcher moved a few steps to lob the ball in softly so Shaya should at least be able to make contact.

The first pitch came in and Shaya swung clumsily and missed. One of Shaya's teammates came up to Shaya and together they held the bat and faced the pitcher waiting for the next pitch. The pitcher again took a few steps forward to toss the ball softly toward Shaya. As the pitcher came in, Shaya and his teammate swung at the bat and together they hit a slow ground ball to the pitcher. The pitcher picked up the soft grounder and could easily have thrown the ball to the first baseman. Shaya would have been out and that would have ended the game.

Instead, the pitcher took the ball and threw it on a high arc to right field, far beyond reach of the first baseman. Everyone started yelling, "Shaya, run to first. Run to first." Never in his life had Shaya run to first. He scampered down the baseline wide-eyed and startled. By the time he reached first base, the right fielder had the ball. He could have thrown the ball to the second baseman who would tag out Shaya, who was still running. But the right fielder understood what the pitcher's intentions were, so he threw the ball high and far over the third baseman's head. Everyone yelled, "Run to second, run to second." Shaya ran towards second base as the runners ahead of him deliriously circled the bases towards home. As Shaya reached second base, the opposing short stop ran to him, turned him in the direction of third base and shouted, "Run to third." As Shaya rounded third, the boys from both teams ran behind him screaming, "Shaya, run home." Shaya ran home, stepped on home plate and all eighteen boys lifted him on their shoulders and made him the hero, as he had just hit a "grand slam" and won the game for his team. "That day," said the father softly with tears now rolling down his face "those eighteen boys reached their level of God's perfection"

Thus this display of God's Perfection by the eighteen boys can be looked upon as the penultimate state of Consolation of Mind. The boys achieved the impossible task of making Shaya forget and overcome his handicap. In the same way the action of Schindler in the midst of the ethnic cleansing in Nazi Germany can also be looked upon as achieving God's Perfection and therefore a penultimate state of Consolation of Mind. The act of the victims of the super cyclone in Orissa state of India of giving new unused clothes to the victims of the earthquake in Gujarat state of India is also a case of achieving the level of God's Perfection. By reversing the same logic, one can also say that the ethnic cleansing that was carried out by the Nazis presented a deeply sunken state of Mind. Another example of the deeply sunken state of Mind is the failure of the administrators to make available food grains that were lying in the warehouse to the starving millions in Orissa and Rajasthan in India. The food grains were rather allowed to rot than distribute them to the hungry in lieu of work related to rain water harvesting, forestation, building of ponds etc. Both these are the extreme cases of Consolation of Mind, both occupying the two extreme ends of human behavior. Mind is the one that lifts or buries an individual to great heights or depths.

The attempt that is made in the book is to traverse the period of time and look at different societies, all of which have suffered in the same way, in the name of God, Education, Secularism and Nationalism. Expediency of politics has always played havoc with the lives of the people of every society. One gets to see the same mistakes and atrocities committed in different geographical locations at different times under different circumstances.

The globalization of the societies has resulted in the shrinking of the world and vanishing of boundaries. Any act of consolation of mind in some remote part of the global village will find ripple effects in every part of the global village. Gone are the days of "us and them" and therefore the need of the hour is to protect pluralism not only in every individual society but also in the entire global society. There is an urgent need to enforce a minimum level of meaningful governance on all the members of United Nations, Common wealth and other such groups of countries. The minimum level of governance must address God or Religion, Education, Secularism or Freedom of Worship, Nationalism and Community Living. These happen to be the critical elements of a happy, prosperous and contented society that will be at peace with itself and others.

The present global scenario is such that the United States and the European Union are weakening each other. The problem is that the vacuum that may get created in the process of rivalry over issues of concern to every one would lead to a terrible state of uncertainty, which would have a far reaching and far worse consequences. In spite of all the blunders committed by the policy makes in Washington the need of the hour is not to allow either the United States or the European Union to become weak politically, economically or militarily. The case of United States is very strange in the sense that in spite of having renowned universities and intellectuals, the foreign policy initiative of United States is very similar to a road in a developing country, full of pot holes! The United States has always shown an affinity towards dictators and has always worked against the strengthening of democracies in other nations. The reason being that the dictators could be relied upon to and could be manipulated into a state where United States could beneficial commercial or military deals, which were always looked upon as the most important goal of foreign policy and therefore serving the interests of United States.

The need of the hour is to ensure the success of multi cultural and multi religious concept or idea of living, especially because the global society has shrunk and therefore the interdependency of the different societies become more important than ever for the stability and the well being of every other society. The WTO framework is creating a dichotomy where a society achieves great economic growth and prosperity and at the same time large number of jobs are lost to to cheaper and more efficient societies. Thus we have a dichotomy of rate represented by a few rich people becoming richer and a large number of job less families. The stress of governance appears to have shifted to the well being of a few and misery for the large population. The increased economic growth rate is a wonder of the science of statistics! Thus the present day frame work is no different from the imperialism of early 20th century where imperialism helped the creation of colonies. In the present day, it has a new name and a new connotation.

The frame work of WTO that allows for businesses to be shifted to other places based on the cost and efficiency of the societies will ultimately lead to an imbalance not only with in a society on account of widening disparity between the few rich who are becoming richer and the many unemployed, but also with in the global society that has shrunk to uncomfortable levels! On one hand we are fighting terrorism and on the other knowingly or unknowingly we are creating conditions that can be exploited by any unscrupulous party for its own ulterior ends. The need of the hour is to work for the well being of the global society in the true spirit of Mahatma Gandhi and the famous Biblical saying, "Do not do to others what you do not want others to do to you", which is most often violated.

Every society, to some extent, practices Consolation of Mind. India is a truly pluralistic society that has multiple religions, cultures and languages, and therefore India makes for a very interesting case study. Further, all societies have similar problems. Therefore the issue is, should we not work towards a better and a safer society than theorize and manipulate the society that creates more suffering than good and put an end to the state of consolation of mind? Therefore the study of the Indian society, which is truly multi cultural, multi ethnic, multi linguistic and multi religious society would bring out the interplay between different kinds of forces, the good, the bad and the ugly. Therefore the book gives the impression of being India Centric. India is a classic example of pluralism under siege. Thus India becomes a classic case study of

(a) The pluralistic state that had given shelter and a place to live, thrive and develop to many people who had fled their lands as far back as 2000 years or more,

(b) India had trading links with the middle east and the Roman Empire as the kingdoms in the southern India, nearly 2000 years ago in the present day Tamil Nadu in southern India, were a maritime society. The Indian society had the honor of

  ➀ providing support and shelter to the Jews and Armenians who fled the middle east unable to withstand the tyranny of the Roman Empire,

- ⑩ receiving St. Thomas, one of the chief apostles of Jesus Christ who helped preach the message of Jesus Christ and founded Christianity in the southern part of India,

- ⑩ receiving the Muslim traders in early 8th Century AD who had settled down in southern part of India, built mosques and lived in peace and harmony with Hindus, Christians and Jews in southern part of India.

- ⑩ receiving the Zoroastrians who fled Parsa in the present day Iran unable to withstand the tyranny of the invading Arab tribesmen

- ⑩ receiving the Tibetans who fled Tibet unable to withstand the tyranny of the Chinese regimes.

(c) Thus India has a very diverse culture and heritage and that the Indian ethos appears to be capable of sustaining and taking with in its bosom all the dissimilarities and diversities that can be there on this earth.

(d) The systematic attempt that is being made by the politicians in the name of religion and caste to destroy the composite fabric of the Indian society.

(e) Therefore, India is a laboratory in which one can study the inter play between the forces that represent the all possible religions and cultures!

In the book *italics* style is used to represent words that are of either Sanskrit or Hindi or Urdu language. The reader is requested to refer to the Glossary at the end of the book to get the meaning of the word.

The author thanks Dr. B.K.Gairola, Deputy Director General and Dr.N.Vijayaditya, Director General, National Informatics Center for the encouragement. The views expressed here do not in any way represent the views of National Informatics Center and/or Government of India. This work would have been impossible but for the support given, and more important the patience shown by my wife, Vidya, and son, Prashant.

New Delhi   II. K. Suhas
27th August 2003

1

God

All the great teachers and saints derive their strength from the same single source. The essentials of the teachings of all these saints, therefore, are same. However, the interpretations made by their fervent followers become so different that it gives the impression that there are different heavens or empires of Gods. Or the God who sent a particular teacher or savior is the only God and the rest are no Gods and therefore are only the pretenders eager to occupy the throne. But then, the inherent violent state of the human being would not be able to accept the concept of one God as this removes the basic desire to be superior to others. This sets into motion the concept of the existence of several Gods and therefore the need to prove which or whose God is superior. It is made to appear that there exists up in heaven a forum of Gods and the powerful amongst them is elected the God Head or the Secretary General of Gods. This is a good enough cause to fight in the name of establishing the supremacy of one's own God. Thus it appears that who ever wins the battle by either killing the followers of the other God or by converting the followers of the other God to one's own God proves the power of one's own God. The driving force appears to be the motto, "Our God Never Fails". The more the number of followers, the better is the position of the God. A truly democratic principle. Vivekananda after his visit to Unites States where he delivered his famous address in the Parliament of Religions said, "If I wanted to, I could have converted the whole of America to Hinduism. What is important is not converting them to Hinduism, but for a Christian to be a Good Christian, a Muslim to be a Good Muslim, a Hindu to be a Good Hindu. That is all what matters as there is only one God and the different religions are different streams from the same source". Basaveshvara, the founder of the Lingayat movement, advocated sensitivity among human beings to understand the needs of fellow humans so that the desire for the oppression of the poor can be removed from one's heart itself. Basaveshvara's ideals were very similar to the Vedantic concepts. He was against the priest class and the rich who built the temples that became the seats of exploitation of the poor. He said, "My legs are the pillars of the temple. My head is the golden pinnacle. The temple built of brick and mortar and marble by the rich and the priests will tumble down. But the moving temple of mine knows no ruin or end"

The problem is the inherent violent state of the human being stemming from the urge to control others, the urge to impress upon others about the efficacy and/or purity of our way of living and thinking. Thus even though we may declare our peaceful and/or pious intentions, the need to feel better than or superior to some body else is the root cause of all the dissension. But when the knowledge/understanding of an activity or subject falls short, the mechanics of manipulation is set into motion. The aim is to remain in power or in a position of influence. There is a lot of difference between

(a) feeling better

and

(b) being better.

The conflict is due to, in the words of J.Krishnamurty, the great divide between "What is and What should be". We project "What Should Be" as "What Is" and we assume that we are in the "What Should Be" status or category and others are not. Further, if my God or my Guru or Savior is not superior to some body else's God or Guru or Savior then how can I feel better?

Thus the hypothesis is that they alone can allow you to get into the God's kingdom and the gates that they are guarding are the only gates to the kingdom. Therefore, if any body is interested in getting into God's fold, then it is necessary to come to their gates and follow the prescriptions faithfully. The desire to help the people to become a part of the God's fold and get them entry passes into the God's kingdom has made a large number of religious minded people to pursue the path of preaching their God's qualities and get others inducted into the fold or flock. This becomes in a way God's own work whereby the people who are aimlessly wandering due to the ineffectiveness of the other God are led into the fold or flock in exactly as a shepherd or cowherd looks after the flock of sheep or a herd of cattle. Thus the job of providing salvation to people has become as interesting and exciting as the job of a sales man trying to sell the consumer durable. This is possibly what made H.H.Dalai Lama to remark that the need of the day is to have a Super Market of Religions so that the individual can go and pick or choose the religion that gives satisfaction. And at the same time one should have the freedom to reject a religion and choose another that would give one the satisfaction without risking one's life. After all, when one changes the brand of coffee or shaving cream or razor blade, one does not loose one's life but is expected to get more satisfaction and happiness. Thus, the bottom line is getting satisfaction and happiness. This unfortunately involves in the consolation of mind of a different kind.

ii

Man has always been a violent animal with a burning desire to control and rule over the other human beings, for good or for bad. J. Krishnamurty in his lectures compiled in the book "Beyond Violence", has analyzed the root cause of the confusion in the society. His conclusion is that we always mistake the state of "what should be" with the state of "what is". Thus those who think that they are pious or have become pious or are in the process of becoming pious are the victims of this eternal confusion between the two states of "what should be" and "what is". Therefore more often than not, such people turn out to be more violent than those who are perceived to be violent. Does this mean that the God men are violent or dangerous to cultivate? Should one keep near to or away from the God men? This is a very difficult question to answer. Here a line needs to be drawn between those who spread the message of love like Kabir, Gyaneshwar, Sankara, Raghavendra, Jesus, prophet Mohammed, Guru Gobind Singh and the like and the present day God men who appear more interested in setting up organized centers of influence with the main aim of becoming brokers of power and exercise influence in the name of God. These have perfected the art of back seat driving. The tragedy is that inspite of becoming the back seat drivers, wielding enormous power and influence; none of these God men have been able to address the problems of the masses. But addressing the problems of the masses is definitely not on their agenda of activities or plan.

In the area of education Christian Missionaries have built some of the finest of the educational facilities in the form of schools for boys and girls even in remote areas. In the area of medicine also, the Christian Missions have been providing relief and medical help to the poor and the needy. There are a few other organizations like the Ramakrishna Mission, CRY, Maharshi Dayanand mission, Arya Samaj, Arya Mahila Samaj, Mahavir Vikalanga Kendra, Shirdi Sai Baba trusts, Sikh Gurudwara, which have done commendable service to the poor and the needy in the area of education and health keeping the self reliance of the poor in view. The aim of charity must not be to make them dependent on the charitable institutions for ever but to make the poor economically independent so that they also contribute to the creation of wealth in their own way. In the recent past organizations like Satya Sai Baba and Mata Anandamayi Math and a few other institutions have set up charitable super specialty hospitals where every one, including the poor, can get the same kind of medical attention free of charge. They also have set up colleges with high standards. The activities of these charitable institutes are all the more commendable because of the fact that the institutions of governance created to help solve the problems of the poor have failed. These institutions of governance have succeeded in providing more cushy jobs for the bureaucrats and help them to further their career with all the paraphernalia as none of the bureaucrats or the institutions of governance are accountable to any one or anything. Therefore it is left to the religious charitable organizations to use their phenomenal influence to help administer love and care to the needy, poor and sick in addition to dispensing the medicine. It is here that the work of Mother Theresa becomes unparalleled. The Missionaries of Charity dispense love to the terminally sick and dying, and add life to their years and provide a means of making them die in peace.

Another area where the Christian Missions have done commendable work is in the area of training the girls from tribal areas for the job of house keeping. This provides economic independence to the girls and therefore the families. Isn't this the best way of serving God rather than building temples and distributing bread etc to the beggars and successfully prevent them from becoming economically self reliant? Why can't some of these rich join together and donate money to the temple trustees of their choice and start training classes and an employment exchange facility so that the students who get trained are successful in getting jobs. Making the poor economically self-reliant is the best form of service to God, who ever and where ever the God is. But this is obviously not a politically acceptable statement as this does not provide the political mileage to the acts of uplifting the downtrodden.

What is laudable is the kind of effort that has been made by the Christian missions to build a chain of schools, colleges, hospitals, old age homes, orphanages, vocational institutes, institutes for supporting, training and finding employment for illiterate girls. Instead of accusing the missionaries of indulging in the number crunching game why cannot the Hindu organizations, who also get huge sums as donations from all over the world, set up organizations to help the poor and the needy to become economically self reliant? Cannot the Hindu Organizations do what the missionaries are doing and then teach the Bhagavad Gita, Vedas etc to those who have become economically self reliant? It is a myth to presume that the money flow for such activities is not forth coming from Hindus. In fact, there are a large number of Hindus who happily donate money to the Christian missions as they know that the money donated would be used for the service of mankind. Many temples and religious groups are more interested in religious activities and not in community welfare activities. The Hindu religious groups have always given greater importance to the building of temples and *ashrams* in an effort to propagate the philosophical aspects of life and not to the material well being of the people.

God must have become the driving force towards the emancipation of mankind through love and social service. But unfortunately, God has become the cause of division of mankind. The history of mankind has recorded the most atrocious crimes that have been committed in the name of God. The pattern of senseless violence is the same in all the cases, be it Protestant— Catholics in Ireland, against Jews in Nazi Germany, against Muslims in Serbia, against Hindus by the invading Central Asian tribesmen, against Hindus in Jammu and Kashmir in the name of freedom struggle or in the numerous Hindu-Muslim riots that take place at regular intervals. There are always theories that give the reasons for such a recurrence of violent attacks against one community or the other. Every act of violence is given the impression of a reaction to some other preceding violent incident. The innocent people belonging to the religions or communities become the victims of this end less chain of action and reaction. It is strange to find that the mind, under the influence of religious bigotry can stoop to unthinkable levels and make people commit unthinkable crimes against others just because they profess to believe in a different religious belief. This division of the society helps in perpetuating communal and caste tension, and thus ensures a firm hold on the masses. Thus the politicians find this division of the society on religion and caste basis extremely useful for manipulating the society. The communal riots that often overtake such a divided society become the handiwork of anti social elements. This gives birth to the deadly blend of religion, politics and anti social elements. Thus, the religious extremists can survive only in pair. That is, the religious extremists of one religion or community need the religious extremists of another religion or community for survival. They always coexist. They represent the two faces of a coin. They coexist and cannot face each other. God and the place of worship are only incidental. God and the place of worship become tools in the hands of the manipulators and the politicians. The situation on the ground can best be expressed by the couplet,

Kasai yahan bhi hain, kasai wahan bhi hain,
Jaye to kahan jaye, har taraf nazara dardnak hain,
Lashen yahan bhi hain, lashen wahan bhi hain,

Khoon yahan bhi hain, khoon wahan bhi hain,
Khoon nahin dohrata lash ka mazhab kya hain,
Ye Khuda, jeene ka tamanna ab nahi hai,
Uuthale hamen, yeh hi munasib hain,
Kasai yahan bhi hain, kasai wahan bhi hain,
Jaye to kahan jaye, har taraf nazara dardnak hain

The translation is,

Butchers are here, butchers are there,
Where can we go, misery is every where,
Dead bodies are here, dead bodies are there,
Blood is here, blood is there,
Blood fails to tell the religion of the dead body,
Oh, God, we have no more desire to live,
Please take us away (from here) as this is the only way,
Butchers are here, butchers are there,
Where can we go, misery is every where

iii

There is an allegation that the poor people are enticed into changing their religion and therefore the service that is provided is not as selfless as it is made out to be. This also happens to be one of the complaints against Mother Theresa. The persons who complain are the back seat drivers and the pipe smoking analysts/strategists who fear the loss of influence due to the flock deserting them. The back seat drivers and the pipe smoking analysts/strategists are no different from the middle men in business.

What the poor and the needy want is not a dose of religion or the setting up of a grand temple but financial independence, ability to stand on their feet, ability to afford to buy food, shelter, education and medicine for the sick. What they need is a help that makes them independent and self-reliant; to live a decent life with their heads held high and a feeling of being required by the society; a feeling of being useful to the society. Providing these, unfortunately, does not provide any tangible gains to the philanthropist as it is difficult to project the greatness of the donor. On the contrary, when this happens there is every possibility of the rich and the influential loosing their influence and hold on these people. Education and spread of awareness are two great liberators of mankind and therefore the politicians and those in power take care to perpetuate ignorance in order to safe guard their positions. The ignorance helps in the manipulation of the fears, known or unknown, to their own advantage. Therefore, building of a monument in the form of a temple or a series of temples definitely help in the projection of the greatness or the generosity of the donor. Also, the distribution of free food also helps to reinforce the thought, in the minds of the receiver, about the generosity of the donor. Thus this kind of an activity provides tangible benefits to the donor in the form of self exultation but helps in creating a dependent and despondent section of society that has no concept of self worth. This paves the way for the destruction of the social fabric by giving rise to unrest and violence.

Further, the religion appears to support the activity of giving money or food or clothing to the poor or the needy as a necessary act for achieving salvation. Therefore, if the rich people are to go to heaven it becomes mandatory that there must be poor and the needy to receive the *daan*, the alms. This makes it absolutely necessary to make sure that the poverty and illiteracy are not eradicated. If these are eradicated and if the people are made self reliant and independent then it would result in the God men, the pipe smoking analysts/strategists, rich and the influential loosing every thing. Some loose following/followers; some others loose vote banks; a few loose entry to heaven; and some more would loose the opportunity to prove their philanthropy and greatness. One is helping the poor in order to save one's soul and in the process try save the souls of others. Therefore, the existence and furthering of poverty is given a religious interpretation and is encouraged. It is unfortunate that the temple complexes and heads of the various Hindu and Islamic groups have not extended this concept of helping the poor to making them self reliant by supporting projects related to rain water harvesting, literacy and forestation. The example set by people like Rajendra Singh and Burra Munda need to be emulated even if it amounts to loosing influence and control over the people at the end of the day! For some, the existence of poverty is an opportunity to save their own souls and possibly other souls as well. Poverty should not always be looked upon as a gift of God and the poor should not always be expected to accept it with contentment as a gift from God. In the words of Dutta Ray, "The poor should not suffer eternally to satisfy some Christian theory of global salvation. People want to live in comfort and not die in peace" But the fact is that the Christian missions have done a lot to provide support to the poor to live with dignity and to die in peace in dignity. They have integrated the act of inculcating a feeling of self worth in their missionary activities. The same cannot be said about either the Hindu religious institutions or the Islamic religious institutions.

But is it not a fact that all of us want to die in peace, in addition to living with dignity? For example, when people ask for some thing to make them independent, they are often told not to be greedy and be contented with what they have. Therefore, the status quo has become the bedrock of religion. Any attempt to rehabilitate the poor and the needy and prevent them from begging either at the places of worship or elsewhere is be opposed at all costs. Any attempt by an individual or a group of individuals to improve their lot is invariably looked upon as promoting a cult of greed or money mindedness, and therefore moving away from the path of God. The attempt is always to make sure that power and money are in the hands of a few and the rest are to follow/obey the commands of the handful. The poverty is more by design than by accident. The driving force is the fear of God's retribution. Consider the prayer by Swami Chidananda of Chinmaya mission:

> This is my prayer to thee, my Lord
> Strike, strike at the root of penury in my heart.
> Give me the strength
> Lightly to bear my joys and sorrows.
> Give me the strength
> To make my love fruitful in service.
> Give me the strength
> Never to disown the poor
> Or bend my knees before insolent might.
> Give me strength
> To raise my mind high above daily trifles.
> Give me strength
> To surrender my strength to Thy will with love.

Here the reference is to two kinds of poverty. The poverty of the heart resulting in ignorance and violence, and the other is the poverty resulting in hunger for food. Religion must aim at removing both and not become an impediment in the economic betterment of a society. Here, one can possibly try to fall back upon the wisdom of the great poet Wordsworth to defend the beauty and necessity of poverty and refer to his words, "Wealth Accumulates And Men Decay". But what is attempted here is to create an environment where the human beings can live a decent life and not end up becoming filthy rich and then start decaying. This nurturing of economic poverty may give rise to a situation where a few may find solace by trying to rescue the soul while the majority of the people wallow in squalor. This is worse than the scenario of the oppressor and oppressed as this is being perpetrated in the name of God. Further, a large segment of the population or society should not be left in a state where they have nothing to lose or gain. The state where people have nothing to gain or lose is a state of status quo. But when this is applied to those who have nothing at all, then the condition becomes explosive that is ready to explode any time. If at all the Indian society/nation has not exploded it is because of the unbelievable level of tolerance and the belief in God that the people have. Any attempt at glorifying poverty as a gift of God would be worse than the cause of the poverty. We are taught to be afraid of God's wrath. Should not love and not fear be the driving force? Can God be so cruel as to punish a person who questions the existence of God or who wants to become independent or who does not believe in him? We appear to have succeeded in assuming that the behavior pattern of God and that of an individual are identical. We have assumed, rightly or wrongly, that God has the same kind of idiosynchrosies as the individual. Are God and the individual on the same mental plane practicing the same laws of judgment? Are the cosmic laws and the laws of the civil and criminal jurisprudence similar? Can God be as cranky and whimsical as the individual? Individual can be wonky. Can God imitate individual? The human being is the only creation of God who can rationalize the irrational, and come to terms with any thing, either ethereal or obnoxious, and live with it. This is made possible due to the ability of man to console his mind into believing even the unbelievable and rationalizing even the irrational.

iv

It is very interesting to know the views, pertaining to the subject of the relationship between society and God, of two great men, Dr.Albert Schweitzer and Dr.Sarvapalli Radhakrishnan. Dr.Schweitzer was a theologist, musician and a doctor of medicine, and Dr.Radhakrishnan was a philosopher, teacher, ambassador and a statesman. Dr.Albert Schweitzer decided to become a doctor of medicine and set up practice in Africa after he saw photographs of the people in Africa suffering due to lack of medical facilities. He left his cushy job in the University that made many of his friends and peers think that he has gone nuts. He set up his practice in Lambarene in Congo, Africa, and used to move around serving the sick. His view was that the theology or the religion must inculcate community service as a necessary element of worship, which put in his words meant, "Reverence for Life". His view was that as long as the well being of the entire society does not become the aim of religion the society would not be a worthwhile place to live. M.P.K.Kutty in his article on Dr.Albert Scweitzer, published in Times of India, summarizes Dr.Schweitzer's thoughts thus:

"Can we only live by destroying each other?" Dr.Albert Schweitzer pondered as an old cannibal asked him why the whites were killing each other in Europe. For three days he thought on nothing else as he was on the move in the jungles. On the third day a phrase flashed upon his mind, clear and brilliant: Reverence for Life. What does Reverence for Life mean? It means that life is sacred, and man's duty is to cherish it. True Philosophy, wrote Schweitzer, must start from the most immediate and comprehensive fact of consciousness, which says: I am life, which wills to live, in the midst of life, which wills to live. A man is truly ethical only when he obeys the compulsion to help all life, which he is able to assist, and shirks from injuring anything that lives.

Ethics are responsibility without limit towards all the lives. According to ordinary ethics forgiveness flows out of sympathy one feels towards fellow beings. In the case of Reverence for Life, all acts of forbearance and pardon are part of one's sincerity towards oneself. One must practice unlimited forgiveness because, if one did not, one should be wanting in sincerity towards oneself, for it would be acting as if one was not guilty in the same way as the other has been guilty towards oneself. Because one's life is so liberally spotted with falsehood, one must forgive falsehood which has been practiced upon oneself; because one has been in so many cases wanting in love, and guilty of hatred, slander, deceit or arrogance which have been directed against oneself. One must forgive quietly and un-ostentatiously.

But what is the position of ethics of reverence for life in situations of conflict? In a thousand ways my existence stands in conflict with that of others. The necessity to destroy and injure life is imposed upon me. If I walk along an unfrequented path, my foot brings destruction and pain upon the tiny creatures which populate it. The mouse in the home is persecuted; insects murdered. I get my food by destroying plants and animals. Each person will have to decide in accordance with his sense of responsibility as to how much of his life, possessions, rights, happiness, time, and rest he must devote to others, and how much he can keep for himself. We all have to recognize that our existence reaches its true value only when we experience in ourselves something of the truth of the saying: He that loseth his life shall find it.

It was this view point that made him feel that Hinduism is a religion/philosophy that has concentrated on the issue of the individual, the God, the relationship between the two and the elevation of the individual to realize God that is in himself. Possibly this is the only philosophy that has dwelt on the subject of the relationship between the worshipper and the worshipped, and the numerous paths that one can take to reach the ultimate goal or the goal of all goals. In his view, Hinduism as a religion does not address the issue of social service for the economic betterment and economic independence of the down trodden. Further, Hinduism as a religion does not address the issue of the deliverance of the downtrodden, under privileged and exploited to make them live a decent life and die a decent death. This, he believes to be the cause of the enormous poverty and sufferings that one has been seeing in this country even after independence.

Dr.Radhakrishnan does not agree with the faulting of the Hinduism's concern for the relationship between the devotee and the God as the cause of the neglect of the large segment of society. He points out that, Hinduism happens to be the only philosophy which has hymns said in praise of the well being of all the people in the society, not just that of the person worshipping the God. Also, this happens to be the only philosophy where hymns are said in praise of plants, vegetation, forests, environment, animals etc much before the modern scientist realized the importance or influence of environment, trees, animals and eco-system on human society. Some of these hymns are

Aum, Vanaspatayah Shantihi
God, May the Trees (Vegetation) live in Peace!
Aum, Aushadhaya Shantihi
God, May the medicinal plants live in Peace!
Aum, Sarve Janah Sukhino Bavantu
Sarve Janah Swastir Bhavatu
Sarve Janah Shantir Bhavatu
Sarve Janah Purnam Bhavatu
Sarve Janah Mangalam Bhavatu
Aum Shantih, Shantih, Shantihi

God, may every one be happy
May every one be healthy
May every one be peaceful
May every one be contented
May good happen to every one
God, Let there be Peace, Let there be Peace,
Let there be Peace

Dr.Radhakrishnan opines that Hinduism, as a philosophy, is possibly the only one which had recognized the importance of peace in a society, the well being of every living being and further the importance of peace for achieving development. The history of the various societies provides us with enough evidences to prove this point. He also draws a line between Philosophy and Religious Practices. The Hindu Philosophy is the oldest practicing philosophies on this earth, with the same hymns that were being recited a few thousand years ago being recited even now with the same intonations and pauses.

Inspite of these hymns said in praise of the well being of the whole man kind, animal kind and plant life, why is it that Hinduism as a religion does not show concern for the economic betterment of the society as a whole? One does not see an organized movement, with roots in Hindu religion, for the betterment of the living conditions of the poor. Neither is there an organized movement, with roots in Hinduism, for creating conditions of financial independence for the downtrodden, poor and those who are too weak even to cry in the same way as the movement that has taken place with roots in Christianity. The number of social service organizations that have been working under the umbrella of Christian Missionary movement for making the poor people, living in far flung tribal areas, villages, cities and town, economically independent is something that the Hindu religious organizations must learn to appreciate and emulate. This does hurt the bloated ego of the *thakurs*, land lords, priests and the heads of the famous, not so famous, notorious, spurious and sundry religious groups, *mutt*. There lies the problem.

An essential element of the Hindu religion is the offerings to be made to the poor or indulging in the acts of charity, either after birth or death of an individual, or on birth days or marriage days or festivals, so that one gets admission to the heaven. It appears that the presence of poor in the society is a necessary pre-condition so that the few rich, who always have been controlling and manipulating the society, can make some offerings to these and go through the gates of heaven. Therefore the existence of poor people is necessary for the elevation of a few to heaven. If there are no poor people there cannot be any charity and therefore how and to whom can one give alms? It is this manipulative mechanics that has come in the way of the general well being of the society. The absence of this concern for the well being of under privileged appears to be responsible for the general well being of the people in the west.

The reason for this is the near obsessive concern shown by the guiding lights of Hinduism for the self emancipation by laying stress on philosophical aspects of Hinduism like discourses on Vedanta, Vedas, Upanishads, Bhagavad-Gita, Puranas, Vedic Recitation Classes. There is no place for the programs for the collective well being of the larger sections of the society making the society a better place to live. The guiding principle followed by the guiding lights of Hinduism appears to indicate that the people must be happy with what they have and not bother about acquiring material comforts. But, what if some do not have even the basic necessities of life in terms of food, clothing and a shelter, as happens with the majority of people in India? The words of cheer that are distributed freely are that it is God who gives every one what he or she deserves. Therefore, if you do not have anything accept the state without complaint, rancor and never compare your state with that of the neighbor as that is what God has willed. The poor must accept it as a gift from God. In the book "Complete Works of Swami Vivekananda, Vol.5", Swami Vivekananda observes: "No religion on earth preaches the dignity of humanity in such a lofty strain as Hinduism and no religion on earth treads upon the necks of the poor and the low in such a fashion as Hinduism......". Swamiji put forth his views on the problem of social emancipation by saying: "...You must remove the evil of hunger and starvation, this constant anxiety for bare existence, from those to whom you want to preach religion..." He was possibly the first religious leader to propound the concept of: "First bread then religion". The result of this concern for the poor was that he was reminded, should we say reprimanded or accused of: "You did not preach our Master in America; you preached yourself!" He did encounter opposition, from with in the Ramakrishna Order, for his concern for the poor and his stress on the removal of the suffering and making them economically independent to lead a decent life and then die a decent death. The problem with religion is that it places importance on salvation and therefore as Mother Theresa had said that her aim in life was not to be a social worker, but to help the poor to save her soul and in the process their souls. At least Mother Theresa did help the poor, possibly the word help does not really describe the work that she did to the poor. There is, possibly, no word in English or for that matter in any other language to describe the work she did for the poor. She built homes for the poor and the neglected, gave them a sense of belonging and love. But the Hindu religious leaders appear to have got stuck to the concept of salvation. This is reflected in the importance given to the Vedic recitation classes, Upanishad Classes, *havan*, gifting of food to the lepers and beggars on the streets. These persons become the vote bank and provide a reason for programs aimed at bettering the living conditions of the poor. These in turn have no option but to eat, defecate, sleep, procreate and live in despicable conditions. It is debatable whether this process will give salvation either to the giver or to the receiver. This will only increase the activities of the underworld and strengthen the hands of those who provide protection to these and thus end up as vote banks. The problem with this kind of approach is that sooner than later these people who have nothing will take to crime and work for the powerful, influential and the enlightened ones creating havoc for the entire society. Therefore, it becomes necessary that the guiding lights of the Hindu religion come to understand and appreciate the problems of these people and find ways of making them economically independent so that they can lead a meaningful and useful life. Otherwise, this nation will become a nation at the mercy of criminals, and no police or administrators will be able to save this country. Inspite of the writing on the wall being so clear, we appear to have psyched ourselves into believing that all is well and all will be well, a la Jaspal Bhatti's style, "*Mahol theek hai*" (All is wonderful). A classic example of consolation of mind.

V

The religious practices are invariably entwined by the social customs that are influenced by the external influences, good or bad. For example, child marriage and widow burning, *sati* are the ones that were no where practiced or even mentioned in the philosophical texts. It is said, that there was a time when even the women were allowed to go through the thread ceremony, which is today a male child specific activity. The thread ceremony is about the invocation of Gayatri *mantra* which, is often called the mother of all mantras

Aum bhur bhuah swah
Tat saviturvarenyam
Bhargo devasya dhimahi
Dhiyo yo nah prachodayat
God, thou art the giver of life
The remover of pain and sorrows,
the bestower of happiness
O creator of universe,
may we receive Thy supreme sin destroying light
May Thou guide our intellect in the right direction

This is considered to be an Universal Prayer which only asks the divine to liberate us from our ignorance and lead us on the right path. There is no appeal for grant of money, power or pelf. Therefore, there is no earthly reason to restrict it to only men especially when Gayatri is one of the Goddesses of the Hindu mythology. This discrimination against women is an indication of the insecurity of the stronger sex or an assumed purity of man. One of the reasons that are often quoted for all the discrimination against the women is the menstrual cycle that a woman goes through. But this is not her creation. This is the nature's way of protecting her and keeping her in a state that would help her create, carry and nurse the young one for nearly nine months. Man does not create and nurse the young one even though he is instrumental in the creation process. Therefore, when a woman plays such a major role in the creation process, how can she be called the weaker sex and discriminated. The roles to be played by man and woman in a society, within or without India, are very clearly and definitely different and therefore the need for discrimination, which always stems from the feeling of insecurity, is difficult to rationalize. In the west, there had been discrimination even from the point of giving voting rights to women. In all these cases, the religious beliefs, fundamental or not so fundamental, appear to play a major role in creating a skewed and irrational state of mind. Thus, the cause of the mess can be related to the state of the mind.

One often hears about fundamental approaches to religion. This is found to raise its head in all parts of the world, irrespective of whether the color of the skin is white, yellow, brown, black or any other shade of color. The basic tenet of the fundamentalism is obscurantism making one believe that the only way God wanted man and woman to live on this earth was the way early man lived and not with any of the advances that have been achieved so far. That is, the fundamentalist concept appears to treat any of the advancements in science and the effects of these advancements as unacceptable to God and not as per God's plans. What were God's plans? This is where the problem starts. The answer to this question, which appears to be a very harmless question would be a few bursts from a sten gun or AK47. When this happens, we can be sure to be face to face with fundamentalism. What causes this fundamentalism to raise its charming head that happens in every society irrespective of the cultural background of the society or geographical location; and what are the conditions that make ideal breeding ground for fundamentalism to thrive and spread its hold or tentacles over the society?

The reasons for this are:

(a) Disinterest on the part of the politicians/planners/administrators to pursue the literacy as a major social program. Once literacy spreads, population problem also gets addressed.

(b) Appalling living conditions

(c) Tendency of the administrators to set up committees to solve problems that never see the light of the day. The administrators work on the basis of one point formula: "Wait till a crisis builds up". This helps in destroying the psychological barrier that is absolutely necessary to exist between the administrators and the rest of the human mass. If this psychological barrier breaks down, then for any thing and every thing, there will be a violence, and violence becomes a way of life in as much as corruption becomes (or has already become) a way of life. This forces people to opt for a parallel administrative structure that operate under different but unwritten laws where the justice is swift and through the dispatch of a bullet.

(d) The administration is not proactive but reactive. Whenever a crisis gets created due to the lethargy of the administration, the end result is the call for more force to quell the mob. Nobody is interested in finding the cause of the problem, much less in finding a solution for the problem. In the end the masses get only a committee to look into the problems and submit a report in addition to the water cannons, tear gas shells, and other elements of law enforcing mechanism. The report in most of the cases does not see the light of the day. The administrative officers get promoted and transferred. A new administrative officer reports, and slowly and surely all is forgotten till another crisis builds up when the history would repeat.

(e) The exploitation is from all quarters and angles: from the religious front, the political front and the criminal front. The common thread connecting these fronts is the corruption.

(f) Unwillingness of bureaucracy and politicians to strengthen the judiciary by increasing the number of judges at all levels. This alone will help the people to have faith in the rule of law as otherwise justice delayed is justice denied.

The bureaucracy, politicians, God men and the dons present a perfectly interlocked system at play. This perfect interlocking of the different constituents has been made possible because of our bountiful and immeasurable amount of patience, and the ability to see the silver lining even when there is none. No other society can boast of such a level of conditioning and consolation of the mind.

vi

The problems that are faced by the Indian society not only relate to the state of women but also relate to the large number of under privileged who are at the bottom of the ladder for centuries with no sign of redemption. The cause of this mess is attributed to the caste system and the oppression that is committed in the name of caste system.

Long long ago the *rishis* had analyzed the human beings and had opined that man/woman can have any one of the three characteristics, namely *Saathvik Guna, Rajo Guna* and *Tamo Guna*. These characteristics are either hereditary or can be acquired by constant practice, disciplining of the mind and practice, *sadhana*. The caste system was based on the premise that it is more natural for these qualities to be imbibed by birth than by constant practice and disciplining of the mind, *sadhana*. The reason for this is the environment that the child faces. The other reason is that the birth of a child to parents is essentially an activity that is prearranged and also an activity that is on one's own accord. This is a very interesting concept that has been described in great detail by Sri Sri Paramahansa Yogananda who has written such brilliant books as "Autobiography of Yogi", "Man's Eternal Quest", "The Divine Romance", "Whispers from Eternity" etc. A similar concept is put forth by the Theosophists who believe in the existence of an ethereal world, very similar to the real world, where what ever is to happen in the real world is decided apriori that later starts unfolding or happening in the real world. Great theosophists like Leadbeater and others have written books like "Life After Death" explaining the relationship between the happenings in the ethereal and real world. The poet saint Kabir has sung a number of compositions describing the relationship between God and the man/woman. One of the compositions is

Karale Singar Chatur Alabeli
Nahale Dhole Sesa Uthale
Sajan ke Ghar Jana Hoga
Karale Singar Chatur Alabeli
Mati Odhan Mati Bichavan
Mati Me Mil Janahoga
Karale Singar Chatur Alabeli
Kahata Kabir Suno Bhai Sado
Lautake Phir Na Ana Hoga
Karale Singar Chatur Alabeli

The translation of this is

Oh, intelligent girl, beautify and decorate yourself
Make yourself presentable, comb your hair and
enjoy what ever comes in your way
You will have to go to your lover's house (this
earthly abode)
Oh, intelligent girl, beautify and decorate yourself
(Remember) Your body is made out of dust,
you will lie on dust,
(In the end) your body will go to dust,
Oh, intelligent girl, beautify and decorate yourself
Oh, brothers and sisters listen to what Kabir has to say
(After enjoying what ever comes your way on this
earthly abode)
Make sure not to return again
Oh, intelligent girl, beautify and decorate yourself

Here again there is a hint that it is the individual who alone is responsible for taking birth and therefore can also decide not to return. One should accept what ever comes and enjoy what ever comes, living from day to day treating every day as a new experience and in the end take a conscious decision not to return to this earthly abode. In fact this is also what J.Krishnamurthy says, "Experience it and forget it; Do not carry the impression of the experience with you". Bhagavad Gita says the same. The various forms of meditations like the Maharshi Mahesh Yogi's Transcendantal Meditation, Ramachandra Mission's Meditation and others aim to achieve this liberation from birth. The aim of meditation is to remove the foot prints of the experiences from the conscious/sub-conscious mind.

Does this mean that we come here on our own volition and desire, and can get out of this place not to return on our own volition? And that we choose the environment to live, parents, friends and foes and the people with whom to interact much before we actually take birth? That is, we cannot plan any thing any more after we are born? The saints had attributed this to the will of God or fate: "Whatever is to happen will happen". Here again there are two views about this. Some agree with the concept of fate or the Will of God. Others consider this as a defeatist attitude and assert that one can change the circumstances through work and perseverance. The famous Russian Philosopher Gurdjieff believes that man cannot plan or do anything. Things just happen. What ever has happened could not have happened in a different way no matter what the efforts or wishes. This is true of every thing in the life of an individual or a society. Things just happen. With a hind sight this appears to be true, even though it is difficult to believe it as it hurts the ego. Consider the break up of Russia. Did any body imagine that Russia would break up so easily? I am sure CIA must have tried very hard to achieve this. It is said that they went to the extent of collecting urine and stool samples of the Russian leaders. Nothing happened even after collecting those precious samples. But when the time came, it just happened. In the same way, may be India will resolve all its seemingly unresolvable problems and the Indian Society would become a wonderful and affluent society to live in the next few years. Who knows, it may just happen. We all live on hope: *Ummed Pe Duniya Kayam Hai.* (as there is nothing else to live on!!)

Therefore the environment in which one is born and is living is entirely of one's choice which is possibly decided by the footprints or impressions that one carries of every thing one did and is doing. That is, one seeks out the kind of environment that one thought would be best suited to one and for which one was yearning for when one was in a different environment or state. Therefore when one takes birth again, one makes sure that one positions oneself in that state for which one was thirsting. But it is an entirely different matter when after positioning oneself in that state, which one thought was the most wonderful state, one starts realizing that one should have been in a different slot and not the one in which one has positioned oneself. This sets the long and seemingly unending cycle of birth and death. This is possibly the reason why Kabir said

> Oh, brothers and sisters listen to what Kabir has to say
> (After enjoying whatever comes your way on this
> earthly abode)
> Make sure not to return again
> Oh, intelligent girl, beautify and decorate yourself

The same has been said by J.Krishna Murty, Bhagavadgita and a few other religious texts belonging to Hinduism and other religions. In fact every saint and wise man has said that man returns to dust. Thus the essentials of all religions is the same and the guardians of the gates of God's Kingdom have conveniently decided to turn Nelson's eyes to this commonality, and focus on the trivial and draw thick lines separating human beings creating sorrow and misery in the name of God. The only problem is that the man does not believe this till he has a foot in the grave and another on the banana peel. The veil of conditioning and consolation of mind that had been assiduously cultivated all through one's life for perpetuating selfish interests starts giving way. The man/woman now yearns for a second chance to do things right and the cycle goes on! This is truly a tragi-comic state of unfathomable proportion.

It is a natural phenomenon that every society, east or west or north or south, has people with well defined characteristics and temperament. These are common to all societies irrespective of the conditioning of the mind. The number of characteristics or the temperament is the same all over, viz., *Saathvik Guna, Rajo Guna* and *Tamo Guna*. These are essentially the broad heads of the characteristics and an individual can have a mix of these characteristics.

In the present modern age, due to a thorough mix up of the characteristics of human mind and the thought of becoming an equal opportunity employer has created a perfect setting for a mess. The state has been putting wrong persons in the right positions or is it right persons in wrong positions, because the wrong person has the right connection to be where he/she is though he/she does not have the right qualification. We have thus become an equal opportunity employers and are building a great nation with an equally great future! This is truly a wonderful act of the mind, a case of consolation of mind.

vii

It appears that the thinking of the human beings has not really changed over the years and the irresistible itch for the misuse of power is a very age-old problem, which has become a tradition. We are after all not different from our ancestors and our time/period is after all not different from their time/period even though we keep hearing from our parents and grand parents that their time were so wonderful compared to the present day scenario. If this were really so, there was no reason for Lord Vishnu to come down to this earth ten or eleven or twelve times to save the society. One interesting thing that comes out of this is that both Vishvamitra and Parasurama, though born in different environment had different temperament. This is the first indication of the fact that the temperament cannot be solely hereditary but is something that one is born with. This is in line with the philosophy of the theosophists who believe that every thing is decided in the ethereal world and is played again in the real world. This is in line with the view of the sages that every thing is controlled by "fate" or "destiny". This also is in line with the Russian philosopher Gurdjieff who believes that every thing just happens and that the individual cannot do any thing and therefore events just keep unfolding as though every thing was preplanned with characters making grand entry and an equally grand exit. *Sant* Purandaradasa, a Kannada poet saint, has composed a number of poems describing the relationship between God and the man/woman. These describe the follies of the human mind in the same way as *Sant* Kabir. Purandaradasa wonders why people try to make grand entry and grand exit when they are just puppets and cannot do any thing other than what has already been willed. His concern was for the "grandness", if such a terminology can be used, which stems from ignorance and ego of the human being that causes one to forget one's limited existence and equate oneself to the unlimited state of God. Therefore the interpretation of the caste system that is being made today appears to be flawed.

Consider the two other great personalities: *Ram* and *Ravan*. Ravan was a highly gifted person. The attempt here is not to glorify Ravan but only to compare the characteristics. Ravan was a great exponent of music and is said to be one of the greatest exponent of a string instrument, *veena*. He was a poet, knew the Upanishads and other scriptures, had the ability and temperament to do penance to please two of the Trinities of Hindu religion: Brahma and Maheshwara. He did not trust Vishnu! Inspite of possessing these wonderful qualities, his downfall was due to the usual human problems: arrogance, lack of respect for others, an eye for other women, an egoistic personality and a feeling that what ever he says or does is correct. Thus, even though he had made Lord Brahma appear before him and had the knowledge of the scriptures he cannot be classified as a Brahman because of the complete absence of *sathvik guna* or temperament. We can define two subsets of *Rajo Guna*:

(a) Negative *Rajo Guna*: the negative aspects being the arrogance, self gratification, deceit, not concerned about the well being of others, egoistic in
nature; all these negative aspects clouding the *rajo guna*

(b) Positive *Rajo Guna*: the positive aspects being humility, willing to give
without expecting anything in return, honest, concerned about others
and the well being of others, willing to accommodate others views; all
these positive aspects influencing the *rajo guna*.

Keeping the above in view, one can conclude that Ravan was a *kshatriya*
with negative *rajo guna* thus making him a *rakshasa*, one with demonic traits.
On the other hand, Ram who was a Vishnu incarnate and was a *kshatriya* with
positive *rajo guna*. One cannot conclude that Ram was a person with *sathvik
guna*, even though he obeyed his father's command to go to the forest for fourteen years. This *sathvik* characteristic would not have been the necessary qualification either to become the King or fight any of the *rakshasa* thus negating
the very purpose of incarnation. A comparison between the characteristics of
Vibheeshan, Ravan and Kumbhakarn (Kumbhee for many) brings about startling differences in the temperaments even though they were born to same
parents. Kumbhee had possibly more of *tamo guna* and Vibheeshan had more
of *sathvik guna*. The reason for the three brothers having different temperaments was possibly because of the differing temperaments of the father, a *rishi*,
and the mother, a *rakshasi*, a woman with demonic traits. How did the two
with such different temperaments ended up getting married is another story.
One can see similar stories getting repeated in the present day modern society
where people love to wear their freedom. This is central to the confusion that
one sees in the present society.

Sir Woodrof Wilson in his book, "In Defense of Caste System", describes the
scientific reasons for supporting/defending the caste system. He cites the
examples of breeding of animals like dogs, horses, cows, mules etc and also the
developing of high yielding variety of seeds of wheat, maze, rice etc to support
the concept of caste system. The attempt of such an exercise is to produce a
high yielding, resistant and therefore a better quality of either animal or seed.
This can be achieved if two varieties with similar desired characteristics are
made to come together. In the same way the division of people was based on
the temperament of the individual:

Spiritual or Ritualistic:	Brahman
Martial:	Kshatriya
Trading or Business:	Vaishya
Mundane work or Physical work:	Shudra.

The class referred to Shudra did not connote "Untouchability". But at "sometime" in the history of mankind in India, the word Shudra which was to classify those who did the mundane jobs needing physical labor got split into two classes: Shudra and the fifth group (*panchama*) which became "Untouchables". Slowly and surely the shudras were also pushed into the class of untouchables depending upon the kind of mundane activities that they were involved in. The reason appears to have its origin in the desire of every individual to have somebody under him/her. Another possible reason was the harsh economic conditions the society might have gone through at "that time" in the history of man kind in India. In the recent past, history tells us that whenever economic conditions become difficult, there is every possibility of the strange concoction of politics and theology creating holocausts by identifying a particular set of people as the cause of all problems. This had happened in Hitler's time, and in Serbia—Bosnia, and Ethiopia, and else where. The birth of the fifth group was not the making of the ancient *rishis* but of the recent past with the connivance of the vested interests. The "recent past" in the case of India is on a different time scale and therefore represents time in terms of many centuries.

Thus, the concept of the caste system was to create an environment where the like minded persons interact to achieve and maintain the highest standards of achievements and the general well being of the society. Thus, the profession of an individual became hereditary for the simple reason that the child growing up in an environment of a specific vocation has a greater possibility of attaining mastery over that vocation. For example a medical doctor's son/daughter tends to become a doctor; a lawyer's son/daughter tends to become a lawyer, a *brahman*'s son/daughter has the characteristics of *brahman*, the son or daughter of a *vaishya* has more characteristics of a *vaishya* and so on. The reason is the environment of growth that is made available to the child. However, this never took away the right of a person to change one's vocation to something different from the profession of one's parent. The original concept of the caste system did not mean that the person with a different temperament had no means of attempting to achieve excellence in another area. There was even a possibility of changing ones level in the society by hard work and training. As a concept, this is perfectly logical and scientific. The desire to have some body under oneself was never the basis of caste system. The four groups that characterized the caste system were interdependent and coexistent, each one doing what one is best at. But this concept got distorted completely and assumed a perverse hierarchical system from which there was no escape and was used to control and manipulate the society. One of the causes of the birth of the fifth group of "Untouchables" is the desire for each one of the groups to have some body under them. This is definitely a despicable desire but unfortunately, is a reality. Unless otherwise one has some one under him/her, one is deemed not to have made any progress in life. The number of persons under one's supervision is considered a measure of success one has achieved in life. This leaves one with no other option but to say, 'Oh, my India, my heart weeps for you". This is a classic case of accepting "what is" and not hankering about "what should be", which in turn shows the extent to which the mind has been conditioned or consoled. We do not have the courage to stand up to our convictions and do what we ought to be doing for the well being of the society.

ix

The concept of arranged marriages where the horoscope matching was done was also based on the principle of matching of the temperaments. The issue is not whether astrology is scientific or not. In all probability, astrology is more statistical in nature and dependent on the ability of the person who studies the horoscope. This activity of horoscope reading is practiced for centuries and it is acknowledged that this in itself does not give astrology a status of science. Today, the very thought of the Horoscope Matching and Arranged Marriages based on the Matching of Temperaments are looked upon with cynicism because we have become rationalists with an ability to ask questions and with no ability to answer any. Further, the institution of marriage has been overtly influenced by the consumerism. The well decorated show rooms displaying a large variety of enchanting goods, electronic and non-electronic, have made the minds and therefore the temperaments restless. There has been a radical change in the thinking process. Thus the new value system is far different from the old value system. Today, the match making is more of the bank accounts and status than of temperaments. We appear to be not thinking about peace of mind. However, the practice appears to be to run after money and then spend a small part of it to get peace of mind. Invariably, the need for peace and well being of the rest of the society is felt at the fag end of the career or life. This is true with the rich and the successful. It is because of this that some wise men have said that the poor need the food and the rich need the God for their salvation because the road to salvation for the poor and rich are different. But the rich in their eagerness to help the poor offer the words of God to the poor and ask them not to be greedy leaving the poor in a state of no comfort. The aim of this advice is more to reduce a rush for a part of the shrinking cake. When they do not have food or clothing or shelter these prescriptions that help only the rich are of no use to the poor. Thus we are in an enviable position where the rich and affluent families are disintegrating still further in the name of career/freedom/creativity/achievement/living full life/and whatnot. The poor and impoverished large families have become discordant and are disintegrating still further in the name of making it big, less by hook and more by crook. In the process, one group is influencing the other in a way that may end up in a dance of death. This throws up a few issues:

(a) Should one lead a peaceful life without any excitement and therefore end up leading a vegetable existence?

(b) Should one run after excitement so as to fully utilize this one life that has been given to us by God?

(c) Should one lead a balanced life with a little of peaceful life and a little of excitement, a God Centric Life?

Wise men have always advocated the third option. But, the young have no patience for the laws of nature and want every thing to happen as per their time scale, which is more in the form of whims and fancy. All scriptures, Hindu, Christian, Muslim, Zoroastrian, Buddhism, Jainism, Judaism and Sikh religions, always advocate that things happen only when they are to happen or when God wills it to happen. Bhagavadgita is possibly the only non-religious scripture that tells us the way to live and think in the modern times. The reason for calling this a non-religious scripture is that this advice on how to live and think was given to Arjuna by Lord Krishna on a battlefield. This makes Bhagavadgita an eternal advice to the people on the ways of living and thinking and our times are no different than the battlefield of Arjuna. But the mindset is that who ever tries to lead a God Centric Life is looked upon as a failure in life. Those who specialize in the Manipulative Management are generally looked upon as smart and successful in life.

A study of the mechanism of governance in India displays the absence of fear either of God or for the rule of law. The bureaucratic response to the super cyclone in Orissa and Guarat earthquake, communal riots in Delhi in 1984, communal riots in 2002 reinforces the view on the break down of rule of law or fear of God. The relief material that poured into Orissa never reached the victims. The high quality polythene sheets meant for erecting temporary shelters were replaced by poor quality polythene sheets. Even after an year, the victims of super cyclone received a very small part of the relief materials sent by fellow Indians, foreign governments and Indian government. What ever reached the victims of super cyclone was due to Non Government Organizations and social workers. In this connection, the judgment of Gujarat High Court on the public interest case filed by Kartikeya Sarabhai on the modalities and transparency that need to be followed in case of relief work is a welcome step. The judiciary did come to the rescue of the people of Delhi by forcing the Delhi government to shift the polluting industries out of Delhi and in the process bring the pollution level in Delhi to a low level. Thus, what should have been a normal process of governance gets implemented through a public interest case making judiciary the eleventh incarnation of God.

This is the eternal conflict that one faces and this is possibly the eternal fight between the Satan and the God or the Bad and the Good. The root cause is ignorance about the way of living and thinking or the absence of proper education. It becomes difficult to define "Proper Education". The reason for this difficulty is that what ever might appear to be proper for one may not appear proper for another. We are back to the same diverse nature of the *Guna* or Characteristic of Mind, which was the basis of the formation of caste system. The Caste System was framed not to show the supremacy of one set over the other but only to classify or group the people with different temperaments. The other part of the confusion comes from the concept of "God Centric Life". In most of the cases, this very concept of "God Centric Life" causes more damage than good. Nobody knows the will of God and therefore what ever is mentioned in the scripture, which is very difficult to comprehend, is looked upon as the word of God. There are many horrendous acts that are attributed to the ageless tradition or sacred principles or tenets, *Shashtra*. It is these acts that create misery. The question that often arises is: "Are God Centric Life and Religious Fundamentalism same?" In most of the cases, the God Centric Life changes over to Religious Fundamentalism when ever the conditions in the society threatens the well being of the few influential segments. The persons who have a vested interest in the task of keeping the links between the Creator and the Created start the Manipulative Management. In fact the concepts of manipulative management are as old as the civilization itself.

Is not God a very personal entity? Therefore should not anything related to God remain at personal level rather than at an organizational level? Hinduism is possibly the only religion that is not an organized religion even though attempts are being made to make it an organized religion. The problem with organized religion is that the thought process of individuals is controlled by one individual or a group of individuals and the process of control is based on the voice of God which only these few are able to hear or discern or comprehend. It is under these conditions that there are possibilities of misrepresentation of God's will or voice. There are a fairly large case histories where God has been misquoted and misrepresented causing untold misery to the innocents. This misrepresentation of God's will or voice or laws of nature is a phenomenon that is as old as civilization and therefore there is nothing to feel perturbed. There is a need to have faith in oneself and stand firm against all atrocities that are committed in the name of God.

There have always been two categories of people in society. The one that rules or wields power either in the form of authority or in the form of money or in form of brute force or in the form of religious dictat. The others, who form a majority, are just silent sufferers who have no option but to pray to God. Those who have power do not in general believe in the fair play and by the time they have a foot in the grave and another on the banana peel, they realize that they should have done everything in a different way and that their life has been completely wasted. The whole life is spent in chasing a series of ladders, attempting to climb the ladder and jumping from one ladder to another. After all we are the descendents of the monkeys, are we not? Some who succeed in climbing the ladder try to kick it and those who are at the foot of the ladder cause a stampede in an attempt to climb it. History has been a witness to cases where even blood has been shed in the process of climbing the ladder or in the process of exercising control over the ladder. Truly, the guiding principle of life is nothing but the survival of the fittest. There are also some who sit in the shade of a tree at a distance and watch this stampede or drama that keeps going on around the ladder without participating in the drama. These are normally called "good for nothing" and are generally looked upon as failures in life. But when the successful ones come to the end of their career or life, after a leading a successful, manipulative life style and now look back at their life/achievements with great regret for having wasted the opportunity, look upon the good for nothings as wise men/women! How does one judge the success of a person's existence on this earth? Does success in life depend on the number of ladders that one has climbed or the extent of wealth that one has accumulated or the number of people one has kicked in the process of either climbing the ladder or holding on to the statusquo? Wise men say that man must always associate himself with *Dharma* and Truth and fight for them, die for them. But the problem in the modern day is that every thing is so confusing because of the media hype and information explosion. Therefore in most of the cases it becomes extremely difficult to understand even the issues let alone what is right and what is wrong. The other problem is related to the issue of the true interpretation of the words of God. These issues are made more complex by the assertion of one group or religion about the supremacy of their God and Saviour, who alone can save the souls. This is the start of the Religious Fundamentalism. The guns, swords, hockey sticks, machine guns, grenades, time bombs and other tools of furthering the words of God come much later.

Thus the question of whether "God Centric Life" and "Religious Fundamentalism" are the same, is difficult to resolve for the following reasons:

(a) God Centric Life practiced by individuals with no interference in the affairs of other individuals is the best thing that can happen to a society as this gives the freedom of worship without desecrating or insulting or victimizing the other people or the other beliefs.

(b) God Centric Life practiced by a society or a group of people in an organized manner, as a group activity, has a distinct possibility of degenerating into Religious Fundamentalism of which there have been a few case histories in United States of America where sects have destroyed themselves. Therefore, the God Centric Life practiced on the lines of (a) above is the preferred option.

History has recorded that those who like to lead a life of non-interference, with no intention of dominating others, end up getting suppressed or even destroyed. History has also recorded that those who destroyed others to preserve themselves did not succeed in achieving their goal. Why should the weak always suffer silently? Why cannot they rise to assert their rights? Why is it that those who are too weak even to cry end up suffering with no respite? Should they keep suffering because of their being too weak even to cry? Should not their unwillingness to revolt and shed blood unlike the European brothers be acknowledged as the strength to be respected and admired? Should not the patience be looked upon as the strength to be utilized for improving their living conditions rather than exploiting them? How wonderful it would have been if those in power get this realization when they are still in power rather than at the end of the day, after the sunset. It is possibly this that makes them to take birth again and it is possibly this that is the root cause of rebirth based on the last thoughts before kicking the bucket. Does not this also represent another form of consolation of mind?

Looking back one finds similar case histories. Devayani, the daughter of Guru Shukracharya falls in love with the Aryan King Yayati and decides to marry him. Even though both King Yayati and *Guru* Shukracharya are Aryans, they are on opposite sides, with Shukracharya becoming the Guru of *Asuras*, and opposing, fighting, destroying and killing the Aryans; all this in the name of principles and *dharma* and therefore God. Shukracharya succeeded in creating an empire that became subservient to him by not educating his followers on the scriptures. Thus he consciously built a society that became ignorant of the laws of nature, *dharma* as enshrined in the scriptures and matters related to God. He succeeded in this by indulging in management by manipulation! When Shukracharya opposed the marriage between his daughter Devayani and King Yayati, Devayani rebels and blasts her father for his manipulative methods. She accuses him of creating a society that is not only ignorant of the right and wrong, but also of poisoning the minds of his followers with his own mix of theories. She questions his authority that has helped in furthering his own cause as a *Guru* without bothering about the well being of the people/society. She also questions him on his dual policy of teaching her the philosophy and the values of Aryans and teaching the *asuras* something entirely different which is the cause of the destruction of every thing that is Aryan. This no way means that Shukracharya was not a learned man or was not aware of the laws of nature. Whatever he did was for avenging the ills that were heaped on him by the fellow Aryans. Thus he found that the best way to avenge is to take recourse to manipulative mechanics! Therefore, the role of the middlemen in the activities related to the relationship between man and God has always resulted in causing untold misery and suffering for the masses. Further, this role of the middlemen existed since the very existence of the society.

Possibly, this is the first instance of a *Guru* successfully breeding a society of misguided persons and also the first time that the daughter blasts her father and decides to marry the person of her choice. Also, when Devayani comes to know that her husband, King Yayati, has fallen in love with Sharmishta, who was long standing associate, firstly as a maid in attendance and later as a friend, and has married her, Devayani slams the door on the face of King Yayati and walks out to stay with her father for the rest of her life. This brings to light the freedom that the women of those days enjoyed and also the courage that they had to express their views irrespective of whether the person who is addressed is the king or a commoner. In contrast, the state of women today is such that the girl child is looked upon as a curse. Inspite of our having had a woman Prime Minister who shook all men, the state of the woman or girl child has not drastically changed. However in the recent past there have been dramatic changes in small pockets that are in the form of islands of hope in an otherwise bleak and depressing scenario. The girl child is always at the receiving end right from child hood to the adult hood; irrespective of whether she is living with her parents or with her husband. The economics of living have played havoc with the thinking and value system of society. More than the economic owes, it is the greed that plays a havoc on the psyche of the people. The boy assumes to be doing a favor to the bride and her parents by marrying her; nothing can be more obnoxious than this thought. It is extremely difficult to imagine and feel the pain and terror that a new bride would go through when she is surrounded by her husband and his close and dear ones holding a kerosene oil tin and a matchbox.

The redeeming factor is the courts have made the dying declaration an unimpeachable evidence. But this does not give solace either to the dead or to

the near and dear ones of the dead. The insatiable greed can be the only explanation to the dowry deaths of which only a few get reported in the print media.
In the modern times, there is a great decline in the value system and the attitude of men towards everything including women. There is a great confusion
about the entity "God" and what can be expected of God and what cannot be
expected of God. Will God interfere in the man's life? Will he take sides with
the just and the oppressed, and fight against the unjust and the oppressors?
One line of thinking is that there is no difference between man and God, and
man can raise himself to achieve the perfection of God. It is this that differentiates man from animal. Therefore, it would be futile to expect God to interfere
in the daily mess that man himself has created.

The wise men are of the opinion that the incarnation of God in the form of
Ram and Krishna is meant to indicate that man must work towards realizing
the power that is within rather than keep looking towards heavens for help.
Ram performs all tasks expected of a son and ends up spending about fourteen
years in forest along with his wife. In the process, Sita is kidnapped by Ravana,
which ultimately results in the killing of Ravana. The process of the birth of
Krishna was extremely painful resulting in the death of six new born children;
all this happening in a jail. The question that often comes to mind is, "Why
should the incarnations of God go through these painful processes when the
very purpose of the birth of the God incarnate is to put an end to the evil
forces?" If the purpose of all this was to kill Ravana, Kamsa and others and to
establish the rule of *dharma,* there was no reason for going through all this suffering and tribulation. God could have sent a thunder-bolt from the skies and
forced the evil minded and unscrupulous ones to kick the buckets in one go.
This view of God sitting and keeping a watch on all his creations is possibly
similar to the role of a Don or an Underworld King or a Drug Lord who needs
to keep a constant watch on his empire. Wise men have said that God has no
intention to wear the crown of a Don or an Underworld King or a Drug Lord
as he resides in every living being. What is needed is for the living being to
remember *Him* and call *Him*; *He* is there with you all the time. That is, God
helps those who help themselves. But the problem is that the statement, "God
Helps Those Who Help Themselves", has been faithfully and conveniently used
for helping themselves without bothering about the neighbor or the society.
Some have successfully perfected this art of helping themselves in the name of
helping animals with fodder. Some have helped themselves with the deposits
of the common man in cooperative banks. These have been happening in the
name of God. The people in power have always been helping themselves very
generously.

Another question that comes to mind is, "Aren't people afraid of committing sin?" This throws up another question, "What is sin?" It is difficult to define sin because sin is dependent on the state of the mind. That is, the concept of sin is different for different people depending on the state of refinement or development of mind. Therefore, there is nothing called sin and the people are in a continuous process of mental evolution, with the physical evolution having come to a stop. Thus man can evolve to be a superman. It is said that the Vedantic concept is a state where there is no sin and where the God does not punish or reward. If this is the case then why should one ever follow the path of *dharma*? This throws up another question, "What is *dharma*"? It is evident that sin and *dharma* are linked, and therefore both are linked to the state of mind or the mental refinement. The wise men have always advised every one to adhere to *sva-dharma* and not keep looking at others and try to imitate others. The *sva-dharma* is in turn dependent on the mental refinement of an individual. The sin, therefore, appear to be linked to whether one is living as per one's *sva-dharma* or not; whenever one does not adhere to one's *sva-dharma* one gets into a conflicting state of mind which leaves the impression of a sin on the mind. It is this impression on the mind that is responsible for coming back again and it is this impression that is carried to the next birth. This also becomes a process of refinement of the mind and therefore the elevation of the individual soul. The practice of *sva-dharma* must be in consonance with *dharma*, the well being of the society, and not be looked upon as a license to jump the gun. Even *dharma sutra* suggests different punishment for people with different mental evolution as in the case of *Brahmana, Kshatriya, Vaishya & Shudra.*

Basaveshvara, the founder of Lingayat movement, says that hoarding more than what one needs is a sin. He was against the Brahminical oppression of the lower castes which was being given the status of *dharma* with the sanction of the scriptures. He raised his voice against the priestly class who had assumed the role of middle men between the God and the rest of the people, and who played a role bigger than the God which has resulted in the saying, "It is easier to please God but not the priest". It is the priest who decides when the dead soul reaches heaven or for that matter, will it reach heaven at all or keep hovering around the house in the form of a ghost. God has no power.

Does this mean that Ravana, Kamsa and others of the modern days are not committing any sin because they are following their *sva-dharma*? Upanishads provide the necessary condition to the following of *sva-dharma* in the form of a rider that states that the activity of an individual must be such that it is beneficial to others or at least not harm the interests of others. The activity must not be for self indulgence alone. The guiding principle of life is, "Try not to harm any one; every evening think of all the acts of omission and commission that one has committed during the day, and try to rectify the damage the next day by being honest to oneself and to others". Bhagavadgita, the sermon on the battlefield, presents the ideal way to live. It advises every one to be a "*stithaprajna*". That is live in the same way as a drop of water on a lotus leaf; not getting attached to every thing one sees or does or creates; not thinking of the kind of fruits or benefits one might get either before or after performing an activity. J.Krishna Murthy puts it in a different way, "Experience it and forget it. Do not carry any impressions". The trouble with this guiding principle is that it makes the climbing of ladders, kicking of ladders and kicking others very difficult or impossible. Therefore such persons end up sitting and sleeping under a tree and watch the stampede that takes place around a ladder deriving some comic relief. Such people are generally called not successful in life; people with no ambition. This reminds one of Robert Schuller's book "Life is tough, God is Great".

In matters relating to *dharma,* sin, *shastra,* religion and God the greatest problem lies in the different mind sets of *guru* who lectures and people who have come to hear the lecture. This confusion is compounded by the different levels of knowledge of the speakers and the listeners. Religion and God are two separate entities and to realize God, one need not know the religious practices or follow the rituals as prescribed by the priests. The *guru* that we find today belongs to a creed of manipulators who masquerade as all knowing *guru*. It is easy to find a boss but not a *guru,* even though the boss would very much like to step into the shoes of the *guru* and demand complete surrender by the subordinate. The word *guru* has been derived from two roots: *gu* signifyng ignorance, and *ru* signifying remover. Thus the *guru* removes the darkness or ignorance in his *shishya,* pupil or disciple. The true *guru* is one who understands the abilities of the pupil or the lack of abilities. In the present age, education is accessible to every one irrespective of whether they have the abilities or not. On the other hand in the olden days, the *guru* was more interested in taking only those who had the ability and inner strength to pursue the path of understanding the knowledge of cosmic principle, *Brahman.* Thus the main difference between the teaching of the olden days and the present days is that those days the teaching was "God Centric" whereas in the present day, the teaching is "Material Centric". We have a large number of people who can read and write and therefore come to be recognized as educated. The words, education and literacy, are being used as synonyms and possibly it is this that made Dr.Radhakrishnan to write, "The need of India is to educate the educated". We have become shallow human beings with no depth in anything. Thus, we now have a new breed of human beings, "ignorant educated". We do not take pride in doing anything in the way it should be done. We have been a part of the "*chalta hai*", any thing is acceptable, set up. Thus in the prevailing environment, the *guru* has joined hands with the politicians and successfully exploited the ignorant who happen to be in majority. This gives the *guru* the mechanism of manipulating the large masses and create a society of misguided and ignorant people in the name of God. An ignorant educated person is more dangerous and vicious than an ignorant uneducated person. The uneducated person is like a clean slate and therefore can be groomed and made into a cultured and sensitive person. The educated man has a preconditioned mind making the process of delearning and relearning an extremely difficult process.

The socialist concept of all men being equal may be valid from the point of view of granting the fundamental rights, enshrined in the constitution, to the people. But, in reality, all men are not equal from the point of the refinement of thought processes or development of mind. We are, unfortunately, back to the concept of caste system as it was framed by the *rishis* and not as is being practiced today. Thus, in the ages of the *rishis*, the laws that applied to people were dependent on the mental refinement of the individuals; a fact which even today, in some limited form, can be seen in the juris prudence. The information explosion that has been taking place has helped the people to know the state of affairs elsewhere and therefore can compare their state with that of the others. This comparison and the thought process that go with the comparison appear to be the root cause of increased awareness. Thus, the people are becoming aware that they are being taken for a long ride by the leaders. In the words of Naipaul, "All that was chaotic was really a great sign of hope". Thus, the information explosion has helped in removing the veil of ignorance of the people or the picture of grandeur that is generally painted by leaders, political or religious. It is this that makes the media, print or electronic, the first target of the leaders, political or religious. The basis of attack is that the electronic and print media are projected as the cause of the process of corrupting the tender minds of innocent people who are in need of total protection from the state. As far as the leaders are concerned, a higher level of ignorance and poverty serve as a surety of survival. Therefore, primary and adult education was never given the priority that they deserved. The Indian society is unfortunately beset with strange problems due to a large segment of the society being kept outside the process of even elementary learning. The end result is that this large segment of the society which had been left out of all activities related to development has now become, rightly so, a drag on the Indian society. Therefore, the segment of the population which was in a way responsible for the creation of the mess is now being asked to pay back with, may be, a little interest. The most unfortunate part of this unfortunate scenario is that the fragmentation of the population of India is on the basis of a distorted version of caste system, which is not the way it should have been. The only thing common to both is the name "Caste System" and nothing else; definitely not the operative principles underlying the two different practices, the way it was postulated and the way it is practiced. One is left with no option but to say, 'Oh, my India, my heart weeps for you".

The essence of the caste system as perceived by the sages from the point of view of community living got distorted due to the desire to dominate others. This process of distortion was intentional and started with the desire to keep knowledge out of reach of the majority of the people. Thus, the concept of knowledge as power was conceived much before the advent of Goebbels of Nazi fame. The mind having committed a terrible error of judgment is now consoling itself to live with the present day reality of equal opportunity policy without the matching component of right aptitude and qualification. This leaves no option to the mind but to console itself by thinking about the past.

ix

Irrespective of whether one is leading a "God Centric" life or not, every one takes the name of God at least once in the lifetime. The question that often arises is, "Who is the better God?" Is my God better than your God or is it that somebody else's God is better than our Gods? Invariably this number game leads to misrepresentation and in some cases even falsification of other's scriptures, Gods, ethos, cultural values, beliefs and for that matter every thing that other religions or Gods represent. One reason for this kind of a thing is the need for the people to retain their identity which makes people feel secure and also to feel good about the assumption that they are safe and better off under the care and guidance of their God. But have the different Gods in whose name the followers have formed different religions said different things or have they said the same things? Or, do the different scriptures, which are often looked upon as the words of God say the same or similar things, or do they speak of entirely different and contradictory things? It is here that the works of Immanuel Vellikovsky come handy. Some of his books are "Worlds in Collision", "Ages in Chaos", "Earth in Upheaval", "Odepus and Akhnaton", "Peoples of the Sea". It is unfortunate that these are out of print. It would be wonderful to see these books reprinted again as the strife torn society, the world over, need to read these books.

Immanuel Vellikowsky studied natural sciences at the University of Edinburgh, history, law and medicine (M.D) in Moscow, biology in Berlin, the working of brain in Zurich and psychoanalysis in Vienna. Indeed a very strange man. Immanuel Vellikovsky, like many Jews of his time in 1930s, migrated from the erstwhile USSR to USA. The other famous one to migrate in this period was Madam Blavotsky who founded the Theosophical Society the headquarters of which moved from New York to Adayar in Madras/Chennai. Immanuel Vellikovsky was a linguist and knew Sanskrit, Hebrew, Latin and a few other languages. He studied the scriptures of different religions, the historical evidences and archeological findings in South America, Siberia and other places. Also he studied the research findings related to great civilizations like the Mayan Civilization, civilizations that flourished in the present day Iran and Jordan, generally known as the Gateway of India; and a host of other mythological texts including the astronomical happenings over the centuries. His interest was to make a comparative study of the scriptures, archeological findings, astronomical positions of the stars and other heavenly bodies and the civilizations that actually thrived during those times. The aim was to understand whether the religious and mythological texts that one society, say Indian society, have been reading from time immemorial correlate with the religious and mythological text of some other society or civilization. For example the Greek Mythology has Hercules fighting with a seven hooded serpent while the Hindu Mythology has Krishna fighting with a seven hooded serpent. The seven hooded serpent appears in different locations all over the world under different circumstances. The other example of similarity is the Achilles Heel. The Greek mythology records that Thetis, the mother of Achilles, dipped the infant Achilles into the magic waters of River Styx making him invulnerable. But the heel that she was holding becomes the only weak point as it could not be immersed in the magic waters. A similar story is recorded in Mahabharata where Gandhari, the mother of Duryodhana, makes Duryodhana invulnerable by fixing her gaze on him after removing the cloth tied to her eyes. Here, the thighs of Duryodhana that were covered from the magic gaze of Gandhari become the only weak points. Achilles was killed by a poisoned arrow shot into the heel that had not been rendered invulnerable. In the same way, Bhim, in a dual of mace, killed Duryodhana by smashing Duryodhana's thighs that had not been rendered invulnerable. The moral that the Greek and Hindu mythology convey is possibly that the attempt of the two mothers to make their sons invulnerable even to death, the only certainty in life, was in vain. It was for this reason that even Krishna says "*Kalaya tubhyam namah*": "Time, I Salute Thee". Thus different societies appear to have certain things as common characteristics in them even though they appear to be different from all respects. The Old

Testament talks of the parting of Red Sea and the Bhagavata talks of the parting of Yamuna River. The Rig Veda talks of the falling of the Life Giving Nectar, *ambroza*, after a fiery destruction by fire from the heavens and the Mayan Civilization records similar happening. The list is unending. The differences are in the names, the way the happenings are presented, geographical locations where these activities are observed, the language in which these are recorded, the way these are recorded, the ethos of the people, the looks, the color of the skin and hair etc.

Consider the case of Islam. The general impression that one has of Islam, which is based on the pronouncements of the over enthusiastic religious leaders and possibly some of the historical acts of some of the followers, is that

(a) the religion does not believe in any border,

(b) the religion is fanatical with transnational appeal and following

(c) the religion is violent with no respect for either women or peace

(d) the religion is possibly the only one on this earth where a large number of wars have been fought in the name of God making every war a holy war.

(e) the religion has no place for the followers of any other religion and that the religion believes in eliminating all the non-believers by the sword or gun or by any means: *jihad.*

The teachings are exactly opposite of what is practiced. For example, there have been different interpretations of the word *jihad.* Some say that this refers to the execution of nonbelievers and is a way of spreading the message of the Prophet. Some others, who are in minority, believe that this has the same connotation as the words of Krisna in Bhagavad-Gita who endorses the war against evil and asks Arjuna not to see his guru in Dronacharya or the great grandfather in Bhishma but to see them as people who are supporting the rule of the evil and therefore are against the dharma. Dharma or the path of dharma does not refer to any particular God or saviour. Dharma refers only to compassion, love, general well being of all creations (living beings comprising of plants, animals and human beings) and peace. This is also the view of Koran, which allows/permits violence as a means of coming out of oppressed state and seeking justice in cases where every thing else has failed. That is, battle is advocated for the sake of establishing the well being of the society when all other means of getting justice are exhausted and not for imposing one's views or theology on people or society that believes in another way of peaceful life. The other interpretation, which is looked upon as a corollary to this is that this battle that is mentioned in Bhagavad-Gita and Koran is essentially a phenomenon that takes place in every day life as this is a war that is going on within as much as without. The war within is to eradicate, not control, the violent tendencies within.

This is also very similar to the process of conversion as preached in Christianity. The process of conversion and the process of *jihad* are similar to the Upanishadic thought of "*Tamaso ma jyotirgamaya*": may light drive away my ignorance. Thus, when ignorance is driven away, a new person is born and this is the concept of "born again Christian". Thus every religion, with no exception, teaches the importance of leading pious life and advocates purifying oneself by striving to drive out the darkness with in one self. Thus conversion never meant changing allegiance from one God to another God as there can be only one God who can be worshipped in many ways and many different forms. This is the reason for Hinduism not practicing conversion of people of other faiths to Hinduism. Swami Vivekananda had said that he could have converted Americans to Hinduism, which would not have served any purpose. He said, what is important is that Christian must become a better Christian, a Hindu a better Hindu, a Muslim a better Muslim. Thus, there has always been a great difference between the teachings and the practice. This has always been due to the desire to control and dominate others, a desire to show ones supremacy over others: a case of consolation of mind.

Consider the history of the church. During the dark age in Europe, Church had an absolute control and hold on the life of the people in Europe. The people had no freedom to say anything that the Church did not want to hear. People were not allowed even to think beyond the interpretation of the Holy Scriptures as interpreted or articulated by the Church. The words of the Church were looked upon as the words of God. Any one daring to question these and any one successfully proving that the words of Church are different from the words of God or disproving the words of the Church was put to stake. There was wide spread Inquisition putting many of the thinkers to stake, burning them alive. This was the state in Europe about four hundred years ago. This gave rise to the birth of Protestant movement and also the Renaissance Movement. Renaissance literally means rebirth. It was during this renaissance period that people started questioning the orthodox views of the Church that were being looked upon as the God's words. It was during the period of Renaissance that many scientific discoveries were made and accepted. These included the fact that Sun was the center of the solar system; earth was round etc.

Thus whenever the priests of Hinduism, Islam and Christianity took upon themselves the role of leading the societies either directly or as back seat drivers using the words of the *rishis*, prophet Mohammed and Jesus Christ for their own ulterior motives, the societies went into a state of dark age. Thus, the problem is neither with God or Jesus Christ or Prophet Mohammed or the *rishis* who gave us the Ten Commandments, Upanishads, Vedas, Bhagavad-Gita, Bible, Koran etc. The problem is with the followers and more so with the middle men who don the robes of piety and become the *mullas*, priests and missionaries and create havoc with the psyche of the followers with their own twisted and contorted version of God and God's words. It is because of this that all those who have been advocating peaceful methods of living have fallen victims to violent acts. The list includes Jesus Christ, Prophet Mohammed, Abraham Lincoln, Mahatma Gandhi.

Believers can rationalize the irrational. It is necessary to de-link "God" from the "belief in God" as the two are completely different. The tragedy of the man kind is that we approach "God" in the same way as we approach any commodity. That is, we fall back upon an interpreter of "God's will" and this interpreter is as good as any intermediary. But the conventional intermediary is in many respects a harmless person who is interested in exploiting the people for the sake of money. This is a controllable evil. However, if the intermediary who has taken upon himself/herself the task of interpreting the "God's will" turns out to be a person with political ambition, then even God will not be able to save the society from disaster. The society in all such cases goes through turmoil and crisis leading to untold suffering, misery and bloodshed. The political evolution of Europe had been driven through this torturous route. First it was the crusades in the name of Christ that resulted in the innocent people being put to stake because they did not believe in Christ. Further, there was another set of crusades, "jihad", unleashed by Muslims in the name of their God. Then came the intervention of Church in the matters of science and art resulting in the poisoning of a number of scientists and artists for refusing to toe the line of thought of the Church. After a few centuries came Adolph Hitler, who claimed to have found the ultimate solution to the problems facing the father land in the elimination of the Jews. Even at this time, the Church did not play any meaningful role to stop this barbarism. Nothing more needs to be said about the religion and the intermediaries between God and the people. History repeats. Man has killed more people in the name of God than in the name of any political ideology.

These acts are carried out to protect the religion and the God. Every believer wants others to believe in and accept his God & his religion to be "the only" God and "the only" religion. The believer cannot comprehend the existence of a "God" in different form or name or an idea or thought. There can be no salvation without the help from his "God" or there cannot be a path other than "his" religion that can lead to "God". This frame of mind has always, in the past and present, caused misery and bloodshed. The believer expects tolerance to his ways from others. That is, the believer has difficulty in accepting any other concept or thought or idea of God or religion, and the believer expects other to tolerate this. When this gets mixed with politics one ends up with a deadly concoction. Thus, when believers from different faiths meet then they are faced with the same problem and the same question. "How can these nonbelievers get salvation?" Thus the urge to save the nonbelievers from being damned for eternity, makes the believers to set about saving others souls. This act creates tremendous hatred and therefore violence. Every believer finds it difficult to comprehend the irrational thinking of the nonbeliever and wonders about the practice of paganism. Since this evokes emotional response, the wily politicians, who are always waiting for an opportunity to come to the center of the stage, rush to save both the believers and the non believers. Law and order and governance come with in the purview of the politician. Thus we have a vicious loop with the believer trying to save the nonbeliever and the politician trying to save the believer, nonbeliever, the God and the religion practiced by the believer and non believer, and therefore the society. The politician enjoys playing the role of an ultimate savior. This possibly explains the close links between politicians and the God-men/God-women. What results from this vicious loop is an eternal mayhem.

Every religion has endorsed the view that the God as enunciated by the respective religious text is compassionate, merciful and treats every one irrespective of whether one is honest, just, sinner etc, alike. He, God, is waiting to be called and when He receives an earnest call from any one, irrespective of whether he/she is just, honest or sinner, He is there to comfort him/her. Thus, the bone of contention is not the entity called "God" but to what extent can one use this entity to reap the benefits of being close to the center of power or influence. Religion has become the best form of business. The other problem with religion is that the history of religion, which is a record of the deeds of a few with distorted understandings and wonky ideas, creates more damaging images and therefore lasting impressions on the minds of the people. These images cannot be set right even by the good and soothing words that one finds in any scripture of any religion. The reason for such a distortion in the understanding of the followers is that the frame of mind of the teacher and the followers are vastly different and therefore the interpretations of the words of the teacher are as many and varied as there are followers. This is the start of all problems. Those who understand the master become minority and are left out in the great race for reaching out and pleasing God. The individual ego becomes bigger than God. Thus the importance or significance of the act of doing what is perceived as God's work becomes bigger than God himself. The tendency has always been to manipulate the religion to fulfill the requirements of the few who are powerful and then justify their actions in the name of religion. This has been the case with all the religions as people have no time to learn and understand the scriptures as this is not a commercially beneficial activity nor do we have the patience to carry this out nor do we find the right kind of teacher or *guru*. Maulana Wahiduddin Khan of the Islamic Center says that it is necessary to distinguish between religion and the followers. Therefore certain violent and oppressive practices by either the followers of Islam or Christianity or Hinduism or any other religion should not get the stamp of religion or should not pass off as being permitted by the religion even though these acts are perpetrated in the name of God. Koran even goes to the extent of asking the Muslims to show equal respect to all the prophets whom Allah has sent to different nations. This is the reason why all scriptures and Prophets, Saviors, *rishis* have said the same thing in different ways and languages and symbolic representations. Thus, the learned and sensitive people belonging to different cultures, religions; speaking different languages and looking different in color and looks have said similar things paraphrasing them in different ways. But they are always in a minority, the majority being the ignorant, audacious and violent, and therefore materially successful. Unfortunately God has been the cause of shedding maximum amount of blood the world over. Consider the following:

> If you can keep your head when all about you
> > Are loosing theirs and blaming it on you,
> If you can trust yourself when all men doubt you
> > But make allowance for their doubting too;
> If you can wait and not be tired by waiting
> > Or being lied about, don't deal in lies,
> Or being hated don't give way to hating
> > And yet don't look too good, not talk too wise.
> If you can dream—and not make dreams your master
> > If you can think—and not make thoughts your sin
> If you can meet with Triumph and Disaster
> > And treat those two imposters just the same;
> If you can bear to hear the truth you have spoken
> > Twisted by knaves to make a trap for fools,
> Or watch the things you gave your life to, broken
> > And stoop and build them up with worn—out tools;
> If you can make one heap of all your winnings;
> > And ask it on one turn of pitch and toss
> And lose, and start again at your beginnings;
> > And never breathe a word about your loss;

If you can force your heart and nerve and sinew
>   To serve your term long after they are gone
And so hold on when there is nothing in you
>   Except the Will which says to them: "Hold on!"
If you can talk with crowds and keep your virtue
>   Or walk with kings nor lose the common touch
If neither foes nor loving friends can hurt you,
>   If all men count with you but none too much;
If you can fill the unforgiving minute
>   With sixty seconds worth of distance run,
Yours is the earth and everything that's in it,
>   And—which is more—you will be a Man, my son!

This appears to be a translation of a few of the Hymns in some of the religious scriptures like Bhagavad-Gita, Upanishads, Koran, Bible or Zarathrushta's sayings or any other, as these capture the essence of life and represent God's words. Well, it is none of this. This is the poem "If" written by Rudyard Kippling. There is another book in Russian written by Leo Tolstoy that is translated to English with the title "The Kingdom of God is Within You". This shows that all those who have time to contemplate and meditate upon the meaning and purpose of life, and who are not audacious, violent, greedy and self centered, and who think about the welfare of the community, think alike irrespective of their religion and conditioning of the mind. Such people have not resorted to the state of consolation of mind.

The following two statements are attributed to two different persons even though they are very similar.

"True value of a human being can be found in the extent of liberation he has found from self"

"However great a culture may be, however noble its philosophy, the glory of a people depends upon the discipline of their action, the beauty of their emotions and the height of their ideal"

The first statement was made by Albert Einstein and the second statement was made by Swami Chinmayananda. Is it not strange that evolved souls/persons make similar statements irrespective of the conditioning of their minds, cultural background, language they speak, the color of their skin and hair, and the religion they practice? Unfortunately there are not many evolved persons; otherwise the world would have been a different place to live.

The change in the living style from the age old quite and peaceful style to the present day hurry, worry and curry style has created conditions that have forced the mind to be stretched to limits that it cannot sustain. We are living in the times of unsustainable levels of aggression and unsustainable levels of greed. This realization comes only during the fag end of one's life when the veil in the form of blurred vision over the debit and credit balance sheets of ones life involving the failures and achievements gets lifted with the vision becoming clearer. But the mind that had all along been trained to console itself into believing the rationality of the irrational finds itself torn apart leading to misery. This misery gets compounded after realizing the harm that had been done to others under the guise of order, discipline, progress, heritage, culture and many such ethereal ideas. We spend all our youth comprising of active years with a mind set that helps us to chase the things that slip out of our control. We do not have time to pause and think. Any slowing down in the pace of life is always looked upon as nothing short of failure in life. Therefore, we can never be content with what we have. We always like to chase what gets away from us. We are never happy with what we have. This is often attributed to immaturity. The result is we console our mind into believing that chasing what ever gets away is the purpose of life.

2

Education

Education, it is said, brings in the light and drives the darkness away. In fact many of the Vedic hymns that we keep chanting refer to this aspect of moving away from the state of darkness to a state of knowing or knowledge. The Sanskrit word Veda stands for knowledge. Thus the ideal condition is to have every individual in a society to be educated so that he/she can understand and know the difference between good and bad in matters relating to one's own life and ones surroundings. The attempt that needs to be made is to ensure that every child, boy or girl, gets an opportunity to go to school so that they learn to read and write and get to know the way of managing their own affairs. The present day concept of education and the education during the times of the *rishi* are different. The education imparted to the young aspirants in a hermitage, long long ago, was more in the realm of the scriptures, *dharma* or *adhyatmik*. The word *dharma* not only relates to religion but also to justice, governance and use of power vested in officials.

Thus in the present day education system aimed at creating a read and write base in the society, the exacting standards characterizing the necessary caliber of the student or *shishya* that were set by the *rishi*, are not possible in all schools, colleges or institutes. These exacting standards are even today practiced in certain premier institutes in India. Thus a mechanism of imparting universal education to all the children and also to the illiterate adults would solve most of the problems of this country. The universal education refers not only to the ability to read and write but also to take decisions to improve their living conditions and enhancement of one's sense of self worth. This alone can become the liberating force and not the laws and legislation. The three problems that one encounters in implementing this laudable scheme are the state machinery including the administrative and the political machinery, education system itself and the all pervading and ever present poverty. Consider the cases of the two states Uttar Pradesh and Bihar. Some of the information pertaining to the two states are given in the table below.

The table below tells the story of the failure of the political and administrative machinery in India. A poet in Lucknow, a city with a long tradition of Urdu poetry, told the whole story in a poetic form:

State	Population (million)	Poverty (percent)	Education (per capita)	Health (per capita)
Uttar Pradesh	132. 32	40. 85	Rs. 150	Rs. 53
Bihar	88. 25	54. 96	Rs. 135	Rs. 36

Table 2. 2. 1   Per-Capita Expenditure

> Kaisi ulti hui huqumat hai
> Kaisa ulta hua zamana
> Jinhe hona tha jailkhane mein
> Unke haathon mein hai jailkhana
> What a lop sided administration
> What a convoluted time
> Those who should have been inside the prisons
> Are the ones who control the prisons

This poem or parody written about a decade back explains the nexus between some of the politicians, administrators and criminals in Uttar Pradesh and Bihar, two of the most populous and important states of India. This is true in most of the other states. The difference may be one of degree. However, the links between some of the politicians and administrators and criminals is very close in Uttar Pradesh and Bihar. Thus the schooling and health that are necessary for liberating a society, are generally neglected issues. This is true even in communist run West Bengal. Further, no in depth discussion ever takes place on the improvement of education and health, increasing employment and removal of poverty. The political parties are more concerned about issues that are of no consequence. Whenever important issues are raised, the issues are hijacked and the attention of the people is diverted to issues that are of no consequence. The hijacking of issues is also due to the presence of a fairly large number of religions, castes and sub castes, and most important of all the presence of high level of illiteracy and a large population of people who are oppressed for generations. Thus the high level of illiteracy reflected by a low spending on education, is a part of the planning process to keep the masses at a level that makes them remain at the receiving end. Those who are powerful do not worry about justice, and those who do not even know their rights due to generations of subjugation and suppression remain in an oppressed state and do not know how to get justice or what their rights are. The case of Bihar, in particular, is very pathetic. This is so in spite of the fact that Bihar (Magadh Empire during 350BC-350AD in the northern India) was possibly the first place on this earth which founded the first known university at Pataliputra. The ruins of this great university can still be seen at Pataliputra, a little distance away from the present day Patna. Further, one of the best known treatise on administration and financial management was written by Vishnu Gupta/Kautilya/Chanakya who also hails from the province of Magadh, the present day Bihar. Why do societies, inspite of reaching the pinnacle of mental achievements, crash into oblivion? Why do societies that once practiced and nurtured an excellent education system turn upside down? Is this because of the famous saying that what ever goes up comes down and whatever comes down goes up? Is this what *Kala Chakra*, the wheel of time, all about? Today the nation is ruled more by misrule than by the rule of law. In fact it is not an exaggeration, if one concludes that this nation has never been governed since ages, but only ruled by different set of people. Does this provide us with the hope that we have no option but to go up as there is no way to go down further?

ii

The fundamental problem lies in the way the schools and the education system work. The present day schooling or the education system was introduced in India by the British rulers, the Christian missionaries and by people like Dayanand Saraswati. The princely states which were under the indirect British rule also set up schools for education of the boys and girls; rarely were there coeducation schools. These schools were located only in towns and cities, leaving the villages to the grace of God. Thus we have a long tradition of allowing people to be at the mercy of God. And God being a very kind entity, people succeeded in living and even today are still living. During the British time, the missionaries who founded the schools were successful in inculcating a value system that helped in building leaders who later on fought against the British rule and winning freedom for India. Possibly the British were honest enough to make sure that certain minimum standard was established in the schooling system and that the bright boys and girls were encouraged. Ramanujan, the mathematician, would have lived and died in some place in Tamil Nadu unnoticed and unrecognized, but for the interest and initiative shown by the British, both in recognizing him and in recommending him to Prof. Hardy.

Our education system, like all other systems, is suffering from archaic laws and regulations. Nusrut Jahan, a patient of leukemia and a student of Jewish Girls School, Kolkotta and studying in class IX had difficulties in going to class X even after securing about 63% marks. The reason for this was the insufficient attendance. This was possibly a valid reason as this is dictated by the book of rules. Rules are necessary for the smooth functioning/governance of schools. Should there not be a mechanism whereby the principal or the director of the institution can waive the book of rules and take a decision for the benefit of the students? What should be the main role of the school or the education system? Should it be to teach the three R's, reading and writing and arithmetic? Or should the aim of the schooling system be to enhance one's sense of self worth? The enhancement of one's sense of self worth is the truly liberating force that pulls people from a sense of despair and frustration. The tragedy is that the much-needed succor came only after her case evoked global sympathy. One of the most thoughtful responses was from Srinath Anekal from Jacksonville from USA. He wrote, "If a baby is born seven months into her mother's pregnancy, we do every thing humanly possible to make the child survive the interim period so that it can lead a full life. Therefore, just like we do not penalize a child for not spending nine months in her mother's womb, Nusrut should not be penalized for not meeting her attendance requirement". The response from Darshana from New York, USA is also interesting. She wrote, "I do think that the principal needs to reconsider her decision. Rules are great to have but common sense counts for a lot more. It is not a question of compassion but that of encouragement and positive example to all struggling students". Thus, the girl deserved to be promoted as she had more than satisfied the criteria required for passing. In the end she did get promoted. But the education system did succeed in causing hurt to the girl. Nobody, the education system or the student, gained anything from this delayed action. However, the student definitely went through immense psychological suffering with the principal holding on to the book of rule as though it was a God given commandment. Thus, the Education System failed to encourage the student who deserved to be encouraged. Of what use is such an education system or such principals or teachers who instead of recognizing merit and encouraging merit end up digging their heads into the book of rules or keep waving the book of rules? Nusrut Jahan died on the 24th of August 1998 in the Assembly of God Church Hospital. How wonderful it would have been if the educationists, education department and school authorities had willingly cooperated and accommodated her request for learning. Shame on the system, shame on the educationists and shame on the school authorities. May her soul rest in peace.

In the west, the children are encouraged to take subjects of the next class if they are found to be good at studies and are found to be capable of coping with the extra work load. Thus a student can jump ahead to go to higher classes. The schools are meant to be places where the capabilities are honed and encouraged. There will always be a few students who are more intelligent than the rest. The school must be capable of encouraging every one of the students. The school must also encourage those who are not good at studies. The schools must strive to inculcate a sense of self esteem and self worth in students. If this is not done then education system will be more damaging than any thing else and would result in inculcating wrong value system on the impressionable minds of the students.

The child psychology is such that the environment in the school leaves a lasting impression on the impressionable mind of the child. The child has a natural tendency to trust the teacher more than the parents. Therefore whatever is taught in the school and what ever is discussed in the school by the teacher influences the mind set and personality of the child. Equally important is the environment in the house, which also plays a major role in molding the character and value system of the child. Therefore there is an urgent need to reconsider our value system with reference to the status that is given to the community of teachers in primary and middle schools. It is recognized that the lot of the teachers has improved a lot from 1950s to 1990s. But a lot more is needed to be done in order to attract the best minds to the teaching profession without which the future of the society will be in the danger of coming into the grips of the persons with prejudiced minds. The prejudice is always due to the incorrect representation or record of history. The constitutional decree that education is a state subject is being utilized fully for changing of the books to suit the ideology of the party in power. This is true of History as a subject to be taught in the schools, what with the numerous invasions and desecration that have been carried out by the invaders. This is not true with subjects like Physics, Chemistry, Mathematics etc as one cannot build ideology on top of these subjects. Therefore there is an urgent need to prevent the breeding of jaundiced minds in the name of education.

iii

Education must create an ability to live in harmony with the nature, surroundings and fellow human beings without creating illusions of one's own importance or the importance of the section of the society to which one belongs. All superficial knowledge including the knowledge of scriptures would result in blurring the vision and therefore does not help the person to live harmoniously with nature. However the wisdom, which can be looked upon as knowledge without ego, provides one with an insight into living in harmony with the nature or the state of righteousness. Therefore there is an urgent need to reconsider the assumption about the way the primary and secondary school education is being imparted. The teachers in the schools must get better and more attractive remuneration so as to make them committed to the building of the personality of the children. More important than this is to attract and retain talent, and the persons with the right kind of attitude to teach in schools. Thus the teachers are in many ways more important than the college lecturers or professors, or for that matter even the bureaucrats. The feudalistic pattern of hierarchy has resulted in placing the teachers, who have a very prominent role to play in the building of a society, some where between the middle and bottom of the social ladder. This is causing more damage to the society than good. The governance of a society or state or nation is directly linked to the kind of responsive citizens that the society has. Therefore, from this point of view, the teachers have a greater role to play in solving the problems faced by any society. The ethos of a society is not something that is enshrined in the past making it a historical entity. The ethos of a society is always something that is current and living in the present. From this point of view, the present scenario that one sees in India is distressing. One of the main reasons that can be attributed to this sad state of affairs is the near absence of meaningful elementary education in primary and middle school. The character building takes place at these levels and not in the colleges. The value system imbibed at this early age will stand the test of time. Therefore there is an absolute urgency to attract talent and upright people to the teaching profession. The day this is done, the job of the police, judiciary and that of the bureaucrats would become simpler and quality of life in this country improves. Therefore repositioning of the teachers in the feudalistic hierarchy is absolutely necessary without which the Indian society will degenerate and will reach a level/state of irreversibility. The society should learn to give authority to the teaching community and also learn to respect the words and authority of the teachers.

Today, unfortunately, the voice of the teachers is neither heard nor respected. On the contrary, the voice of the shady and unscrupulous moving around in imported cars, with cellular phone in hand, is heard and respected. The consequence of this is there for every one to see. The answer is not just increasing the police force or increasing the administrative posts. The answer lies in changing the mindset of people. But changing the mindset of people is an extremely difficult task as the adults are conditioned animals. In the words of Radha Burnier, the President of Theosophical Society, people have difficulty in living in harmony with nature, surroundings, environment and neighbors because of the prejudices that are ingrained into their minds due to conditioning of mind from childhood. These prejudices relate to one's

(a) Status in society

(b) Riches

(c) Importance, real or imaginary

(d) Religious bigotry

The list is a long one. To begin with, the child has no prejudices. But as the child grows up, the environment in which the child grows up makes sure that the adult value system is imposed on the tender and unsuspecting mind of the child. When the child reaches adulthood, the transformation and therefore the damage are complete.

The value system practiced is such that those who have the urge to climb, on any thing and every thing, are looked upon as successful in life. These are the "Go Getters". They shall not stop till they get what ever they want. This process of incessant upward and onward movement is often referred to as 'Rat Race'. Unfortunately there is no place for nice guys in such a rat race. This has been echoed by an Indian and an American in different ways and under different circumstances. B. K. Nehru has chosen "Nice Guys Finish Second" as the title of his momentous autobiographical book. While the script writer of the film Godzilla makes a character tell his girl friend, a struggling biologist, "This is doggy doggy society. Here nice guys finish last". Thus, surprisingly, two persons with entirely different mental conditioning, living in two different continents with different cultural identities, with different value system have identical views.

The answer to this problem is, "Change the dismal state of the teachers". The money spent on this will be more than recovered. The reasoning is very similar to the one put forth by J. R. D. Tata when he appealed to the Government of India to spend generously on Family Planning Program and to treat the family planning project as a development project and not as a social function. But the Government of India always looked upon the expenditure on Family Planning

Program as a social welfare program resulting in a perennial shortage of funds with no meaningful goals to achieve. The same is true with the education. The trouble is that both the programs of Family Planning and Education are such that it becomes difficult to quantify the gains if certain expenditure is made on them. Thus the statistics bound experts in the Government have difficulty in writing lengthy notes/paragraphs on the green sheets, the noting sheets that are green in color, justifying or negating such projects. The result is that these projects are given annual grants that do not make any impact but satisfies every politician, that some thing great is being done for the country.

Sl. No.	Indicator	1950-1951	1960-1961	1970-1971	1980-1981	1990-1991
1.	Health and Family welfare	RMP per 10,000 population				
		1. 7	1. 9	2. 8	3. 9	4. 7
		Birth Rate Per thousand				
		39. 9	41. 7	36. 9	33. 9	29. 5
2.	Education and Literacy	Literacy Rate %				
Male		27. 16	40. 40	45. 95	56. 37	64. 1
Female		8. 86	15. 34	21. 97	29. 75	39. 3
Total		18. 33	28. 31	31. 45	43. 56	52. 2

Table 2. 2. 2   Indicators of Indian Economy

iv

India had been following the socialistic development model that was practiced in Russia, Hungary, Czechoslavakia, Yugoslavia etc as these were perceived to be people friendly economic models unlike the harsh capitalistic models of the west. But in India, unlike in these socialist countries, stress was not given to either education or family welfare. The selected indicators related to literacy, family welfare for the five year plans, starting from the first five year plan (1950-1955) to the eighth (1986-1991), provide very interesting insight into the plan process. These indicators have been taken from the book, "Indian Economy Update, Vol. 6", Ed. Raj Kapila and Uma Kapila, Pub.: Academic Foundation, New Delhi, 1997; Page 367. A summary of all the plans is given in the book "India 1991" Edited and Compiled by Research and Reference Division of Ministry of Information and Broadcasting, published by Publication Division in 1992. The objectives of the various plans are summarized in the Table 2. 2. 3.

From these tables it is clear that the planners gave importance to the distribution of wealth without giving much thought to the process of creating an environment that would demand change, progress, creation of wealth and distribution of wealth. Thus the entire planning process was initiated in the reverse order. This also helped in perpetuating the feudal system. Thus the rules and regulations, acts and laws, were never changed to reflect the aspirations of Free India. The restrictive practices, as practiced by the British rulers, were perpetuated. This did help those in power to get a feeling of being in power. The conditions in the nation did not change. Only the power changed hands. When this country was under the British rule, Indians were told about the things that were good for them. They had their loyal servants, the ICS otherwise called the brown sahibs, to support and ratify what ever they did or said.

Sl. No.	Plan	Objectives
1.	First Five Year Plan	(a) to correct the imbalances in economy caused by the 2nd
	1950-1955	world war and partition of the country (b) to initiate a process of all round development. Highest priority was given to agriculture and power projects. 44. 6% of the outlay (Rs. 23,780 million) was allocated for development of public sector.
2.	Second Five Year Plan	Special stress given to industrialization, iron and steel; heavy chemicals like fertilizers, heavy industries and machine building industry.
3.	Third Five Year Plan	(a) self sufficiency in food grains
		(b) expand industries like steel, chemicals, fuel and power, machine building plants
4.	Fourth Five Year Plan	The 1965 war and severe drought resulted in the delaying the start of the fourth plan. (In between came the East Pakistan/Bangladesh refugee problem and the 1971 war. This was the start of the plans going haywire.
		This also was the start of the interest in the Science of Futurology or the Science of Predicting the Events in the Future without taking recourse to planetary positions or parrots or tarot cards.)

Table 2. 2. 3   Objectives of Five Year Plans

After India got independence, the ritual was repeated. This time the politicians, the administrators and the planners who were supposed to be think tanks told the people what is good for them. The people were assumed to be ignorant and gullible and therefore had to be protected from the evil influences from outside. Thus, the only way to keep protecting the people was to keep them ignorant. The only way to keep the people ignorant was not to create facilities for spreading literacy whereby they could read, write and understand the wonderful way the nation was being administered.

The result of this meticulous planning process was

(a) The wealth was distributed even before it was created.

(b) A large population was allowed to remain illiterate to the extent that they have no understanding of their rights; much less how to exercise their rights. This is true even about the middle class who would rather let bygones be bygones.

(c) This helped maintain the feudalistic nature of the society that existed much before the The Britishers came to India, which was perpetuated by the The Britishers in their own interests.

   (i)   This process of preserving the feudalistic nature of the society was of great help for

   •   The administrators who could feel their enhanced status in the society

   •   The politicians who could project the concept of *thakur*, the village head who is very rich and the *mai baap*, benefactor (in reality, very cruel, calculating, manipulating and unscrupulous)

   •   This in turn helped the politician to create new unforeseen and not thought of vote banks.

   •   The vote banks were based on the plank of uplifting of illiterate masses: The issue should have been the eradication of illiteracy and make the people aware of their rights to demand justice rather than economically uplifting the illiterate masses.

   •   The vote banks on the basis of religion, caste and sub-caste: The British regime had successfully created the division on the basis of religion. The politicians fine tuned it. Local politics is all about caste and sub-caste.

   •   The preserving of these vote banks reinforced the need to keep the masses illiterate and foster the caste and subcaste divide. If the people become literate and start reading and writing, then a generation of leaders will loose influence and position.

- Thus the local leaders who are adept at handling the local issues that are essentially caste based end up mapping these thought processes on to the nation and become national leaders. It is this unfortunate mapping process from the local to the national level that has been the bane of this country. We have leaders whose vision for the country is nothing more than the vision of their village or constituency. We have only a handful of men and women who treat India as a constituency. The reason attributed to this state of poverty of thought is that the nation is said to be in the grip of a political churning.

Thus the overall situation is such that the preservation of the politicians at the local or the national level is the only important agenda and the essential requirement for this is the preservation of the vote banks. What appears to be happening is that the vote banks are getting split and reorganized under a different label and a different leader as part of the political churning. The common ingredient for all this so called churning action is the preservation of illiteracy and ignorance. Without these two all important ingredients, neither can the vote banks be stable nor can the leaders/politicians survive. Thus, often we hear of the people being ignorant and gullible, and therefore a genuine need to protect them. Take any scandal into account, one hears the standard explanation that the opposition is trying to mislead the people.

V

The best solution for uplifting of a society is to spread literacy so that people become aware of their rights and understand the way they are being taken for a long ride. Once this is achieved, the progress becomes automatic as the demand for change would come from the society or the intended beneficiaries themselves and not from the generosity of the leaders as this would be feudalistic and therefore is manipulative in nature. But no political party is interested in taking up this task of spreading literacy in right earnest as the political bosses know that the day the people become literate, the people also would understand the ways of the working of the politicians. The spread of basic education/literacy would also help in checking the pilfering of allocated development funds that result in the intended beneficiaries not getting any thing. Thus the spread of basic education/literacy and the future of the politicians are unfortunately linked in an inverse manner. Greater the spread of education bleaker will be the future of the politicians. The elbow space for the politicians to manipulate any thing and every thing is inversely proportional to the spread of education and awareness amongst the people. This does not in any way mean that the western society is a clean society with no blemish and no corruption. One finds corruption every where, in every society. The only difference is that in the developing societies, the level and extent of corruption eats into the well being of the people. The very basic and minimal requirements of the people for existence, let alone a dignified living, become out of reach of the people. Therefore the issue that needs to be addressed is not to cleanse the polity of corruption, which is an impossible task, but to ensure that the basic amenities are easily available to the people without any hassle and without having to go through any permit system.

Thus the most unfortunate thing that happened in this country was that the planning process for the improvement of the society/people started from the reverse side. This conclusion is definitely not a case of hind sight providing the answer to what went wrong. People like J. R. D. Tata had advocated that the government must look at family planning and basic education as a development activity and not as a social activity. Generous financial benefits were recommended to be given to all those who adopted family planning and a certain level of basic education. Their argument was that this would help in

(a) controlling the population which is essential for a fair distribution of wealth

(b) controlling the negative aspects of an uncontrolled population growth that would water down all the progress that might be achieved

(c) controlling crime and other illegal activities that are associated with uncontrolled population growth and absence of basic education

(d) improving the quality of life due to an increased level of basic education

(e) increase the success rate of the plans as a demand from the people will force the proper implementation

(f) the planned projects would be people driven rather than planners driven who have no knowledge about the ground reality.

The planners were bitten by the socialist bug. Unfortunately this made them see only the state owned steel plants, large mechanical industries, dams etc but not the stress that the socialistic countries gave to health, education and fitness. Thus our plans were neither communistic nor capitalistic in nature. The plans were socialistic in nature resulting in the accumulation of the ills of both the systems. The basic education was neglected. Further in the communist or capitalist societies the education had a result or goal oriented nature from the point of utility in real life. Compared to this our education system was not of any help to the students to cope with the demands of the industry. The curriculum is heavily loaded with every thing with the stress on memorizing rather than on understanding and applying the knowledge to solve practical problems. Since the education does not help the students to think independently, they find it difficult to find the bearings after coming out of schools and colleges. The result is that the government is burdened with the additional task of finding jobs for the innumerable people who come out of colleges with degrees in hand 'that have no relevance to ground reality.

Consider the British Education System. From the times of Isaac Newton to the times of Stephan Hawking, they have been able to maintain a very good standard of education. There is an opportunity for students, irrespective of their nationality, to complete courses well ahead of the normal schedule. The British society over the many centuries has been able to hold on to more or less the same standard of education. Thus, the structure or the system that does the identification and provides encouragement to the deserving people with merit has been nurtured over these long years and this in turn has paid handsome returns to the British society. The checks and balances that are in position have been very broad based and effective in providing avenues to the students who have shown extraordinary capabilities. This has been left untouched to a great extent by the political system that invariably corrupts any thing and every thing that it comes in contact with. This possibly reflects the integrity of the people in charge of education system who have shown their inability to bend. One of the reasons for this may be the low population and therefore less pressure on the system. The other reason is that the very framework of the education system is so framed as not to stipulate the qualification of graduate or a postgraduate for any and every job.

vi

Many of the ills in India, including the pathetic state of the education system, can be traced to the increasing population. Had the spread of education been looked upon as a development project, the number of educational institutes would have increased resulting in an education system supporting the increased demand on it. The absence of such an allocation on education has become the root cause of the problem of non-governance. Therefore, today we seem to have consoled our mind into believing that the root cause of our misery or problems is over population. This is a case of barking up the wrong tree. If education had been made as a part of development project, then there would not have been a population explosion. Thus the root cause of the ills of the nation is not population explosion but sub-minimal expenditure on basic education. Further there have been many committees that were set up to look into the matter of revamping the education system. Every time the work load and the subjects taught in the primary, middle and high schools were increased, one definite thing that happened was the students getting a stoop on account of carrying those heavy books. The work load during the initial days of the child in the school must never be heavy. The child must be allowed to grow at his/her own pace and the syllabus must be increased slowly. The child must be made to understand the environment in which the child is living. Today the stress is on covering everything in the class with less or no stress on making the child understand the usage of the knowledge being imparted in day to day life. The child may be capable of grasping every thing and repro-ducing in the examination hall. This cannot become an excuse for burdening the child. After all the childhood is the best part of one's life and care must be taken to make sure that the child does not become neurotic or end up becom-ing a case of stunted growth. On the other hand the syllabus at the college level, after the mandatory 10+2, must be made extensive to provide an in depth knowledge in any chosen, specific subject. The syllabus must be aimed at producing students with requisite skills to take on the real world challenges in science, technology, research & development from the beginning.

It would be advisable to make 12th grade as the compulsory basic education level. This would mean that if one is interested in pursuing a career of a Secretary, then one need not have to finish B. A or B. Sc and then apply for a job of a Secretary. After completing 12th grade, one can join course for a year that trains one to become an efficient secretary. Today, we have secretaries who are graduates or postgraduates who neither know how to handle the files, nor know typing or shorthand, nor know how to make atom bombs. Houses are built and we have difficulty in getting a good plumber or an electrician even though we are made to pay through the nose for the man power that we get. The plumbers and masons do not understand levels. If one is interested in Law, why study literature? Why not study Law after 10+2 instead of studying B. A and then study for Law? We have created a perfect mess and claim to have the largest scientific man-power. A person who is interested in getting a job in a bank need not have to be a graduate in Arts or Science.

The other basic problem of Indian education is that the education till 12th is unfortunately driven by the needs of higher education. That is the courses are loaded with mathematics, physics, chemistry and biology. Thus, the aim of the education is to ensure that every one is driven to become either a scientist or an engineer or a doctor or a chartered accountant. There is a need to provide a mechanism for the children to get educated and yet not get into the hassle of going through the mathematics, physics, chemistry and other courses. We have a system that prescribes that the child must have the knowledge of mathematics, physics, chemistry and biology as the basic requirement to be recognized as an educated child. There is a need to come out of this mind set and recognize that a child can opt for other branches of learning and still be recognized as an educated child. This is sadly missing in our system and the educationists have let the children down in an effort to pursue their own intellectual dreams.

There is nothing new about this kind of reorganization of the education system. Many experts and educationists have advocated a reorganization of the system and giving more thrust to the practical aspects of each discipline. The many proposals for reorganization refer to the deepening of knowledge in any given area rather than creating a situation where the student ends up spreading thin ending up neither here nor there. The student ends up knowing a little bit, which is more on the jargon level, of every thing that helps neither the student nor the employee. Thus, our education system has resulted in creating people who have half baked theoretical knowledge and no practical knowledge. Further, in view of the lack of practical knowledge, they lack the confidence for starting their own enterprise. Therefore, it is humanly impossible for the society to sustain the large population of graduates and postgraduates who have been trained in arts, science, engineering, medicine and provide them with jobs. The entry into colleges for graduation or post graduation must be only for those who are interested in acquiring more knowledge and not for earning a livelihood. This would mean that there shall be no age bar or limit for getting admission into a college. The age limit that is exercised in the present system is not fair as there are a fairly large number of persons in their late thirties and forties who have a natural urge for studying, researching and acquiring knowledge. The present system unfortunately shuts the door on the faces of all persons using age as a single criterion without bothering to recognize the capabilities of individuals. This is the difference between our education system and the American education system.

However, this unemployment amongst the educated has become a convenient issue for the political parties as this keeps cropping up every time there is an election. The issues of eradication of poverty and providing employment to the ever increasing masses of graduates and postgraduates appear in every political manifesto. However, no political party has the political will to address the key issues of population control and reforming the education system. In the past a few committees/commissions on education reforms have been set up. These commissions did a lot of study and made a number of suggestions for revamping the education system. Unfortunately, like all other good things, their reports have been received and preserved to gather dust. The last report was from Prof. Yashpal. Every one has suggested that the education in the colleges must be more practical oriented. Many have wondered at the futility of asking a graduate in science to do the job of a secretary. The reason for the lack of political will to discuss the issue of education reform is that it disturbs the vote banks and therefore the equilibrium with in the society. Any attempt to educate people would prove counter productive as far as the politicians are concerned. The reason is that the person who has been taught to think will not just think but also asks uncomfortable questions. This creates problems. Therefore, it has always been the unwritten principle followed by the political parties to keep education out of the development activity. The argument is that the people need food, clothing and shelter and not education. This is very similar to the famous slogan *"Roti, Kapada aur Makan"*, "food, clothing and shelter"

vii

The case of Kerala youth makes an interesting and illuminating evidence of the apathy of the administration towards problems facing the nation. It is well known that Kerala, a southern state in India, has achieved 100% literacy, *saksharata*. *Saksharata*, literacy, is in the area of reading and writing so that even the lowest of the low will not put his/her thumb print on a paper that contains clauses that are not in the interests of the individual. This is commendable and is a sure way of overcoming the damages that the middle men have the ability to inflict on a society. This is one end of the ladder of literacy, if one may use such a terminology. When one looks at the other end of the ladder of literacy, the view one gets becomes depressing. The view that one gets is depressing because of the fact that there are many educated youth, graduates and post-graduates, in Kerala who are working as bus conductors. There is nothing demeaning or degrading to work as bus conductors. The question is "Should one be a graduate or post-graduate to become a bus conductor?"

There is nothing wrong in a bus conductor being interested in the works of Bernard Shaw or Shakespeare or Milton or Charles Lamb or Lord Byron or Wordsworth or Goethe or Sophocles or Valmiki or Kalidasa or Bana or Vyasa or for that matter the works of any literary figure. In fact this is commendable and deserves appreciation that the bus conductor has such a highly developed taste and faculty. But it would be unfortunate and frustrating for a person to be asked to possess a degree certificate to work as a bus conductor. The difference between the two is that in one case the graduation or post-graduation becomes the necessary qualification to become a bus conductor because this is the only way of filtering the innumerable applications that the state receives for the position of the bus conductor. In the other case, the bus conductor develops an interest in literature or any other subject and pursues the study of the subject of his/her interest. In this case, there must be no limit or bar on the age for studies and as a corollary, there should be no limit or bar on the age of the applicant for a job. That is, when ever a person feels inclined to pursue studies there must be avenues for doing so with out having to face age bar restrictions. The open universities have addressed the issue of age bar by offering distant education programs. However, a lot more needs to be done in the area of content of education with special reference to relating the job requirement with education qualification.

Therefore, the general level of education must stop at 10+2 level. Even at this level, certain level of general grounding in biology, botany, chemistry, physics, mathematics, computer science, commerce, economics, literature, management etc can be given to facilitate the student to pursue the growth path based on his/her interests. There must be an option for a student to pursue a career in any other area other than the science & commerce. Therefore the education up to the level of 12th must be of two streams,

(a) one the general stream where the student can pursue any other field other than the science, engineering, medicine, commerce, economics, sociology etc with more stress on vocational disciplines

(b) other, which is the conventional stream with stress on science and commerce aimed at helping those students who are interested in becoming scientists, engineers, doctors, economists, chartered accountants etc.

This must be followed by the redefinition of the qualification requirement for the run of the mill jobs. The job requirement can be met with the basic 10+2 supplemented by one or two year diploma in the particular area. The advantage of this is that this reduces the enormous pressure that is getting developed on the education system that is making more and more children neurotic and are becoming victims of speech and other mental problems. The fear of failure to qualify and therefore to get a decent job appears to be creating a generation with mental problems. This is augmented by the parental and peer pressure. The end result is that we are, knowingly, becoming responsible and party to the child loosing the childhood, which is the best part of one's life. In return the parents are also becoming neurotic because the child's failure will make a lot of difference in the kitty party or office. The mother will have a major problem in executing a master stroke in the kitty parties and the father has problems in the office answering queries about the child's future. Thus, the urban society is fast becoming a society that is mentally sick and neurotic. To add to the problem we have special reservations for every body except those with merit. We have reservations for backward classes, other backward classes, scheduled castes and tribes and women. This has resulted in a situation that is going to pave the way for a grand catastrophe.

viii

The issue is not whether reservation should be there or not. There is no dispute in the assessment of the sociologists that the reservation is the only mechanism for emancipation of the section of society that had been left out of the main stream for long years. But the problem is not going to get solved by introducing reservation in every sphere starting from admissions to colleges, jobs and promotions. Reservations at the admission level help the students to get into the main stream. But diluting the standards to a level where the product that comes out of the institution would become so bad that the very concept of reservation would help neither the candidate nor the organization/society. Providing a job or giving a running promotion does not in any way help the person to contribute to the society. It is necessary that the candidate be made to realize that the process of competing with others and improving one's knowledge and skills is as important as reservation at the first level.

Thus, generations have been reduced to a state of dependence on jobs created by the state and this state is not economically sustainable. The jobs so created are ineffective in creating any meaningful wealth and therefore the government is always starved of funds to keep supporting this program. Even though this program has always been found to be ineffective in improving the living conditions of the people, the program has always benefited the politicians both in terms of creating and retaining vote banks. We have a strange state where the distribution of wealth is given prime importance and not the creation of wealth. We have no concept of creation of wealth as we expect the government to provide for all our aspirations. But we always expect the government to have all the resources under the sun, moon and the other planets to take care of every thing. The need to educate the people on matters of governance is not felt because of the large population of believers who believe that the good things of life come free. It is hard to realize that "Lunch cannot be free". This thought is limited to the literate masses that have been pampered due to their proximity to the center of power and due to their organized ways of holding the nation to ransom. It would be unfair to assume that the illiterate masses want a free lunch. The illiterate masses are any way living below the poverty line and therefore do not get a decent meal a day to eat.

On the contrary, it is the organized literate masses of the urban India that are cornering the major share of the cake and they are the ones who are getting almost every thing at subsidized rates, if not free. It is this state that encourages mass migration of people from rural to metropolis. The tragedy is compounded by the incapability of our administrators to realize the need for large number of metropolitan centers and plan for the same. The result is that the few mega-metropolitan centers have reached a state where they can no more support the burgeoning population. Thus, we have a perfect setting for crime to take an upper hand with the police being caught between the underworld and the politicians. Many a time, one hears that the conditions were far better during the British days. Was this because the population was not as large as it is now? Was it because the administration was run by a handful of British officers assisted by a set of hand picked Indians whose integrity was unquestioned? Was it because the mechanism of balancing between different groups and sub-groups that has become a part of democratic structure did not exist and therefore the basis of all appointments was merit and integrity alone? The answer to this dichotomy is that we have successfully consoled our minds into believing that that the best way to liberate the poor is to elevate a person from that class, caste or community to a higher position irrespective of whether he/she deserves the position or not.

To add to this sad state, the President of India in his Republic day address to the nation appealed to the private sector to reserve posts for the scheduled caste and tribes. What is conveniently forgotten is that the private sector is the only hope for India to be able to stand up to the western competition. The industries and other enterprises in public sector, state sector and the joint sector are being sold. Therefore the extension of the reservation policy to the private sector in the name of social justice is a sure way to spread sickness. This is very similar to distributing wealth without creating it in the first place. Further, there is enough evidence for those who are willing to see that whenever same facilities are given to the children belonging to deprived classes and those who are fortunate enough to enjoy the privileges the performance of the children has been the same. The need is to encourage merit irrespective of the religion, caste, region or community. Further, in many cases, one has seen that the children belonging to the deprived classes have out performed even those from the privileged sections of the society. Therefore, it is necessary that the leaders come to terms with the reality and stop demeaning the children by branding them as belonging to the scheduled caste and tribes. On the other hand, the leaders must ensure and fight for similar facilities to the children of the deprived classes. It is recognized that the children of the deprived classes may not be able to speak English at all or may not be able to converse in the same way as those children who are born with privileges. But then, if the same conditions are provided to the children from the nursery class, then there is a fair chance that one finds not much variation in the performance in the different children. This does not mean that all the children will score high marks. For that matter, even the children born to privileges do not score high marks. One does find laggards even amongst the privileged children. Therefore, the need of the hour is to stop consoling our minds into believing that reservation is the solution to the problem. The solution lies in providing equal opportunities to all the children at the nursery level, and allow the children to get into a competitive spirit. The need of the hour is not to label the children as belonging to a particular caste or creed. The need is to help them to inculcate a sense of self worth, which is sadly missing in our education system.

3

Secularism

Man has committed more number of crimes and injustice in the name of religion than in the name of anything else. During the 9th to 11th century came the marauding and rampaging and fanatical tribal chiefs on horse back from central Asia who went about the business of killing and plundering and leaving a permanent scar on the Indian psyche with utmost precision. On the other side of the ocean came the Spanish invaders who discovered the continent of Americas and went about destroying the two great and rich civilizations of Aztecs in Mexico and the Incas of Peru. Both the fanatical riders on the horse back and the Spanish invaders in ships took away the gold and silver to become an affluent society and therefore a civilized society. Then came the infamous Adolph Hitler who claimed to have found an ultimate solution to all problems by exterminating the Jewish community. Around this time, there was the wide spread practice of slavery of the black men and women bought from Africa on the cotton fields of America. The end of this slavery and the unification of America required a war to be fought by a man of the stature of Abraham Lincoln. The imperialism practiced in Europe resulted in the division of Africa amongst the powers in Europe. A strange way of subjugating the week societies for the sole purpose of ensuring the well being of the strong ones. There have been cases of a number of tribal wars waged in Africa with the sole purpose of establishing the supremacy of one tribe over the other. In the process of this many innocent men, women and children have been put to death. Then came Pol Pot who put millions of Cambodians to death for opposing his utopian ideas. The generals in Pakistan found a different kind of a solution by evicting more than ten million people belonging to minority communities from East Pakistan that ultimately resulted in the birth of Bangladesh. The government in Pakistan perfected the process of ethnic cleansing by bringing in mercenaries into Kashmir in the name of Jihad and drove tens of thousands of Hindus from the Kashmir Valley. They called it freedom struggle giving the honor of the greatest freedom fighter to Adolph Hitler. In the Balkans, Milosevich also practiced ethnic cleansing by putting to death thousands of Muslims. In the beginning of the 21st Century Osama bin Laden set up the Al Quida network and declared jihad against United States of America by destroying the World Trade Center. Jihad has also been declared against Israel and India indicating very clearly that only Islam has the right to prevail on the earth and nothing else. This definitely cannot be a part of any kind of revelation.

In all these cases, many innocent men, women and children belonging to one tribe or one religion or one school of thought were systematically put to death. This often gets the sanction or the blessings of being an ultimate solution to all problems faced by the society. But even after this, the problems continue and the search for a new solution goes on. The framework of World Trade Organization, WTO, is no different. It stipulates the member countries to open their markets to the developed countries for all commodities including agricultural, diary, poultry and fisheries products. The impending unmitigated disaster to the ethos and concept of community living on this earth is clearly written on the wall for all those who are willing to see and observe. This disaster becomes acceptable as this is in the interests of the developed and powerful countries. In contrast, the thought of Kautilya, Vishnu Gupta, who wrote the first treatise on economics, taxation and governance, is worth noting. He decrees, "In territories acquired by him (king), the conqueror shall continue the practice of all customs which are in accordance with *dharma*, and shall introduce those which had not been observed before. Likewise, he shall stop the practice of any custom not in accordance with *dharma* and shall also refrain from introducing them".

There is another form of distortion of facts or misinformation that is often attempted by dictators for the purpose of giving the people a sense of pride. With this comes the perception for the need to reform the nonbelievers. Both the sense of pride and the need to reform the nonbelievers are exercises in controlled violence. This becomes a case of controlled violence because the violence is directed towards the nonbelievers only. The subject of non-belief may be religious or ideological in nature. Further, the sense of pride in their beliefs and the need to reform others provide an undying anchor to the believers. Thus, the believers become zealots who take upon themselves the task of setting the aberrations of life right. These aberrations of life are attributed to the imperfect state of the belief that the non-believers had adopted. This becomes the basis of the activity that is aimed at liberating the other people who entertain a different set of beliefs or ideology. All through this activity of liberating others, the underlying assumption that has become the driving force is the irrational assumption of perfection of one's own state. This process of liberating others invariably takes recourse to the cleansing process. In the history of mankind this kind of liberation or cleansing has been seen many times resulting in elimination of local prevailing cultures and implanting of new cultures through violent methods. One can see the evidence of this on the lands of Mesopotamia, Mexico, Peru, Hawaii, North Americas, Korea. The list is never ending. In some cases, the cleansing process had been initiated within the society without an external intervention or cause. The examples of this are Adolph Hitler, Pol Pot of Cambodia, etc.

ii

The case of the Vikings of Norway is very interesting. In an article "The Amazing Vikings" published in the Time magazine of 22nd May 2000, Micheal Lemonick and Andrea Dorfman present new evidences that have emerged from the archeological excavations in Europe, Canada, Greenland and Iceland. The popular belief about the Vikings is that they were brutal with a great reputation to kill, destroy and plunder. They were believed to be nothing less than barbarians. But the reality appears to be far different from this popular folklore. All Vikings were Norse but all Norse were not Vikings. The word Viking refers only to those Norse who went on raids. It has now been found that they were explorers who reached North Americas nearly 500 years earlier than the Spanish explorer Columbus. They founded the oldest surviving parliament much before Britain changed from feudalism to democracy. They were master craftsmen and had created exquisite designs in gold, silver and bronze. Further they had trade links with countries as far away as Rome, Baghdad, the Caspian Sea, Africa etc. The historians and experts knew this for decades but for reasons best known to the experts these facts about the Vikings were never acknowledged. One reason for not acknowledging the finer aspects of Vikings must have been the unwillingness of historians in Oxford and Cambridge who were the only ones to write history or make history to acknowledge that Britain was after all not the mother of Parliamentary Democracy! They were not willing to show or depict Britain in a less exalted state, a classic case of Imperialism. In fact, Britain was in a state of abject feudalism when Scandinavia, under Vikings, was a flourishing democracy. Thus around 8th to 16th Centuries, there was a society in Europe that was far more developed both in skills and in governance that the other societies like the British and the Spanish societies. These were backward, feudalistic and underdeveloped. The

Nordic society embraced Christianity only around 10th century and therefore in all their activities involving the attack or plunder of other societies the spread of religion was not the driving force. The spread of religion as the driving force to conquer other societies started much later and had its roots in Spain.

In India, there have been many liberating processes that have taken place without imposing any religious norms on the people, which is unique only to India. The mighty kings who conquered other kingdoms declared that their new religion, Buddhism or Jainism, to be the state religion. This was an example of the state supporting the spread of the religion of the king in both the eastern and western world. The one great difference between the support given by the king/queen for the spread of the religion in India and elsewhere is that in the west coercion/violent methods were used while in India the option was left to the people. In Europe, crusades were launched for spreading Christianity and Islam causing widespread suffering and death for the non-believers. The people had either to fall in line with the wave or be put to stake and killed. On the other hand in India the king provided funds for the spread of religion and for the setting up of religious institutions. However, the scenario changed with the invasion from central Asia and Persia that left a permanent scar on the Indian psyche. In the south, the activities of the zealous Portuguese missionaries who indulged in the same kind of activities like putting nonbelievers to stake as was done in Europe during the times of Crusades created more problems not only for the Christians but also to the people of other communities.

The spread of Buddhism, Jainism, Advaita and Dvaita philosophies in India present very interesting case studies in human behavior and the relationship between the king and the religion. These case studies throw light on the Hindu psyche that prevailed during that time. The spread of Buddhism was a phenomenal success and Buddhism became the religion of India. It must be remembered that there never existed a political entity called India during those times. In spite of this, the spread of Buddhism across the Indian land mass was through peaceful process of debates, *tarka*, and not through violent methods involving the use of the sword or putting people to stake. In the same way, when Adi Sankara propounded the Advaita philosophy and traveled all over India on foot, from Kerala to Badrinath, Varanasi, Puri and Kanchi engaging in discourses and debates, many of the people who had embraced Buddhism came back to Hinduism. In both the cases there was neither violence nor the lure of economic betterment. Thus these cases of the spread of philosophies/religions in India were unlike those that were witnessed in Europe or China or far east or Americas, where local prevalent ethnic cultures were wiped out by the new settlers or kings through the use of violent methods. The spread of the message of Mahavir or Ramanuja in India also followed the same peaceful process. In all these cases coercive or violent methods were never used for spreading the philosophies. This was true even in those cases where the king adopted one of the religions or philosophies as the state religion or philosophy.

Adi Sankara established the supremacy of the Advaita philosophy in India. Possibly he was and is the first person to walk around the length and breadth of any country to spread a philosophy without resorting to coercion and brute force of the sword. He established, in the words of Swami Chinmayananda, the unassailable strength of the Hindu philosophy and the unquestionable superiority of the rich Indian heritage. Jainism, which is one of the three Indian philosophies that do not accept the supremacy of Vedas, was founded in the period of 599 BC to 527 BC. Mahavira is looked upon by the followers of Jainism as one of the archetects of the Jain philosophy. The other two Indian philosophies that did not accept the supremacy of Vedas were Charvaka and Buddhist philosophies. Jainism was (and even now is) practiced by a fairly large population in addition to being adopted as the state religion in south of India in the same way as Buddhism was adopted as the state religion in the north of India. Thus, the Indian society is possibly the only society in the world that had different religions and philosophies coexisting for over 2,000 years. In addition to this, India gave shelter and a place to flourish to many refugees who fled from the country of their origin trying to escape from the tyranny of the invaders. These people who fled their motherland and sought refuge in India are the people practicing Zoroastrian Religion and the Tibetans practicing Buddhism. The people of Zoroastrian faith fled their ancestral home in Persia in the face of the invasion by the Arab tribesmen who had become Muslims. No wonder that the French scholar, Romaine Rolland, has said that if there is one place on the face of earth where all dreams of living men have found a home from the earliest days when man began the dream of existence, it is India.

The name Persia, the present day Iran, is derived from the name of the place Parsa of which Cyrus the Great was the Lord. Some of these people fled their homeland to escape from the Arab tribes, who had been converted to Islam, on the horseback with a sword in the hand who invaded Persia that is often referred to as the Gateway to India. Mohammed the Prophet in the 7 AD had founded a new religion known as Islam and the Arab tribes were converted to Islam. These Arab tribesmen were united into political group and had invaded many parts of western Asia and eastern Asia, Europe and Africa. This also resulted in the spread of Islam. The people of Zoroastrian faith who took refuge in India are the well known Parsi (derived from Parsa, a place in Persia) community who have created wealth for the country.

Some of the Church historians, like Holger Kersten and Dr. Elma R. Gruber the authors of "The Jesus Conspiracy" and "Jesus Lived In India", have recorded that Jesus Christ lived in India for a period extending from his childhood to his appearance in Palestine. These years that he spent in India refer to the missing years that have not been documented for reasons unknown. These Church historians have also opined that Jesus Christ came to India along with some of his followers including St. Thomas who was one of his chief apostles. They also have documented that Jesus Christ lived in Kashmir where he was martyred. The interesting point here is not about whether Jesus spent his last days in India or not because this is controversial and therefore very explosive in nature with far reaching consequences and repercussions. The point of interest is that there are two theories that are going the rounds about the advent of St. Thomas Christians and the visit of St. Thomas to Kerala. One set of church historians opine that St. Thomas along with Jesus Christ arrived in Kashmir. Jesus Christ along with a few faithful followers decides to stay on in Kashmir. St. Thomas decides to take the land route and travels down to south preaching the message of Jesus Christ. Another set of church historians like Dr. Susan Viswanathan who is the author of "The Christians of Kerala", and Father A. Philip, Bishop Vincent M. Concessao opine that St. Thomas arrived at the port of Kodungallor in AD 52 and set up seven spiritual communities. He visited many other kingdoms and returned to Mylapore in Chennai in AD 72 where he was martyred. Further the museum at Taxila, near Islamabad in Pakistan, records that St. Thomas visited the Parthian King Gondopheres in AD 40. The fascinating part of this episode is that Christianity came to India much before it went to Europe or USA or for that matter even Rome. This means that St. Thomas succeeded in spreading the message of Jesus Christ and could convert a fairly large number of people in present day Kerala to Christianity. These Christians are known as St. Thomas Christians and have been living together with the other communities in peace and harmony for nearly 2000 years. All this was achieved without any violence either in favor or in opposition to his teachings. This is in stark contrast with what happened in Europe and the role of the church, which resulted in the period being called Dark Age. The Buddhists, Hindus, Jains, Christians, Jews and Armenians (the last two took shelter in India unable to withstand the atrocities of the Roman Empire) have been living in peace and harmony for about 2000 years. The mosques were built in south of India in 750 AD to facilitate the Muslim traders from the Arabia. Thus, India has been the place where people of different religious beliefs have been living together in peace and harmony for hundreds of years till the advent of the Secular Politicians.

What is more fascinating than this is the fact that St. Thomas Christians have been the victims of divisions inspired by the Anglo Saxon missionaries inspite of their singing of the hymn

> Lord bind us together
> In bonds that cannot be broken

These St. Thomas Christians have a heritage of about 2,000 years and therefore can be looked upon as one of the first Christians in the world and definitely as the first Christians outside of Bethlehem or Israel or Palestine. The Portuguese traveler, Vasco da Gama has recorded that when he landed at Calicut in Kerala, he was greeted by people who claimed to be practicing Christianity for about thousand five hundred years. This would certainly mean that during that period, about 2,000 years ago, there were essentially five religions that were coexisting and being practiced in India, viz., Hinduism, Buddhism, Jainism, Judaism and Christianity. Further, historians have recorded that there existed a maritime link between the Chola Kingdom (the present day Tamil Nadu) and the Roman Empire and the middle east. This maritime culture of the Cholas was responsible for the establishing of trade connection between the Chola kingdom in south of India and the Roman Empire and the Middle East countries. This resulted in the visits of a few Muslim traders to southern India either for direct trade with the traders in the kingdom or on their way to far-east or on their return from far-east. These visits and the settling down of some of the Muslim merchants in Gujarat and Malabar (Kerala) led to the building of the Muslim places of worship to facilitate the Muslim traders offer prayers.

Thus the building of mosques in these areas was done with the willing approval of the local rulers and was not as a consequence of invasion and the destruction of temples as was to be the case in the northern part of India. Thus, the mosques came into existence in the southern part of India earlier than in northern part of India. The mosques in north of India were due to the invasion from Central Asia, Persia and Afghanistan. Thus, it may be said that the Hindus, Jains, Jews, Christians, Buddhists and Muslims lived in harmony for over a thousand years. Further, in addition to the Arab Muslims who settled in some parts of the southern India, people of Armenian origin also made southern part of India as their home land escaping the oppressive regime in Rome. It needs to be qualified that the Buddhist influence that existed in India got diluted and possibly wiped out due to the advent of Adi Sankara in 8 AD. Sankara propounded the Advaita philosophy and went round India on foot giving discourses on Advaita philosophy and taking part in debates on philosophy. The word philosophy is derived from two Greek words meaning "love of wisdom". The Muslims in Kerala and Gujarat became one with the local population and started speaking local language and adopting local tradition. They did not try to preserve their identity or preserve their Arab roots by continuing to speak in Farsi or Urdu. Till recently the Muslims in Kerala and Tamil Nadu felt at home speaking in the local languages. But today, the scene is slowly changing due to the advent of Secular Politicians. Walls are getting erected between communities in the name of secularism and at the instance of politicians who have found secularism a good weapon to beat and swindle the society. Secularism has become a useful tool to get the votes and divide the votes. In both the cases, the winner is the politician and the losers are the society and the nation. But then who cares? If this is not a case of consolation of mind, what else can be?

Around the middle of the 20th century, the communist regime of China annexed Tibet for security reasons. The security in question was not of Tibet or people of Tibet but of the Chinese. The Tibetans fled from their ancestral home of Tibet to escape from the communist regime of China. Thus, India had been able to absorb people with different cultural background and of many religious thoughts and coexist in a peaceful manner providing freedom to every one to practice his own faith. The main reason for making this happen or possible in India is that Hinduism is not a religion in the same sense as other religions. Dr. Sarvapalli Radhakrishnan in his book "A Hindu view of life" provides a detailed explanation as to why Hinduism is not a religion but a way of life. It is this freedom and broad based ethos that makes Hinduism a tolerant entity that can adapt to changing times.

The European society did not have this kind of broad cultural values because of the strong influence of the Church on science, literature, statecraft etc and also because of the out going and aggressive out look of life which believed in dominating and subjugating other societies and cultures. The era of Renaissance in Europe is often referred to as a case of coming out of darkness. Every body refers to Africa as a dark continent. It appears that the darkness in Europe was far more oppressive than the darkness of the Dark Continent, Africa. The darkness in Europe was because of the Church and lasted from about 476 AD to 11th Century. During this period a new form of governance called Feudalism came into existence in Europe. Soon after this period the Christian Crusaders launched a series of religious wars against Muslims from 11th to 14th century to regain control over the Holy Land, particularly Jerusalem. There was a time, not long ago, when the then Shah of Iran, later deposed and now dead, who was a great friend of America and especially Dr. Henry Kissinger, said, "The westerners must remember that we had a great civilization here when they were learning to climb the trees". In all fairness to the late Shah of Iran, one must acknowledge that he spoke the truth and nothing but the truth, even though the westerners tend to believe that the civilization was founded in the west. The television serial by British Broadcasting Corporation on the History of Civilization, which covers only the west, is a clear indication of this.

The Renaissance movement was responsible for the European society becoming secular. The word secular meant a separation between the church and the statecraft. Thus, the civilized societies in Europe got into a state where the church/religion and the statecraft got separated only in the last few hundred years even though time and again the intermingling of religion and statecraft can be seen in the history. On the contrary the state in India was far more refined and developed than that represented by the word secular which in the European frame work meant separation of statecraft and religion. Therefore, it is unfortunate that the word secular was borrowed and introduced in the Preamble to the Indian Constitution.

The word secular is, unfortunately, alien to the Indian society. Even during those times when the kings and therefore the state adopted a particular religion as the state religion as in the case of Buddhism, Jainism and Islam, the people did have the freedom to practice the religion of their choice. If this were not so, the many invasions that this country had faced and the rule by kings who practiced a religion other than Hinduism would have resulted in the Hinduism as a religion and as a way of life being reduced to a minority state or would have been wiped out. This did not mean that there were no forcible conversions to other religions. The state of the St. Thomas Christians is attributed to the coercion tactics of the missionaries of British and Portuguese origin. The problem with the St. Thomas Christians was possibly that they had become indegenized and had adapted themselves to the Indian way of thinking and living while practicing the teachings of Jesus Christ. This became incomprehensible to the missionaries of Europe who were influenced by the concepts of crusades against other religions. Thus the over zealous Christian missionaries representing the Queen, the head of Protestant Church and the Portuguese missionaries representing the Catholic Church had difficulty in accepting these St. Thomas Christians of more than one thousand five hundred years of standing as fellow Christians. The St. Thomas Christians were one of the oldest living Christians, older than the European or British Christians. Further, the Jewish Aramaic speaking communities were present in Kerala since the first century AD corroborates the writings of Holger Kersten and Dr. Elma R. Gruber, the authors of "Jesus Conspiracy" and "Jesus lived in India". However with hind sight one can say that the word "secular" that was introduced in the Indian constitution will take care of the mess that is created by the secular politicians. They had the vision to foresee that men of straw would fall back on setting one religion against the other with the sole intention of capturing power to rule the society/nation and not govern the society/nation. But they might not have visualized the possibility of creation of a deeper damage on the psyche of the people by these men of straw in the name of secularism.

iii

The History of any society makes interesting reading. The historical records clearly indicate that till as recently as the end of 2nd world war, the people of Europe had no religious tolerance or for that matter any tolerance at all for any thing other than their ownselves. The political evolution of Europe was violent. The European history comprises of the activities of wild Huns, the Goths, the Vandals, the Romans, the Vikings, the attack of Mongols on Byzantine Empire and the Turks in addition to the great advances in fine arts like painting, music, literature and science. It also includes the dark ages leading to Renaissance, the religious wars between Christians and Muslims, the colonization and subjugation of other people for their own good and well being. The modern history possibly begins with the invention of the guillotine in France, the mass upheaval in Russia killing the Czar and his family and the arrival on the scene of the concept of the supremacy of one race over the rest of the world leading to a global war. This does not negate the cultural heritage of Europe in the form of Goethe, Socrates, Aristotle, Leonard da Vinci, Vincent van Gough, Beethoven, Morzat, Bach, Paganini, Galileo Galilee, Copernicus, Schubert, Wagner, etc. The Ancient Greek heritage can be looked upon as the founder of the modern democratic principles such as the government of the people, trial by the jury and equality under law. In addition to this, they also discovered the annual monsoon winds in the Indian ocean which helped every other European country to reach India and then rule India for a long time. The list of great cultural achievements is indeed a very long one. The details of the sea borne trade are described by an unknown sailor or merchant of Alexandria, Egypt in a book called *Periplus of the Erythraean Sea*. According to this book a sailor named Hippalos made the first trading voyage to India. Welcome to India.

Europe has also been a witness to some of the organized upheavals that are possibly responsible for the kind of discipline that one sees in the European society. In most of the cases the changes that have been brought about in European society have been a consequence of the demand for a change that has been projected by the people and not the rulers. Thus, the rules and regulations that one sees in the European countries are citizen friendly and the administration is transparent. At the same time they are security conscious. That is, the open system or environment that one sees in Europe does not in any way mean that it is so open that any one can walk in. The environment in Europe, in spite of being a witness to two world wars and organized revolutions in France and Russia, does not treat every citizen as a suspect. The one main reason for this state is that the mass upheavals that were witnessed in Europe resulted in translating the wish, desire and dreams of the people into laws. The laws and regulations were not handed down to the people by a handful of influential persons as normally happens in a feudalistic society. Thus even the prisoners in these societies have rights that are respected by the law-enforcing agency which is unthinkable in a feudalistic society. In fact the criminals know their rights and demand compliance from the law-enforcing agencies. Thus the societies that have gone through organized upheavals have better chances of becoming successful democracies than the feudalistic societies trying to become democracies. Even when a feudalistic society makes an honest attempt to make a transition to a democracy, the vested interests make sure that the fear of God, fear of Lord, fear of landlord, fear of leader etc are nurtured. This leads to the establishing of a feudalistic democracy that has a natural tendency to become a dynastic democracy. That is, the leaders are born in one and only one family. In a dynastic democracy the people who think they are the leaders run to the door or house of the real leader and say "Hukum, Sircar", "Command me, Oh. Leader." All solutions will come from the house of this leader. This is an enduring case of consolation of mind.

India has not witnessed any organized upheaval. The history of India starting from the Maurya dynasty in 321 BC speaks of rise and fall of many dynasties till the advent of the Mughals and finally the British. The Mauryan dynasty/empire lasted for about 135 years with Pataliputra, the present day Patna, as the capital. When the Mauryan empire declined, a Brahminic dynasty of the Shungas with the capital in Ujjain came into existence around 180BC. In 100 AD another empire called the Kushanas, a central Asian tribe, came into existence in the north western region covering the area of Sinkiang up to Varanasi. The Gupta Dynasty/empire came into existence in 320 AD and lasted for about 180 years till about 500 AD. This empire also had Pataliputra as the capital. The Mauryan empire was essentially the first empire to unite a large part of India. The Gupta dynasty had lost control over the southern part of India, which was under the control of the Pallavas. It is acknowledged that the golden period of Indian history is the Gupta period starting from 300 A D to about 500 A D. Here also, each Gupta king enlarged his kingdom by waging wars and demanding allegiance from the conquered provinces/people. All through this process of changing dynasties and the expansion of the kingdom by any given dynasty, India was dotted with ethnic and dynastic divisions with people not speaking one language and people not practicing one religion. The many invasions by kings never destroyed the diverse identities of the separate kingdoms. The people were neither destroyed nor were they forced to renounce their religion or beliefs or heritage or way of life to embrace a new religion or a new heritage or a new way of life. How ever the king or the emperor sought to enforce universal rule and demanded acceptance and allegiance from the conquered people, nobles or kings. Thus the word "Secular" as used in Europe for the purpose of de-linking the state-craft and religion has no relevance in the Indian context. The Indian ethos has always been democratic with great respect for the freedom of the individual. This changed for the worse with the invasions from Afghanistan and Central Asia when the stress was more on the destruction and loot and forcible conversions to the religion practiced by the invaders. The most unfortunate thing about this is that the reason for these invasions is the petty rivalry and jealousy amongst the many kings of the numerous kingdoms that dotted the north western region of India. In many of the cases the Indian kings invited these invaders to help them to settle petty scores without realizing the damage that is going to be done to the nation or society as a whole.

This part of the Indian history is possibly very similar to the history of Britain. In about 449 A D the British king named Vortigern invited the Germanic tribes comprising of Angles, Saxons and Judes to come to England and help him drive back the invading Picts and Scots. The Germainic tribes accepted the invitation (who does not) and came to England. The allies quarreled and started driving out the native Britons. Thus the origin of the quarrel amongst the allies can be traced to Britain. By the end of 500 AD the Germainic tribes had occupied the whole of England up to the borders of Wales and Scotland. The word England is said to be derived from the two words Engla and land meaning the Land of the Angles. The descendents of Alfred the Great, who was the king of Wessex, were the first to use the title of the King of all Britain and the present day monarchy have their roots in Alfred the Great.

In fact, till recent times the history of a society or the record of the evolution of a society was always looked upon as the biography of the king or the queen who ruled the society. This is true of both the east and the west. Further, it was assumed that it is the right of the historians in Oxford and Cambridge Universities to write the history of the different societies. In many of the cases the perception of these professors of what the kings or queens did or ought to have done became history. In many cases, the different conditioning of the minds of these professors, different from the members of the society that they tried to chronicle, gave rise to a strange twist in the recorded history. The historians of Oxford and Cambridge have given the title of greatness to the Greek King Alexander and have called him Alexander the Great. The imposition of greatness on Alexander is more due to his ability to invade a fairly large land mass between Greece and India, and vanquishing the opponents and subjugating a large number of civilizations till he reached the borders of India. He achieved all this at a very young age. Therefore if one looks at his achievements, one is struck by the fact that this young brave, ferocious king had till his end built only garrisons in different parts of land mass spanning Greece and India, and nothing else. He captured and burned the city of Persepolis in 331 BC, the capital of the Persian Empire. Alexander the Great burned the city of Persepolis built by Darius the Great, the greatest of the Persian rulers, possibly in retaliation of the burning of Athens by Darius the Great. The one and the only ambition of Alexander the Great was to avenge the humiliation that was meted out to Greeks by the Persians and to conquer the world. His end came in Babylon in 323 BC far away from his home land Greece. He arranged marriages between Greek nationals with the prominent persons of the provinces that he conquered and thus helped in consolidating the empire. But, his untimely death brought about a rift between his quarreling generals that resulted in the destruction of the Greek Empire. It is extremely difficult to comprehend the achievements of King Alexander the Great. However, one thing that becomes clear is that the conquests of Alexander the Great were not motivated by a desire to spread the Greek religion or culture. Neither were the conquests of Cyrus the Great or Darius the Great were motivated to spread their Zoroastrian religion. The conquests by Alexander the Great, Cyrus the Great and Darius the Great, and the burning of Athens and Persepolis were essentially acts that were propelled or motivated by a desire to conquer and subjugate other societies. Thus a belief in their own supremacy and therefore the belief that every thing else must be subservient to them was the basis of these conquests. The same is true with the conquests of the Kings of Japan and China and the destruction of the Korean heritage.

However one thing that becomes very clear is the western society respects brave and ferocious kings who invade other societies and subjugate them. This also happens to be the history of Japanese kings who invaded Korea and destroyed the cultural heritage of Korea as this is the only way of subjugating another society. Similar things have happened in India. King Asoka invaded another kingdom killing and destroying every thing that he came across. But the sight of the misery that he created changed his heart and he embraced the

Buddhist religion and gave up waging wars. He also helped in the spread of the Buddhist religion in Sri Lanka, Indonesia, Malaysia and other far eastern countries. In spite of all this the historians of Oxford and Cambridge have never used the word great to characterize King Asoka, who gave up war after victory. Are the achievements of King Alexander more profound than the achievements of King Asoka who renounced war after victory? Magadh province, the present day Bihar, has produced many great kings. The Mauryas and the Guptas of Magadh, Krishnadevaraya of Vijayanagar Empire are possibly the dynasties that set up empires/kingdoms as great as the Roman Empire. The one difference is possibly that the kings of Magadh and of the Vijayanagar Empire were not as cruel as the Roman Kings. There were no fights between hungry lions and human beings, slaves, captives, or dual unto death. This pacifism definitely did not appeal to the historians of Oxford and Cambridge to recognize our kings also as great kings. This is another case of consolation of mind, which can also be looked upon as a case of conditioning of mind.

The only deficiency of many of the kings who

(a) gave up war after victory

(b) built the first university in Pataliputra near present day Patna

(c) built the Vijayanagar empire

(d) built the Bamiyan Buddha statues and other Buddhist Viharas in Afghanistan, Kazakistan etc along the famous silk route

(e) created Hindu temple complexes, Buddhist Viharas, Jain piligrim centers

was that they did not invade other kingdoms with an intention of imposing their ways of life on the vanquished. Also, they did not entertain the idea of ruling the world as Alexander did. Therefore the military command structure and the army that the kings in India built or created was not as huge and remarkable as that built by Alexander. This is possibly the one and the only reason for attributing greatness to Alexander. It is truly amazing that during those days, Alexander had perfected the command structure to such a level of perfection as to be able to travel all the way from Greece to the border of India. This is amazing because the commanders of the huge army had to ensure that the army on the move needed to halt, rest, chart the course of journey and also keep the morale of the men high all the time. This is unparalleled in the recorded history of man kind. Compared to this feat of Alexander, the invasions planned by the Indian kings were very small in magnitude and in some respects trivial. However, the contribution of the Indian kings to the harmonious living by people of different faiths is unparalleled in the recorded history of man kind. It is said that the beauty lies in the eyes of the beholder. In the same way the greatness of a person also lies in the eyes and mind of the beholder or chronicler. Mind being conditioned, the response to what one observes is dictated to a large extent on the value system imbibed as part of the conditioning. This helps in consoling the mind into rationalizing what ever happens around oneself. It is sad that the greatness of the Indian Kings is being realized and understood only after the destruction of the Bamiyan Buddhas by the Taliban ruling elite. The western mind that had been consoled for centuries into believing that the desire to live in peace and to coexist is more a case of weakness than a case of greatness was rudely shaken by the Taliban regime that enacted the acts of destruction.

Why does invasion or ethnic cleansing keep happening at regular intervals all over the world? This reinforces the thought that it is no God's commandment that all crooks shall belong to one religion or shall have a particular color of the skin or shall speak a particular dialect or shall live in a particular part of the earth. The basic cause of all these acts that have been recorded in the history appears to be the need or the desire to become rich and to get more returns on investments that are as low as possible or to have absolute control over others. The cases recorded in Mexico or Peru or America or India or Korea clearly support this point of view. The desire to have more wealth has been the characteristic of all times. The wealth has become a means of controlling people and is looked upon as necessary for wielding power. Thus, the extent of economic wealth that one has or a nation has, dictates the power or influence that the individual or the nation can exercise. Therefore having wealth has become extremely important in the society and this is the cause of the rat race. We, in free India, are committing far greater atrocities in the name of secularism, socialism and different kinds of "isms" than when we were under the British rule. A number of private armies, *senas,* have been marching round this country indulging in vandalism. Incidentally the word "vandalism" is derived from the word "Vandals" who along with their other friends "Huns" and "Goths" used to attack the mighty Roman Empire. They were in some way though not fully responsible for the downfall of the mighty empire. The various "senas", private armies, have been killing innocent people with the sole intention or purpose of preventing any change in the state of equilibrium in the society. The state of equilibrium refers to the poor remaining poor and the rich remaining rich or getting richer. The size of the cake remaining more or less the same or increasing at a slow pace cannot meet the demands or the greed of the fast increasing population. Thus, this conflict of interest is given the color of poor versus the rich; high caste versus low caste, one religion versus the other etc. Any attempt at disturbing the precious state of equilibrium would immediately invite the wrath of the powerful ones who feel threatened.

What justification do we have to be doing all that to our own people and in our own country, even after fifty years of independence? In what way are these acts less callous than those perpetrated by Col. Dyer?

In the present day scenario the words secular and secularism are being used to win the votes and come to power. These people do not seem to have an understanding of the tradition of religious freedom that existed in India. Even now, there exists to a great extent the freedom to pursue one's religious beliefs. But this freedom is now laced with fear, the fear of getting killed. This phenomenon is new and foreign to the Indian ethos that had always believed in pluralism even long before the Europeans invented the word "secularism". Most of the powerful and affluent societies that control the international affairs have evolved from a violent upheaval, religious or ethnic, involving the destruction of the value system or heritage of some other society or community. This is possibly the root cause of the tilt that one sees in the international affairs; the tilt towards China or the tilt towards Pakistan. Both the societies have no respect for other religions or heritage or for anything other than their own selves. It is a pity that the Indian leaders/politicians seem to be creating more misery and pain and worst of all a severe irreparable damage to the national psyche by indulging in manipulation of the worst kind involving religion, God and the places of worship. Keeping the past glorious tradition in view, one finds the contemporary Indian scene as created by the few powerful, unscrupulous and influential ones incomprehensible and unacceptable.

4

Nationalism

It would be wrong to assume that all the Britishers were honest or all the Britishers were callous. There were people like Col. Dyer who had a convoluted thought process. The point that is being made here is that the British rulers who came to India to rule and therefore to exploit the people and the riches of this country did have a section who did encourage the natives. National Congress was started not by an Indian. The Home Rule movement was started not by an Indian. This section of the British society was not paralyzed in the same way as a fairly large section of the honest administrators and some honest politicians in the present day, after fifty years of independence. This state of paralysis is what makes the situation pathetic and hopeless. This state of hopelessness does not in any way mean that there are no honest politicians or administrators. This only means that the small number of the manipulating, unscrupulous and corrupt politicians and bureaucrats have successfully held the nation to ransom. It is this that makes all the difference between the *Swadeshi* rule and the British rule.

But were not the British rulers the experts in exploiting people? Were they not the authors of the divide and rule policy? Were they not the people who set one kingdom against another, one community against the other to serve their partisan interests? Did they not kill, possibly the word kill is not the right word, the innocents in Jalianwalabagh? But are we any different? In all the general elections, the selection of the candidates and the voting pattern are always based on caste and religion. The concept of secularism, whatever it means, is the main issue in all elections. The issues of development, literacy, health, drinking water, decent living conditions, power, transport are only secondary and therefore of no great concern even though every one talks about these at great length. Thus, even after fifty years of independent rule:

(a) We have fine-tuned the process of exploitation of our own people and thus have perpetuated what the British rulers did in the past, which is more horrendous than the actions perpetrated by the British in India.

(b) We have successfully honed the political activity on the basis of not only the religion but also on caste and sub-caste. This is worse than what the British did in India.

(c) We have problems related to boundary and water sharing between states that are allowed to remain unsolved so that these can be raised at times to serve as red herring. These serve to take the heat off the real issues and divert the attention of the people to non-issues. This is very similar to the strategy followed by British rulers to prevent different kingdoms within India from joining hands and putting a united opposition to the British rule.

(d) We have frequent incidents of the burning of the houses of underprivileged people and the killings of one community in the same way as Col. Dyer did in Jallianwalabagh or the mass hangings of freedom fighters from the Banyan tree.

The list is a very long one. There can be a justification for the British rule to perpetrate such atrocities in India as they were the aliens from a far away land and were the rulers of India with the sole intention of exploiting and suppressing the people. The aim was nothing more than to use India for the benefit of England, the land of Engles. They were here to uphold supremacy of Her Majesty's kingdom and government, be it racial or cultural. Consider the history of foreign rule in other countries. History, like religion, is a very explosive subject. Generations have been brainwashed by making children read books that give distorted view of history. Unfortunately, history of political evolution of a society or nation and that of religion are not separated and it is this act of omission (which, in some cases, may be an act of commission) that does more damage to the fabric of the society. A comparative study of the value system of the British, Spanish and the Japanese rulers would make interesting reading. The Spanish explorers backed by the king and queen of Spain discovered America, West Indies and the American Continents. They also discovered two great civilizations of Aztecs in Mexico and the Incas in Peru. Here they found vast quantities of gold, silver and precious stones. So, they conquered these lands, destroyed these civilizations and brought gold and silver back to Spain. Spain became very rich and therefore by default consider themselves to be a part of civilized society. After all, what makes one civilized is the riches one has or one can flaunt, irrespective of how the riches were acquired. When the Japanese invaded Korea, they brought ruin to the Korean heritage and culture, and inflicted physical abuse on the Korean women. Today, Japanese consider themselves to be highly civilized. Therefore with this as the background one finds that the value system practiced by the British rulers was far better and superior and sensitive than the value system practiced either by Spain or Japan.

Consider an interesting proposition. Assume that Col. Von Dyer, a German officer, commands a platoon of French soldiers/policemen near Paris to fire on unarmed men, women and children who have assembled in a park surrounded by houses or boundary walls and therefore with no escape route in as much the same way as the Jallianwalabagh. The question is "Would the French soldiers/policemen fire upon fellow French unarmed citizens on the command of the German officer even when the Germans have occupied the whole of France in about two and a half days?" The answer is very simple. The German officer would have been killed on the spot by the French soldiers/policemen. The French soldiers/policemen would have preferred to die than to shoot at the unarmed fellow citizens. Subhash Chandra Bose during his days in the Presidency College in Kolkotta assaulted a British faculty member when the faculty member made some indecent remarks about Indians. Subhash Chandra Bose was removed from the college. Later on he was successful in completing the ICS examination in London. He willingly forsook the cushy job of an ICS officer and refused to work for the British Government saying it was below the dignity of an Indian to obey the orders of the Englishmen who had no business to be ruling India. Therefore arises the question "Could not the Indian personnel who accompanied Dyer shoot and kill Dyer rather than killing innocent unarmed men, women and children in Jallianwalabagh?" What made the Indian personnel insensitive to the screams of the men, women and children? Were they blind or short sighted so as not to be in a position to see the result of their actions? Did not even one Indian person accompanying Dyer get the urge to turn the gun/rifle at Dyer and pull the trigger?

The Germans would never have trusted the French or Austrian or any other soldiers/policemen and given them arms. On the other hand the Englishmen were so sure of the nature of the Indians that they had only a few supervisory staff from Britain and the rest of the subordinates who hunted down the revolutionaries or hung the revolutionaries and kept the Union Jack flying high were the Indians. They had no hesitation in giving arms to the Indians to fight the Indians. They had full faith in us till possibly Mohandas Karamchand Gandhi came on the center stage. The Englishmen made use of the absence of nationalism to the fullest extent possible and therefore they were here because we allowed them to be here. India was culturally one, with similar or same religious/philosophical thought process through out the country. The British rule established a single administrative entity called India. The concept of India as a nation or as a single political entity came into existence only because of Mohandas Karamchand Gandhi.

Thus, India was never a single political entity until the East India Company and later Queen Victoria took control of the whole of India. Here the administrative mechanism was such that

(a) As far as the British were concerned, India was looked upon as a single Administrative entity

(b) But as far as the Indians were concerned the legitimacy of the provinces and the associated distrust between the rulers of different provinces were assiduously maintained by the British, to be used later.

This was achieved by exploiting the all pervading distrust and hatred amongst the various princely rulers that had been the cause of the invasion by Ghouri, Abdali, Babur etc. History tells us that these were invited to come to India by the Indian princes to help them in establishing supremacy over other princes and settle scores. This is similar to what happened in Britain in 449AD. The British king Vortigern invited the Angles, Saxons and Jutes to help him drive the Picts and the Scots out of Britain and in the process was driven out of Britain.

The assumption that the British ruled India by the divide and rule policy is not a completely distorted version of the ground reality. Our kings and queens were willing to be divided. No two kings were willing to sign pacts with each other to come to each other's help if attacked by British East India Company. All the efforts of Hyder Ali and his minister Purniah of Mysore to forge alliance with Peshwas and others failed. On the other hand the kings and queens were willing to sign pacts with the British East India Company to come to each other's help if attacked by any other Indian king or queen. How can any one blame the British for this? If at all any body is to be blamed it is the kings and queens of India

(a) who had difficulty in seeing beyond the boundaries of their small kingdoms

(b) who had great suspicions about the designs of the neighboring kings and queens,

(c) who had great visions of their imaginary/non-existent greatness.

Thus the British East India Company successfully used the weakness of Indian rulers in establishing their rule and furthering their interests. The greatest failing of India was the absence of the feeling of oneness, even though culturally India was one. Thus nationalism, as a characteristic, was not the strong point of India. Regionalism was the main forte of the kings and queens of India even though many of them did not have the necessary financial and military clout to hold on to their identity. They needed an external support in the form of a prop from the British East India Company to survive, which the East India Company gladly provided. What better opportunity could they, East India Company, ask for in order to further their interests and strengthening their grip on this country? The added advantage was the absence of a unified political entity called India.

The greatest service that the British did to India was to create a unified administrative entity called India with governance from a capital city with a number of provinces providing support. It is to be acknowledged that this was not an intended service to natives but a necessity for the British rule to succeed. However the support structure at the grass root level of *taluk* and village level were those that had been established by the Indian kings for administration, revenue collection, law and order enforcement etc. Some of these positions that had been created by the Indian rulers were the *daroga, patel, talukdar* etc The British rulers retained this localized structure of administration and made use of them by keeping them happy. This not only saved their time and made their lives simpler but provided an effective means of administration as the grass root level requiring interaction with the population comprised of the local Indians. In order to cater to the ambition of the educated and the influential Indians, they created not only the provincial cadres but also the national level cadres. However, they strengthened the supervisory structure which were manned essentially by the British officers. The provinces were independent with in the framework defined by the British. Thus, even though the local administration was overseen by the Indians, every one was subservient to Her Majesty's government in Delhi and London. Thus the British laid the foundation for the freedom movement in the form of creating the unified administrative entity called India. This unified administrative entity had two faces. The first face was the monolith represented by the British authority in the form of a Resident in every princely state and he fulfilled the role of the watch dog. Every major decision that was taken by the local administration represented by the king, the king's court, senate and the Dewan was wetted by the Resident. The other face was invisible till India got independence. This unseen or hidden face of British administration was the right given to the princely states to negotiate terms of acceding to and becoming a part of independent India with the newly formed Indian government at Delhi whenever that eventuality arose. The reason for calling this the hidden face is that the transfer of power at Delhi did not necessarily mean that the control over the entire administrative entity called India got transferred from Britain to India. On the contrary, Her Majesty's hold or control over the princely states, prior to 15th August 1947, was complete and absolute.

The creation of an administrative entity called India was done by Lord Clive, Lord Wellesley and Lod Dalhousie through wars and manipulations. But the common factor for the success of British in controlling the entire subcontinent was the distrust and therefore disunity amongst Indians. The British rulers encouraged this characteristic of Indians and made full use of it to their great advantage. They kept the spirit of nationalism under control using various acts of commission and omission. The various acts of commissions were similar to

(a) giving awards/titles for the loyalty

(b) giving business opportunities in return of loyalty

The various acts of omission were similar to

(a) massacre at Jallianwalabagh

(b) hanging of people from the Banyan tree

The depressing thing, about these acts of omission was that all these were done by Indians under the over all guidance/supervision of the British officers. Would such a thing been possible in France, Germany or Italy? It has been noted that even in Europe there were people who were collaborating with the invading Nazi troops. It has been observed by sociologists and behavioral scientists that under similar conditions different people with different conditioning of mind and cultural back ground behave or respond in more or less identical/similar way. But it must also be acknowledged that in Europe the feeling of nationalism was much more prevalent than the desire for climbing the ladder of social acceptability. It is this that resulted in the British ruling India for over 250 years. The situation/conditions in India were unfortunately different till Mohandas Karamchand Gandhi came to the center of the stage. Once Mohandas Karamchand Gandhi took over the reins of the freedom struggle he could hone, polish and rekindle the spirit of nationalism in the fellow Indians. This process of rekindling the spirit of nationalism will go down in the history books as an unprecedented phenomenon for having been responsible for an oppressed society to win back its freedom in a non violent way preserving the friendship and respect of the oppressors. On the other hand the political evolution of the countries belonging to the P5 or the G8 groups has been smeared with blood.

It is this difference in the way the freedom was won and the way the political evolution took place that has made the difference between India and the other developed and affluent countries. We have remained a feudalistic society. The demand for a change has not come from the bottom. The change is effected in a controlled manner, controlled in a manner that suits the feudal lords. The change will come only if the persons in power feel that there is a necessity to give the relief to the people and not because the people are genuinely in need of a relief. Thus the change is more a personal favor of the feudal lord in power. This is the fundamental difference between a feudalistic democracy and a democracy by the people, for the people and of the people. Thus the feudalistic democracy is more often said to be a democracy by the system, for the system and of the system. Here the system represents those who are in power and the survival of the system and therefore of those in power and in most of the case the holding on to the status quo becomes a one point program. This in no way means that no progress has been achieved. But what could have been achieved with the inherent talent, patience of the people, willingness to work that exits in this country and the money that has been spent on development could have been much more than what has been achieved.

The Concise Oxford Dictionary of Current English, 7th edition edited by J. B. Sykes (1985) defines "nationalism"

Nationalism: patriotic feeling, principles or efforts; policy of national independence

That is, the actions of a society are based on the national interests. If this is coupled with the ideal of not hurting the interests of another society that would make such societies great civilizations and are looked upon as societies that have a highly developed and refined cultural value systems. The Indian society had not only given shelter and refuge to people of different faiths from different countries who fled their country, unable to bear the tyranny, which was mostly religious in nature, of tyrants but gave them the freedom to practice their faith, prosper and flourish. In return these people created wealth for India and integrated themselves with the society. It is difficult to classify whether these actions of the Indian society can be called nationalistic or not. The main guiding principle of the Indian kings and queens had been *pran jayee per vachan na jayee:* may death come to me but may I not fail in keeping my words. Even the *asuras,* the people with excessive *rajo guna,* were bound by the word of their mouth. Unfortunately this principle of dying for one's word cannot be called nationalism, definitely not in the modern society. This principle was lost with the advent of modern civilization, more so with the advent of the invaders on the horse back whose main interest was to plunder and ransack whatever they could lay their hands on. The new value system represented the survival and furthering of the fittest and the strongest, and not that of the noblest.

ii

The case of Prithvi Raj Chohan, the 11th century king of Indraprastha near the present day Delhi, is very interesting. Qutubudin, the slave of Muhammed Ghouri, was sent by Muhammed Ghouri to bring his brother Mir Hassan who had been given shelter by Prithvi Raj Chouhan. Qutubudin had come to Indraprastha as a mercenary and not as an ambassador. Inspite of this, Prithvi Raj Chohan sent Qutubudin back with a warning to Muhammed Ghouri. Looking from all angles, this turns out to be patently stupid action of Prithvi Raj Chohan. Even Krisna of the Bhagavadgita fame had used all the tricks in the bag to kill those who were on the side of evil. Bhishma could be killed only when he dropped his bow when he came face to face with Shikhandi. The *guru* Dronacharya could be killed only when he dropped his arms after he heard about his son's death, which was a lie. The end of the great warrior Karna came when he was killed while he was trying to extricate his chariot out of a pit. He was standing on the ground and was unarmed. Thus all these great men were killed when they were not armed. The justification for this was that these great men fought the war favoring evil. On the other hand, Prithvi Raj Chohan refused to kill Qutubudin when he was caught as a mercenary. The reason for this was to show the valor of the King himself and also to warn Ghouri not to make any silly attempt at attacking Indraprastha. Further, Prithvi Raj Chohan refused to chase Muhammed Ghouri and kill him after the first battle when Ghouri was wounded and was being taken away from the battlefield. The reason for this action was that the *dharma* did not permit the killing of an unarmed person, especially when he was wounded and was being taken away from the battle field. A second discourse on dharma by Krishna for the benefit of Prithvi Raj Chouhan would have saved him and India. This could have been a sequel to the first discourse on the Kurukshetra battlefield. This could have included an explanation for all the things that Krishna did to tilt the outcome of the Kurukshetra war in favor of *dharma* and in the process save *dharma*.

There are three interesting cases in the recorded history of India where being just and honorable did not evoke similar responses from the opposing parties. They are

(a) Prithviraj Chohan showing mercy to both Qutubudin and Ghori and not killing them, even though his minister, Chandavaradai, advised the King to kill them as they were men with evil intentions.

(b) Jawaharlal Nehru taking the issue of aggression in Kashmir to United Nations against the advice of Sardar Patel.

(c) Rajiv Gandhi sending Indian army to Sri Lanka for Peace Keeping Operations against the advice of some of his ministers.

All these have turned out to be tragic decisions. Prithviraj Chohan and Rajiv Gandhi paid the supreme price for daring to trust the untrustworthy by loosing their lives in an extremely ruthless attack. As regards referring the aggression in Kashmir to United Nations is concerned, India is still paying the price for it. The developed countries equated the aggressor and the aggressed and put both on the same plank. Nothing can be more dishonest and horrendous than this. The single mistake committed by all these persons was that they assumed that being just, sincere and honest would evoke a similar response from others. Nothing can be more simplistic and fatal than this. But all these are classic cases of consolation of mind, a state where one believes that just actions beget just actions. Nothing can be far from truth.

Kurukshetra is often called Dharmakshetra as the out come of the war decided the fate of *dharma.* It was on the battlefield of Kurukshetra that the forces in favor of *satya* (truth and therefore *dharma)* and the forces in favor of *asatya* (falsehood and therefore *adharma)* came face to face for a showdown. How could Prithvi Raj Chohan, a descendent of Pandavas, commit a blunder in interpreting *dharma sutra?* The prevailing confusion was more confounded by the king of Kannauj, Jaychand, who looked upon this as an opportunity to take revenge against Prithviraj Chohan. This resulted in Ghouri plundering Indraprastha that must have given immense satisfaction to Jaychand. The king of Kannauj had a personal score to settle with Prithviraj Chohan. This is definitely not nationalistic. But on second thoughts, possibly this is nationalistic from the point of view of the Kingdom of Kannauj. The reason was that there never existed a political entity called India even though an attempt at establishing a centralized political entity called India was made by Chanakya during the early 3rd and 4th Century AD. Thus the well being of the small kingdom was looked upon as the goal of nationalism. This was justified as the kingdom, however small it might have been, represented the nation for the people and the king.

However, the king who was considered the representative of the people got transformed into a feudal lord. In both the cases the king was looked upon as a person who reflected the personality of God. Therefore the rule of the small kingdom was only in the interests of the king himself and not of the people or the kingdom or the region. The kingdom was the nation, and was looked upon more as a personal fiefdom. Thus monarchy was nothing short of feudalism on a grand scale. Finitely a few exceptions to this observation that the kings were nothing more than feudal lords, misusing wealth that the state accumulated. Some of the Indian kings have invited not only Ghouri, but also Babur and Abdali to settle personal scores. The results of these invitations and invasions are as much a part of India as we are. Therefore why are we wasting our efforts and energy in talking about Babri Mosque or for that matter any other mosque? This will only vitiate the atmosphere taking the entire society comprising of all people of all religions to stone age. This is similar to what happened in Britain in 449AD. The British king Vortigern invited the Angles, Saxons and Judes to help him drive the Picts and the Scots out of Britain and in the process was driven out of Britain. Can the natives of Britain set the clock back? This is classic example of the saying that those who do not read history are destined to repeat the history. It is difficult even to comprehend that Prithvi Raj Chohan, descendent of Pandavas, did not know about Mahabharata and the teachings of Krishna. The result of this fatal error was the building of Qutub Minar and the success of Ghouri in the plundering of Indraprastha. This also opened the doors of India for many more to walk in and plunder. Can we fault Qutubudin and Ghouri for whatever happened?

iii

A comparison between the Indian ethos and the ethos of the policy makers of developed societies would bring out startling differences in the thinking processes. USA conducted swift retaliatory strikes on the terrorist camps in Afghanistan just because two or three Americans were killed in an attack on US embassy. This is a classic example of American nationalism. France invaded and defeated China and obtained extra constitutional rights for trade and commerce just because a Christian missionary was killed in China. Contrast this with the way India was and is being bled by Pakistan backed terrorists with the tacit approval of US and other European countries while our bureaucrats and politicians are possibly debating on the interpretation of the *dharma sutras*.

Consider the after effects of the Gulf War of 1991 and the more recent war, Desert Fox, in Iraq. Maggie O'Kane in an article in the Guardian describes the extensive use of ammunition made from depleted uranium which after explosion result in millions of fine radioactive particles spreading in the atmosphere. It is well known that the depleted uranium has a long radioactive chain. Thus Iraq has become a testing ground for these new weapons and a fairly large amount of depleted uranium has been left on the Iraqi soil. Thus USA and Britain have unleashed a genetic plague in Iraq because Iraq had an ambition to possess or possibly possessed chemical weapons. This is very similar to the logic expounded by France to get better trade rights in China. Nobody can match or excel the spirit of nationalism as displayed by the policy makers of the developed societies. They are always busy investigating the cases of child labor in some developing countries and therefore do not consider this issue of genetic plague caused by them that has resulted in the birth of genetically deformed babies a serious issue to waste their time.

All the actions of

(a) Destruction of the Red Indians (the famous cow boy statement. "A Good Indian is a Dead Indian"),

(b) Destruction of the Aztec and Inca's civilization

(c) Destruction of the Korean heritage and culture

(d) Attack on the Jews

(e) Support given to the ethnic cleansing in Kashmir resulting in tens of thousands of Hindus leaving Kashmir till 11th September 2001

(f) Unleashing of genetic plague in Iraq

(g) Support given to the ethnic cleansing in East Pakistan (the present day Bangladesh) resulting in more than ten million refuges crossing over to India

were a part of a well orchestrated plan to further the interests of a particular segment of a society or nation and performed as a part of Nationalistic Movement. The will to preserve and further national interests is looked upon as "Nationalism". Thus the members of the G-8 have perfected the art of justifying their right to talk of the ills of child labor on one hand and initiate genetic plague that would result in the birth of deformed children on the other. This is due to the violent political evolution of these countries that explains this characteristic of the willingness to do any thing to further their interests. Thus the Indian ethos of "*Sarve Janah Sukhino Bhavatu*", may every one be happy, does not have any relevance in the thought process of the developed nations. It is this basic conflict in the ethos of India and the developed nations that is responsible for India getting side lined. On the other hand, China and Pakistan do not have such an ethos as India and therefore are more easily accepted as friends of the rich and the powerful, G8 and P5.

British Medical Association has indicated in a study that it is possible to genetically engineer biological weapons that can target one ethnic group while leaving the others untouched. This is done by using the naturally existing distinction between the DNA (deoxyribonucleic acid), the self-replicating material present in all living organisms for targeting to produce harmful, to put it mildly, outcome. The genesis behind this is the work carried out by the Human Genetic Diversity Project for the purpose of identifying the cause of diseases/illness in certain ethnic groups. The research, which is laudable in many ways for having increased knowledge about the importance of understanding the nature of diseases from a genetic engineering point of view has now fallen into the hands of the military strategists. The California Institute of Technology is doing pioneering research work in the area of finding a Genetically Engineered solution for dreaded cancer. Researchers believe that it is possible to synthesize Genetically Engineered solutions for such afflictions as spastic state, autism etc. These are hall marks of the Brave New World of Aldous Huxley. But, the genetically targeted biological weapon is some thing that even Adolph Hitler had not dared to imagine. Further, key Defense officials of United States making a statement that the scientific community has come "very close" to making ethnic-specific genetic weapons displays the attitudes of cold-bloodedness that surpasses the Nazi thought process. Does not this make Adolph Hitler a Humanist for he attempted to give plain, simple and instantaneous death to the ethnic Jewish community. But the thought process of the Defense officials of USA proves that concept of nationalism can justify one to take any decision however dreadful the thought process may be, leave alone the nature of the weapon.

We, in India, seem to have perfected the art of showing the other cheek to the enemy to such an extent that we have become an emaciated society unable to stand up and even fight for our own survival. Any one from any nation can come here and give us advice and instructions on how lead a peaceful life. The set of instructions also contain valuable tips on how not to stand up and fight for our rights that would result in the messing up of the international peace. We gratefully accept this advice. This is definitely not nationalism.

The case of Pakistan is interesting from the point of view of nationalism. Pakistan had been sending terrorists trained in some of the camps in Pakistan and/or in Afghanistan for creating disturbance and communal rioting in India. This reminds one of the famous statement of the Chinese premier Zhou Enlai, "All diplomacy is a continuation of war by other means". But the question that comes to one's mind is, whether Pakistan was carrying out diplomatic initiative or a proxy war? In the international diplomacy there is hardly any difference between diplomatic initiative and proxy war. This had been going on for nearly twenty years. The Indian government, with great difficulty, had been fighting an undeclared war at the expense of men, money and material. Pakistan gifted India's territory in consideration for the help that was offered to Pakistan that culminated in the explosion of atom bomb. This is nationalism from the view point of Pakistan. Thus, while India was very busy taking about *dharma*, Pakistan was systematically carrying out acts that were nothing other than subversion, which became a single point program of Pakistan. All the western powers, as a routine practice of nationalist policy, turned Nelson's eye to this as they were being greatly benefited by the business relationship with China. This again is nationalistic approach from their view point as this brought in revenue on quarterly basis from the business links with China. When Advani, the home minister, talked of punishing the terrorists and even indicated that India will adopt the principle of hot pursuit to address the problem of terrorism from across the border, the State Department officials termed the reaction of the home minister as rash and hot headed. India was told to discuss the matter and sort out the issue and not to create disturbance in the Asian region by resorting to the use of force. This response of US government was also in their national interests as the aim of the response was to support their ally, Pakistan, and to rein in the democratic India which always had problems in toeing the line of thought and action of Democratic America. The greatest democracy on this earth, the God's own country, the most powerful country on the earth cannot stand the sight of countries who can hold their heads high in dignity. Thus, policy makers of US prefer to support a few amenable leaders than those who have difficulty in bending their frames or nodding their heads in constant succession. All these acts of US are in the interest of protecting the national interests of US.

Thus the human rights issue comes much later or for that matter it is no issue at all as long as the business relations are going right for the most powerful democracy. The prime importance is to defend its national interests. The national interest predominantly includes the quarterly financial report of the American Corporate. Any thing becomes acceptable if it makes the financial figures in the quarterly reports attractive. All through the twenty odd years, when India was being systematically bled by the terrorists from Pakistan, the western media was busy playing the role of a great sage asking India to negotiate with Pakistan and solve the problems. Thus the western media was doing the role of a nationalist, protecting the interests of the western countries by not calling a spade a spade. Terrorism in the name of religion is being practiced by Pakistan making India the victim of this campaign and with the explicit support of the western media. The rule of the game is that as long as the fundamentalism and the terrorism does not hurt the interests of western countries and is creating suffering and misery elsewhere, far away from their borders, it is a news that is fit to be seen on the television. That is, as long as the misery is out side the first world there is no harm in supporting it by not condemning it or stopping it. The bottom line is that it should not be in the civilized, cultured, affluent and peace loving western countries, normally referred to as the "NORTH". They cannot see their blood being shed as they had shed enough of it earlier.

But God's will was something else. Wise men have said, "Do not do to others what you do not want others to do to you". This is said to be a biblical saying. In addition to this biblical saying, *Bhagavan* Krishna had said on the battlefield of Kurukshetra that the fall of a man or a society takes place only after the thought process or the mind fails. On a fine day or was it night, the two American Embassies in Africa were bombed by the terrorists trained in the camps located in Afghanistan and backed by a person trained by US. This was not acceptable for the US government. There was a sudden realization that terrorist attacks really hurt. Not that they had no idea that attack always hurts. They always thought that others are born to bear and grin, but not the Americans. In fact the US foreign policy had always had great respect for dictators all over the world. It is difficult to comprehend the reasons for the greatest democracy always feeling comfortable with dictatorial regimes. Can the reason be that the American government has no time for the slow process of decision making of the democratic structure? Or is it that the dictatorial regimes find it easier to be in synch with the policy makers in Washington? Or is it that the American policy makers find dictatorial regimes more amenable for manipulation and therefore can make the dictatorial regimes toe their line of thought? Or is it that the policy makers in Washington find that the dictatorial regimes to be more efficient than the democracies?

In most of the cases it is found that the dictatorial regimes can help the US Government to wage proxy wars or help in fighting the proxy wars. In fact US has been a willing partner in the process of most of the ethnic cleansing that has been witnessed in different parts of the world. In the year 1971 more than ten million Bangladeshis who could not speak Urdu, the national language of Pakistan crossed the border into India. US supported Gen. Yahya Khan and sent the 7th fleet to Bay of Bengal. US had even urged China to attack India in order to keep pressure on India. The same is true with Vietnam and now with Serbia and Croatia. US supported Pakistan's proxy war that resulted in the Kashmiri Pundits leaving Kashmir and become refugees in their own country. Thus the moral stand that they take, whenever they take it, becomes a mockery of every thing they stand for. But then who cares as long as it serves their national interests? It is this policy of the G8 countries that has made Ariel

Sharon, the foreign minister of Israel who is now the Prime Minister of Israel, as quoted in the Israeli newspaper Yediot Aharonot, observe that after Yugoslavia Israel could be the next target. The bombing in Yugoslavia has neither succeeded in forcing an outside solution on the contending parties nor has resulted in easing of the conflict. This bombing has resulted in thousands of refugees fleeing their countries. This act was justified as part of the strategy to force Milosevich to step down from power. The only saving grace, if it can be called that, is that the refugees are neither Americans nor British. Milosevich, the Yugoslavian dictator, was accused of human rights violation because of the seven hundred fifty thousand Albanian refugees. Compare this with the support given by US/Britain to the generals in Pakistan when more than ten million refugees crossed over to India in 1971. Does this not make Milosevich a decent man? The value system of the western policy makers is extremely profound to be understood by common people.

All the policies that were being pursued by United States of America went out of the window on 11th September when they realized terrorism hurts very badly. Britain supported United States of America in all the policy issues including the need to rein in Pakistan. They jointly put pressure on Pakistan to rein in Pakistan and allow the American forces to use Pakistan as a staging area for bombing Afghanistan. United States of America and Britain understood the view point of India on Kashmir and supported India. It is unfortunate that the destruction of World Trade Center was required to make the policy makers of these two nations understand the issue of cross border terrorism that had been going on in the name of freedom struggle. Nothing can be sadder than this. At the same time this displays the extent to which we console our minds. We seem to have moved away from the Biblical saying, "never do to others that you do not want others to do to you". The Kashmir problem is the creation of Britain under the Prime Minister Lord Atlee. Philip Noel-Baker of Britain misled not only his Prime Minister but also United States in order to strengthen the position of Pakistan over Kashmir. In all fairness to United States of America, the Secretary of State, Marshall, disagreed with Noel-Baker's plan of putting Kashmir under UN Control. This was a classic example of pursuing national interest by even misleading one's own Prime Minister and the world at all costs. This was also a case of the empire striking back at India, which was the root cause of Britain loosing its glory. Britain has always misled United States of America and the world to fulfill its ambition of being at the center of power or at least close to it. The Economic Times carried a wonderful caricature by Manjul where a British official advises Tony Blair "Don't try to go to the root of the problem. You will find us there"

History of man has been a record of consolation of mind.

iv

In the epic Mahabharata, Krishna always advocated a peaceful solution in favor of *dharma* and in favor of those who stood for *dharma*. However when the negotiations with Kaurava clan failed, every member of the Pandava clan advocates war as the only option. Even at this juncture, Krishna advocates that one should never give up making attempts for finding peaceful solutions for any conflict. War should be the last option and if an opportunity comes in the way of stopping the war even at the last moment, every effort must be made to hold on to that opportunity. This may result in bruising of the ego of some important people. That should not become the reason to start the war. For example, Draupadi, the queen of Pandava kings, reminds every one of her untied hair and the vow of Bhim to rip open the heart of Dushyasan, his cousin, and bring a handful of his blood for applying to her hair. At this stage, Krishna reminds every one that the vow of Bhim or the untied hair of Draupadi thirsting for Dushyasan's blood, are not so profound and important as to start a war resulting in shedding the blood of thousands of people on the battlefield. The vow is not so profound as to make women and children weep over the dead bodies of their loved ones.

However, in the modern day civilization where man is always short of time, violent methods appear to have become a part of life. One can extend the argument of Krishna and question the gains achieved by US and Britain by initiating the policy of supporting the dictators and turning a blind eye to the atrocities committed by their allies in other nations. Lord Wavell set in motion the formation of Pakistan and the ethnic cleansing that got associated with it. These actions are justified as they happen to serve the interests, what ever they are, of the powerful countries, and of those who happen to be around and at the center of power in the countries that are not so powerful. But the question is, should not nationalistic actions/goals that bring misery to thousands of people with thousands of people becoming refugees be damned as satanic however beneficial and however lofty the professed goals may be? This indeed is a utopian thought.

In the case of the dictatorial regimes, the cacophony is replaced by a single voice giving an impression of a happy, smiling and disciplined society that has an efficient decision making mechanism. This possibly explains the close links between USA on one hand and China and other closed societies including the oil rich countries in middle east on the other. In many of these cases the dictatorial regimes are more interested in self-preservation and therefore have limited global aspirations. This fits into the global perspective of USA, especially when these regimes are willing to play any appropriate supporting role. Thus the dictatorial regimes can easily mesh into the global game plan of US Government and therefore become valuable allies in the pursuit of the national interests of US Government. The difference between India and Pakistan lies in the capability of Pakistan to mesh easily with the global ambition of US Government and also the willingness on its part to play the game. After all, wasn't it Pakistan that helped Dr. Henry Kissinger to hop step and jump to Beijing from Pakistan? But the bombing of US embassies was unacceptable and did not merit any peaceful discussions with any one, least of all with the terrorists. Giving advice to others is definitely easier than following the same advice. Giving advice to others is always in the national interests. Asking others to show restraint even when innocent people are being slaughtered by the terrorists who are supported and funded by an ally is also nationalism. Raising the issue of human rights to condemn reaction or counter action against terrorists by a nation that is besieged by terrorist attacks is also nationalism. This is more so if an ally is backing the terrorists, which in turn helps to rein in the nation that refuses to toe the line of thought of the big brother. The P-5, G-8 and the Security Council did make references to the Kashmir issue providing encouragement to the transnational (or international) terrorism. These actions of the developed and the powerful countries were nationalistic as this helped them to keep the ally happy and increased the business from China, and helped to rein in India.

Both Henry Kissinger and Ms. Madeleine Albright are truly nationalist in their approach to the problems. Their nationalism can be demonstrated by the fact that their actions have always been in the interests of US. These actions might have created misery elsewhere. But the interests of US were of prime concern in all the foreign policy initiatives that these Secretaries of State initiated. They are:

(a) Henry Kissinger was an active supporter and strategist of the policy of carpet bombing of Vietnam and the use of Agent Orange. This resulted in the defoliation of the land, creation of thousands of refugees with in their own land and creation of large number of orphans; disabled men, women and children. The end result was a totally devastated nation; defeat of the mighty US and in the end the death of Air Marshal Van Thieu in US. These were the outcome of the actions that were supposed to serve the interests & well being of US. Isn't the survival and victory of the people of Vietnam, in spite of the massive carpet bombing by US, the greatest achievement of mankind in 20th Century, greater than the landing on moon? This was the view projected in one of the films of the famous director Satyajit Ray. There will definitely be disagreement with this point of view.

(b) When the ethnic cleansing in East Pakistan was going on with more than ten million refugees crossing over to India, Henry Kissinger was busy with the famous Pakistan tilt. The US Seventh Fleet was moved to the Bay of Bengal with the intention of supporting the Pakistan military leaders who were a party to the ethnic cleansing. It is strange and ironical that Henry Kissinger, himself a witness to ethnic cleansing, could become a party to ethnic cleansing.

(c) US supported Ferdinand Marcos of Philippines and he took asylum in US and died there.

(d) Madeleine Albright advised the Indian government to show restraint even when ethnic cleansing went on in Jammu and Kashmir with thousands of Hindu pundits becoming refugees in their own country. The philosophy of US appears to be that the creation of refugees in any part of the earth, other than US, is permissible and if it serves US interests, then one should not hesitate in creating misery elsewhere.

(e) Madeleine Albright sent an invitation to the Yugoslov president Slobodan Milosevich to come to the table for discussion by bombing. This created unrelenting exodus of refugees. In exactly the same way as Henry Kissinger, Madeleine Albright herself was a refugee and a child of war torn Czechoslovakia. Like Henry Kissinger, she also has become a party to ethnic cleansing and human catastrophe in Serbia. This has been echoed by no less a person than the conservative columnist Arianna Huffington.

Is it not strange that the two persons who come from two different regions but had been witnesses to ethnic cleansing and senseless wars have been responsible for creating misery and suffering in other regions and societies? What makes those who were the victims of ethnic cleansing or witnesses to the humanitarian catastrophe become active proponents of similar things elsewhere? One reason may be that the suppressed frustration of the younger formative years comes out as a volcanic eruption and is displayed by utter lack of concern for the suffering of large population in the pursuit of goals that are larger than life.

All these actions of Henry Kissinger & Madeleine Albright were in the national interests of US. Thus literally speaking, the national interests of US have been taken care of by an attempt to force the thought process and way of living of American strategists on others. The consequence of this strategy has always resulted in creating misery and suffering in other societies and is looked upon as justifiable in the interests of US. On second thoughts, does Henry Kissinger's hop from Islamabad to Beijing merit supporting the misery and ethnic cleansing in East Pakistan, the present day Bangladesh? What kind of US interests are served by creating an ethnic cleansing involving the exodus of *pundits* (Hindus) out of Jammu & Kashmir and become refugees in their own country? Can this be called an out come of the freedom struggle? Can a freedom struggle be launched where members of one community or religion are systematically driven out or killed or attacked? The west has got to answer these questions in the years to come. The attack on World Trade Center on 11th September will definitely bring about a change in the thinking of these countries or societies or for that matter civilization, if one can use such a term at all. Is the need to contain and rein in India an extremely important activity in order to establish peace in this part of world? Do they, the US and the British policy makers and strategists, believe that a society

(a) that allowed St. Thomas to preach Christianity and convert people to Christianity nearly two thousand years (older than the European Christians),

(b) that gave shelter to Armenians, Jews, Zoroastrians etc who ran away from their homes unable to withstand the atrocities of invaders either from Rome or from the Middle east and Central Asian countries

(c) that allowed the Muslim traders from Arabia to build mosques in southern part of India (the Mosques were built in India much before or around the same time as they were built in Iran, Afghanistan, Pakistan),

(d) that gave shelter to the Tibetan Buddhists who fled from Tibet unable to bear the atrocities of China, which is America's greatest friend and ally (at a time when European and US leaders were avoiding H. H. Dalai Lama till Richard Gere of Hollywood fame came under the influence of H. H. Dalai Lama),

(e) that allowed the building of churches, mosques, fire temples, pagodas etc

is a great threat to peace? India had given shelter to more than ten million refugees from East Pakistan, the present day Bangladesh. The Indian government had introduced the refugee relief stamp to mop up resources to support the millions of refugees who had crossed over to India.

India did not indulge in the kind of bombings of the refineries or chemical plants that US or NATO had resorted to in Vietnam or Iraq or Yugoslavia. More than three thousand Indian personnel died in the process of liberation of Bangladesh. The policy makers and strategists of US appear to be sitting in a rarefied atmosphere, which alone can give rise to such amazing thought processes. Does US believe that China & Pakistan will help in the establishing of peace in this part of the world? Does US believe that bombing of Yugoslavia/Serbia/Croatia will help to establish peace in that part of the world? Milosevich has been brought to stand trial for the war crimes. But who would set right the effects of ecocide caused due to the bombing of chemical and other plans in Yugoslavia? Now that Yugoslavia has voted to join Russia, does US perceive a greater threat to peace and therefore merit more intense carpet bombing than the one in practiced in Vietnam? It is clear that the process of protection and furthering of national interests as perceived by these leaders is in no way different from Adolph Hitler's perception of the supremacy, protection and furthering of the Aryan Race. Unfortunately, history has shown that time and again similar strategies have been planned by various societies to force an absolute control over others and to ensure national interests. Some of these are:

(a) genocide practiced by Nazis in Europe

(b) the extensive use of Agent Orange in Vietnam

(c) carpet bombing was perfected resulted in the defoliation of large tracts of land in Vietnam

(d) use of weapons made from depleted uranium creating a genetic plague in Iraq

(e) bombing of refineries, chemical plants in Yugoslavia/Serbia/Croatia resulting in ecocide and genetic plague

(f) ethnic cleansing of East Pakistan (present day Bangladesh) and Kashmir in the name of freedom struggle

(g) declaring jihad against America, Israel and India by Osama bin Laden and his Al Quida group

The mind has a strange way of convincing itself about the right or wrong based on the value system that has been imbibed. Is it that we become civilized if we are rich and powerful, and wear the finest of the silks and brooches? What right do we have to force our views on others or our way of living on others? What kind of progress is this and what kind of civilizations are these? Why has violence become a way of life and is looked upon as the only way of life? Whoever does not conform to the ways and views of the rich and powerful is declared the heretic and non-believer. Why is it that mankind has always chosen different reasons and motives to subjugate other societies and destroy them? We have changed our ways of living but our thought processes have not. Even though we believe we are different and made progress, we have always been the same and brutal.

General Padmanabhan has categorically stated that most, nearly sixty percent, of the terrorists killed in the encounters were foreign mercenaries. Here the foreign mercenaries refer to nationals who are not the citizens of India. Thomas Pickering, the under secretary of state for political affairs, has advised India not to resort to hot pursuit in Kashmir and Pakistan. This statement came soon after US attacked the terrorist training camps in Afghanistan. This attack on the terrorist training camps is made to protect the national interests of US. This also sends signals to all terrorists that they can have a field day as long as they do not hurt the American interests. The terrorists also understand this. It was this understanding of the US policy that made the terrorists in Kashmir kill the Norwegian hostage and not any other. There appears to be a perfect understanding between the terrorists and the policy makers in Washington.

Violence has become a part of life in modern age. We have become insensitive to views and sufferings of others. We have become so self centered as to believe that none has the right to have a different belief or different way of life or practice different religion, different from the one that we hold on to. We have consoled our minds into believing that the hall marks of civilization are the riches, quarterly corporate reports, silks and brooches. In the Process, knowingly or unknowingly, we have become soulless and dead inside. The tragedy of India is the absence of a structure of governance based on nationalism and furthering of national interests. The three most disastrous declarations made by the Indian policy makers are:

(a) The statement in 1962 by Jawaharlal Nehru in the parliament indicating that the Chinese will be thrown out of the occupied territory. These appear to have come from the thought process of Krishna Menon. It is a pity that he did not know the status of the Indian military at that time and did not realize the consequences of such a statement. The need of the hour, keeping the strength and preparedness of the armed forces, was negotiations and not an emotional outburst.

(b) The statement of the then president of Srilanka praising Rajiv Gandhi for his wisdom in sending Indian army for peace keeping activity. The rest is history.

(c) The statement by Goerge Fernandes indicating China to be number one enemy of India. The defense ministers are expected to keep their emotions under control and work for building the strength of the armed forces, and not make foreign policy statements.

These actions were definitely not in national interests and therefore not nationalistic.

The recently published book "The Fate of Tibet" by the French Scholar Claude Arpi contains startling documentary evidences regarding the mess created by Jawaharlal Nehru and Krishna Menon. The Chinese invasion of Tibet and the Chinese involvement in Korea took place around the same time. This had put pressure on China to mend and solve its border dispute/issues with India. During this time, H. K. Richardson, who was the British representative in Lhasa, Tibet, was requested by the Indian Government to continue working as the Indian representative. He filed a series of reports with copies being sent to India Office, London. These present a strange picture of Zhou-en-Lai making attempts after attempts to resolve the border issue with India in a phased manner. Nehru and Krishna Menon were more interested in Panch Sheel and Korea than in the resolving of the border issue. This made Zhou-en-Lai ignore both Panch Sheel and India, and the rest is history. The other interesting thing that happened was when Dalai Lama left Tibet and took refuge in India in 1959, Nehru and Krishna Menon were more interested in propagating the view that China must be made the permanent member of Security Council. They were more interested in strengthening China and helping Korea, rather than helping solve India's border issue with China or for that matter championing the cause of Tibet. The west had great difficulty in fathoming the strategy being followed by India that helped neither India nor the cause of Tibet. This will possibly go down in the history as a case of idealism bordering on lunacy that resulted in the killing of thousands of young men in the Indo-China war in 1962.

V

Gone are the days of military conquests that resulted in subjugation of societies. The regime of World Trade Organization, WTO, is in. Here the military subjugation is replaced by the subjugation of societies through the scale of economic and manufacturing operations. In principle, the free market concept gives access of every market to every one. Further, the societies that are less organized to cope with the international competition in terms of finance, range of quality products, services and infrastructure are given time to change and make preparations to take on the competition. The challenge before the bureaucrats, politicians and planners is to rejuvenate and reorganize the small and medium scale industry as they have neither the advantage of scale of operation nor the financial staying power. It is necessary to improve the governance of the society from the point of view of providing the basic necessities like food grains, health facilities and schooling. Unfortunately every issue including those connected with human suffering and misery becomes an issue mired in controversy with the condition of the people remaining same or becoming worse. There are a large number of examples like the super cyclone in Orissa and the earthquake in Gujarat to authenticate this. Even after one year, the people affected by the cyclone have not received any help to restart their shattered life. The generous help that came pouring in appears to have vanished without leaving any trace. After this comes the news of the food grains rotting in the ware houses and people of a few districts in Orissa and Rajasthan facing starvation due to drought. Amartya Sen, the Nobel Laureate, has observed that the cause of the infamous Bihar famine was not lack of food grains but absence of distribution mechanism. It is sad that even after fifty three years of independence, the problem in Orissa & Rajasthan is the same as that in Bihar during the British rule. The pressure on the system is so intense that in spite of the best efforts of the government machinery, the mechanism of governance has become so rusty, inhuman, insensitive that the food grains that are in plenty are rather left to rot but not distributed, free of charge or under food for work program, to the starving people. It is sad that the democracies in Asia and Africa present a picture of cacophony and give the impression of not being capable of looking after their societies. In the Indian context, the use of the word "impression" is justified because there are three visible faces of India. One face is represented by a set of people who are as competent as the best in the west. The second face is represented by a set of people who keep bungling and are largely responsible for the misery and suffering of the large majority of the population. The third face is the large majority of the population who constitute the poor and illiterate masses. The misery and suffering of people becomes an opportunity to score points. Thus the final image that emerges is one of chaos with multiple players actively taking part in undoing every good that the others are doing. The viewpoints, often called ideologies, become more important than reducing or removing suffering and misery of people.

It is recognized that the liberalization has brought in quality products and has made the "money for quality" concept a dominant factor that has created difficulties for many of the *swadeshi,* protected and indigenous industrialists. Before the coming of the multinationals with their quality products, the Indian consumer had been taken for a ride by the *swadeshi* bandwagon. The Indian industrialists who produced sub standard goods were definitely not nationalistic. This speaks volumes about the national psyche of the many of the *swadeshi* industrialists who had been taking the consumers for a ride and at the same time some of these industrialists were systematically making the units sick by bleeding the industry. They did not loose any thing. The loss was to the share holders who had reposed trust in them and to the financial institutions who had invested public money. If this is the attitude of our industrialists, are we justified in blaming the British rulers for exploiting and in some cases swindling us?

Consider an electrical three pin socket and a three pin plug top. Invariably they either do not fit in or they make a very loose fit. Should not have the Directorate of Small Scale Industries inculcated and enforced into these small scale industries the concept of adhering to the standard and made it mandatory that no product without the Indian Standards Institution stamp shall be allowed to be sold? Unfortunately, this becomes unacceptable. It is recognized that making the ISI stamp a mandatory requirement violates the fundamental right of making easy money by selling some thing. Adhering to standards always involves extra effort to hold on to quality standards and therefore involves expenditure both in terms of trained man power and holding on to the exacting standards. Therefore, this comes in the way of making easy money. The market had always been a sellers market and therefore any thing could be sold. Therefore this act of creating a mechanism where any one can start an industry and manufacture any thing and sell it was looked upon as encouraging small entrepreneurs. Thus any attempt at forcing the adherence to standards and quality was looked upon as discouraging the small entrepreneur and hence a violation of the sound principles of democracy. With the liberalization of economy any multinational can, on the basis of the quality of the product and scale of operation, out price the small-scale units throwing them out of business. Thus the entire small-scale sector is in the process of pulling the shutters down. This has resulted in the patriotic *swadeshi* band wagon clamoring for protection so that they can sell sub-standard goods at a premium. Now, the entry of Chinese goods has affected these sub-standard goods even more. It would be interesting to find out the reasons for a company like Premier Automobiles that had a wait list of a few years for its car, going sick. The patriotic *swadeshi* band wagon has much to explain to the share holders. There are many such companies that have been systematically mismanaged to the great benefit of the few promoters. This clearly indicates a lack of vision and pride in making things that speak of quality with a "Made in India" tag. Thus the nationalistic fervor to come out with a world class/quality product is missing in many of the entrepreneurs, though not all enterpreneurs.

The finance and the industry ministries have been very generous in giving sops to the small-scale sector but appear to have remained unmoved about the urgent need to change the quality of the product that is churned out of the small scale sector. The sole reason is the kind of pressures that keep operating make it impossible for any well meaning government machinery to take a stand on this, let alone implement it. Here, the need is definitely not one of getting ISO 9000 certification. Given the scale of operation, it is not economically viable, in spite of financial incentives, to ask for or expect ISO 9000 certification. However, it is necessary to make it mandatory that any thing that is sold in India must carry the ISI mark in order to ensure that all similar products, say a three pin socket, have the same minimum quality as prescribed by ISI. This ensures that every Indian company, small scale or medium scale or large scale, must, as a mandatory requirement for marketing its products in India, put the ISI mark on the product. However, the individual companies can add to this base level of quality and that should be the differentiating criterion between the products and the pricing. Thus as an example all the three pin sockets manufactured in India will be guaranteed to have the minimum quality standards as specified by the ISI Code. This ensures that the consumer is not taken for a ride nor will the consumer be pushed to a corner and made to take a painful decision between choosing the *swadeshi* product with no quality and a foreign product with quality and a comparative price tag. Can the Government of India make the use of ISI Stamp mandatory for selling products in India irrespective of whether are Indian or foreign brand? But CII and similar organizations have not bothered to lobby for such a legislation making one wonder whether the intention is to create a situation where the manufacturers of sub-standard goods would continue to take the consumer for a ride in the name of patriotism and nationalism. Fortunately for the consumer, the opening of the markets has changed the situation. The prices of white goods have fallen and the quality of white goods has improved due to competition and the value for the money has been the norm of the day. But the small scale industries are finding it difficult to stay in business due to the opening up of the market and obsolescence of technology.

The tragedy is that the communities every where, either developed or developing, are facing the brunt of the liberalization of economy and market, and the WTO stipulation. The death of Kevin Flanagan, a software engineer in Silicon Valley, USA as as tragic and unfortunate as the death of any farmer or small enterpreneur in India. Both are the victims of the system that believes in opening of markets and providing the best of products/service at the cheapest prices. In fact Black Will, US Ambassador to India defended the business process outsourcing as per the WTO guidelines stating that this helps the consumer to get the best services at the best (lowest) prices. The question therefore is, how can the consumer benefit when jobs are being lost and people are dying? Flanagan Sr said, "Kevin could not understand why Americans are losing jobs. He understood it economically, but not emotionally" Therefore, the question is, if the people are losing on account of the WTO regime, will the collapse of the society be far behind? The WTO regime appears to be benefiting only the quarterly reports of the corporate houses and therefore the super rich, and definitely not the common man.

In 1970s a German Transportation Expert was invited to visit India and give recommendations on the ways and means of opening up the Automotive Sector. He was taken around the nation and was taken to the premier automobile manufacturing companies. His observation was that India must stop manufacturing the cars and instead lower the tariff and import the cars and get the scale advantage. The existing car manufacturers can fold up and start the manufacture of critical components. Thus the consumer would get a better quality, fuel efficient cars at prices cheaper than the current prices of the outdated models. This was good news for the consumer but bad news for the *swadeshi* band wagon. But does the good news for the consumers translate into a nationalistic stand? Does the good news for the consumers necessarily mean good news for the country? Does the good news for the consumer result in the country becoming a trading nation like Hong Kong or Singapore with no manufacturing capability of any kind and therefore with no meaningful scientific and technical competence? This makes the issues more complex.

Here there are a few important inputs that need to be taken into account before arriving at any conclusion. These inputs are more technical and less emotional. These are

(a) wealth generation capacity of the society

(b) prevailing level of expertise in terms of both technical and managerial that is available in the society

(c) the ambition level of the society: whether to be a trading nation or to be an industrial nation

(d) the vision of the politicians and the willingness to take matching decisions to effect changes in the society

(e) the willingness of the industrialists to change from a protected environment and face the competition from the multinationals

If one takes a helicopter view of any society, one finds that the problem has always been with the kind of leaders who ruled the country. This is true for all nations. We did/do have good people but they were/are surrounded by the unscrupulous ones who stage managed every thing to suit their personal ends. Even after fifty years of independence they are busy

(a) eliminating poverty

(b) supplying drinking water

(c) providing basic sanitation

(d) eradicating illiteracy

(e) creating basic infrastructure

The track record of the industrialists is equally pathetic. Except for a few industrialist groups like the TVS Group, TATAs, Reliance Group, Anand Mahindra Group, Kumarmangalam Birla Group, Bajaj Group, Godrej, Larsen and Toubro, Infosys, Satyam, Hero Group, Hindustan Computers Ltd, Wipro etc many others appear to have the expertise to make the industry sick and believe in making a fast buck at the expense of the shareholder. The interest of the shareholder and a willingness to increase the value of the share holders investment appear to be the last priority. The desire or the urge to create a product for the world market and put the label of "Made in India" on it is missing. Majority of the industrialists believe in jumping on to the *Swadeshi* band wagon and take the people for a long ride by producing some sub-standard goods and making money, and ultimately make the industry sick taking the share holders for a ride. The root cause for this is the freedom given to the entrepreneurs to go public and mop the share capital even when the company has not started functioning. It must be made mandatory that the

(a) company must make profits consecutively for at least three years

(b) the company must be forced to present its accounts/balance sheets for a minimum of five consecutive years

before it is allowed to be listed on stock market and allowed to raise share capital. The assumption here is that the company must be making profits at least for three consecutive years before it is allowed to go public.

In addition to the mess that has been created in the name of encouraging small scale sectors, the signing of the agreement on WTO regime and not using the grace period to brace up for the impending challenge will create a bigger problem. In the editorial of The Times of India dated 9th December 1998 under the heading "*Dhobi* List for WTO", the editor commends the report of the Parliamentary Standing Committee on Commerce released in the last week of November 1998. This report, for the first time, talks of the pathetic nature of the way the Indian delegations to the WTO meetings perform. This is mainly due to the scant respect that an expert receives at the hands of the bureaucrats. This results in the list of members in a delegation, look like a "*Dhobi* List" in the words of Times of India editorial. All *Dhobis* (washermen) unite, you have nothing to lose but your clothes. Look at the Electricity Boards, Various Public Sector Corporations, Public Sector Undertakings etc. One always finds the bureaucrats occupying cushy jobs with all the paraphernalia around them. The experts are expected to be subservient to them. Can't the experts after a certain stage in their career head these organizations? The concept of the bureaucrat being the most patriotic person serving the cause of the nation with every one else being suspect is unfortunately of British origin and it is time that these concepts are given up. During the British rule, the entire country was managed by a handful of British officers who needed to have points men for controlling the administration process. However, in the present circumstances, after over fifty years of of independence, there is a need to recognize the importance of bringing the experts to administer the nation.

India does not, unfortunately, have a good record of protecting its interests in a pro-active manner. The recent refusal of US to honor the Kyoto Protocol because of the economic slow down is a classic example of protecting their national interests. Thus, in the national interests, which are often termed short term parochial gains, US has blindly and willingly sacrificed the long term gains with no respect for community living. This is nationalism for United States of America.

The case of Mohandas Karamchand Gandhi not getting the Nobel Peace Prize makes an interesting case study. The recently released diary of Gunnar Jahn tells the story. Gunnar Jahn was the head of the Resistance movement during the Nazi occupation of Norway. He later became the Head of the Norwegian Nobel Committee after the World War II. His opposition to Gandhi being awarded the Peace Prize was an indication of his gratitude to the British Empire for the help extended to the Norwegian Resistance Movement. Thus he did not want to embarrass the British Empire by becoming a party to the awarding of the Peace Prize to the man who was responsible for defeat of the British Empire in India. This was nationalism for Gunnar Jahn.

The greatest enemy of India is neither China nor Pakistan or any other nation. We are our own enemies. We are possibly the only society on this earth (or may be in this universe) who love to bind or hurt ourselves. We love to fall down again and again. We take great pride in falling down. We have perfected the art of pontification of the process of falling down. There is nothing wrong in falling down. Every society has problems and has taken a few falls. There is no society that is free from ills or has not committed blunders. But there is no society like the Indian society where doing the right thing is looked upon with suspicion. This is definitely not nationalism. We have become the only society that indulges in consolation of mind to an extent that we are caught unawares every time and we have consoled our mind into believing that this happens due to our goodness!

5

Politics

Politics is management of people. Therefore management is always politicized and politics gets a whiff of management. Politicization of management always creates an environment for manipulation and therefore feudalism.

There are two different styles of management:

(a) Boss is the Organization

(b) Every One including the Boss work for the Organization

The profound principles of management that govern the style represented by "Boss is the Organization" are:

(a) Boss Knows the Best

(b) First Serve the Boss & then the Organization

(c) Boss is the Most Honest and the Rest are at Different Levels on the Ladder of Honesty.

Thus, much before the IT hype, the binary system of 0 and 1 were in use as a part of management scheme. That is, the Boss was always 1 and the rest were zeros (0). This system of management was also called the feudalism and had its origin in Europe.

With the passage of time, Europe was rocked by upheavals that changed the structure of the society from the feudalism to a democratic structure where the Ladder of Honesty was dismantled. The era of feudalism was put to an end and buried deep into the earth, in many cases with stains of blood. Thus, the rule of every citizen being honest till disproved was put in place. With the advent of capitalism, the market driven economy started dictating not only the management issues but also the business decisions and therefore the government policies. Thus the concerns of the European society shifted from the "feudal lord centric" to "societal welfare centric". This shift also resulted in the shift in the value system and therefore the mind set. One can argue about which of the two shifts came first. Did the shift from "feudal lord centric" to "societal welfare centric" occur first or the shift in the value system and therefore the mind set occur first. The circumstances that make life difficult bring about a change in the thinking. Therefore the "Consolation of Mind" keeps changing with time and this mechanism of change has been the prime reason for the adaptation of human beings through difficult and trying times.

In the past, the changes that swept the developing nations always followed a time lag of a few centuries or decades with reference to the developed societies. This was more because of foreign domination and feudalism that prevailed in the developing societies. On the other hand, in the recent past, some of the nations that were once classified as developing have made great strides and boast of facilities that are either on par with or in some respects better than those in the developed societies. Malaysia is an example where the infrastructure facilities are better than even those in the western developed societies. In this regard, India is a unique exception. We believe in debating on issues even if the issue that is being debated involves the life and death problems of the people. These life and death problems might be due to drought, floods, cyclone or earthquake. Relief will not reach the affected people till the issues are thoroughly debated to the satisfaction of all the parties who are interested in debating. In this process of intense debate, the food grains would end up rotting. But the idealism and the search for the best way to serve the people is so intense that preserving of the idealism becomes more important than preserving the food grains let alone giving it to poor people. The relief material will not be allowed to be distributed amongst the people till all members and parties have a satisfying debate and every person's and party's ego is satisfied with the outcome of the debate. The intended beneficiaries would have successfully consoled their minds into believing that their interests are being debated and taken care of, and would patiently await the arrival of the relief. The wait invariably is an eternal wait, forcing the people to live on hope. The cultural shock that the people of the first world and third world experience when they interact is not only due to the cultural differences but also due to ways of managing the affairs. The two are interdependent and extremely difficult to compartmentalize.

Any change in the state of an entity needs a cause, and further there is always a resistance to any change as stated by Sir Isaac Newton. Therefore, for any change to take place the cause must be substantial enough to break the initial resistance to change. Thus those societies that have gone through violent upheavals have undergone far reaching changes resulting in a complete turn around in the value systems. On the other hand, in the case of the societies that have gone through changes in a peaceful manner, there is really no change in the value system of the society. The change has been only in the system that controls the society and therefore the change in the method of control or governance gives the impression of a change in the value system of the society. For any meaningful change in the value system, it is necessary that these upheavals are initiated by the members of the society and not by an external source or cause as happens in the case of an invasion. This change has in turn been responsible for a change in the way the affairs of the society are managed. On the other hand, those societies that had not been subjected to an upheaval have been very slow in accepting changes. The upheaval in a society can be considered to be of two kinds. One that is more lateral or horizontal and the other that is more vertical. The lateral or horizontal upheaval is one where one dictator replaces another. The vertical upheaval is one where the people revolt and wipe out the ruling class resulting in the replacing the old ethos with a new ethos. On the other hand when the cause of upheaval becomes external to a society, then the society goes through a death like feeling resulting in the loss of the will to fight, survive, recoup and progress. The society becomes emaciated and too weak to cry. India is in such a state as can be seen by the following:

(a) Nation has abundant stocks of food grains and children, men and women in some districts of Rajasthan, Orissa, Maharashtra are starving and under nourished. We have allowed the food grains to rot. We have a debate on introducing the genetically engineered and Vitamin A enriched rice! We find it below our dignity to acknowledge the existence of problems of governance and talk about e-governance.

(b) The victims of super cyclone are still waiting for help from central and state governments.

(c) There is water drought in many states and the mechanism of governance is yet to respond.

(d) The people of earthquake hit Guarat write letter to the President of India in their blood to draw his and government's attention to their suffering. This becomes a one line news item and all is forgotten.

If these had happened in any of the Anglo-Saxon societies, there would have been a revolution. But we Indians have consoled our minds into believing that God would come down to the earth to save us from the clutches of those who govern us. Did not God come down to earth twelve times including Buddha and Jesus Christ, to save the people?

Compared to the Indian society where peace has been the way of living for centuries, the European, Chinese, Japanese & Korean societies have, through centuries, witnessed upheavals that were caused both by invasions and by revolts against the oppressive rulers. The invasions have always resulted in the suppression of the conquered society and therefore the will to put up a fight against oppression is under check, though not for long

ii

The Indian society is possibly a classic example of evolution. The following information was published in a German Magazine about "WORLD HISTO-RY—FACTS ABOUT INDIA".

(a) India never invaded any country in her last 10,000 years of history.

(b) India invented the Number System. Aryabhatta invented zero.

(c) The World's first university was established in Takshila in 700 BC. More than 10,500 students from all over the world studied more than 60 subjects. The University of Nalanda built in the 4th century BC was one of the greatest achievements of ancient India in the field of education.

(d) Sanskrit is the mother of all the European languages. "Sanskrit is the most suitable language for computer software" reported Forbes magazine, July 1987.

(e) Ayurveda is the earliest school of medicine known to humans. Charaka, the father of medicine consolidated Ayurveda 2,500 years ago. Today Ayurveda is fast regaining its rightful place in our civilization.

(f) Although modern images of India often show poverty and lack of development, India was the richest country on earth until the time of British invasion in the early 17th Century.

(g) The art of navigation was born in the river Sindh 6,000 years ago. The very word Navigation is derived from the Sanskrit word NAVGATIH. The word navy is also derived from Sanskrit 'Nou'.

(h) Bhaskaracharya calculated the time taken by the earth to orbit the sun hundreds of years before the astronomer Smart: Time taken by earth to orbit the sun: (5th century) 365. 258756484 days.

(i) Budhayana first calculated the value of pi, and he explained the concept of what is known as the Pythagorean Theorem. He discovered this in the 6th century long before the European mathematicians.

(j) Algebra, trigonometry and calculus came from India; Quadratic equations were by Sridharacharya in the 11th century; The largest numbers the Greeks and the Romans used were 10^6 whereas Hindus used numbers as big as 10^{53} with specific names as early as 5000 BC during the Vedic period. Even today, the largest used number is Tera 10^{12}.

(k) According to the Gemological Institute of America, up until 1896, India was the only source for diamonds to the world.

(l) USA based IEEE has proved what has been a century-old suspicion in the world scientific community that the pioneer of Wireless communication was Prof. Jagdeesh Bose and not Marconi.

(m) The earliest reservoir and dam for irrigation was built in Saurashtra.

(n) According to Saka King Rudradaman I of 150 BC a beautiful lake called 'Sudarshana' was constructed on the hills of Raivataka during Chandragupta Maurya's time.

(o) Chess (Shataranja or AshtaPada) was invented in India.

(p) Sushruta is the father of surgery. 2,600 years ago he and health scientists of his time conducted complicated surgeries like cesareans, cataract, artificial limbs, fractures, urinary stones and even plastic surgery and brain surgery. Usage of anesthesia was well known in ancient India. Over 125 surgical equipment was used. Deep knowledge of anatomy, physiology, etiology, embryology, digestion, metabolism, genetics and immunity is also found in many texts.

(q) When many cultures were only nomadic forest dwellers over 5,000 years ago, Indians established Harappan culture in Sindhu Valley (Indus Valley Civilization).

(r) The place value system, the decimal system was developed in 100 BC.

QUOTES ABOUT INDIA:

(a) Albert Einstein said, "We owe a lot to the Indians, who taught us how to count, without which no worthwhile scientific discovery could have been made".

(b) Mark Twain said, "India is the cradle of the human race, the birthplace of human speech, the mother of history, the grandmother of legend, and the great grand mother of tradition. Our most valuable and most constructive materials in the history of man are treasured up in India only".

(c) French scholar Romain Rolland said, "If there is one place on the face of earth where all the dreams of living men have found a home from the very earliest days when man began the dream of existence, it is India".

(d) Hu Shih, former Ambassador of China to USA said, "India conquered and dominated China culturally for 20 centuries without ever having to send a single soldier across her border".

All the above is just the tip of the iceberg, the list could be endless. But, if we don't see even a glimpse of that great India in the India that we see today, it clearly means that we are not working up to our potential and that if we do, we could once again be an ever shining and inspiring country setting a bright path for rest of the world to follow. But the first requirement is to come out of the state of consolation of mind that we have forced ourselves into.

iii

Is politics in this country coming in the way of inspiring the young ones to build a new nation with old values? Has politics by setting one religion against the other, one tribe against the other, one caste against the other for the sake of votes ruined the very multi cultural fabric of the nation? At the very outset it is necessary to acknowledge that the politicians are a much maligned lot. They are not as bad as they are portrayed in as much as the medical community is not as clean as it is portrayed. There are doctors who steal kidneys and are a party to to the spread of spurious medicines. One finds black sheep in every profession. There are definitely a large number of politicians and bureaucrats who are honest and just. The political evolution of India appears to have succeeded in replacing the erstwhile feudal lords, the kings and *nawabs*, by a new set of feudal lords, the middlemen. Thus, the present scenario is that the management style practiced is represented by the concept "Boss is the Organization". This is true with many of the developing countries. The feudal lords position themselves on the pedestal and no matter what, the pedestal is looked upon as sacred. Thus, politics and the political activity center round this pedestal and the person occupying the pedestal is made greater than the party or the people or the nation. Thus, the political movement makes sure that institutions are not built, and if they have been built, make sure that they are pulled down. Thus, the survival of the political chieftains becomes more important than any thing else, including the well being of the people. Thus, unfortunately, the prime importance of politics every where is to perpetuate ignorance and create an air of uncertainty with reference to security, trade, caste and religion, instead of bringing together the people and harness their energies for building a better environment and therefore a society. This helps in building what are known as vote banks.

Therefore, the society becomes "feudal lord centric" and can never become "social welfare centric". However, even here the socialistic and communistic thought process proclaim the state to be a "social welfare centric" state. But, in reality, the socialists and communists also function as feudal lords. On top of this, there is no accountability either on the relevance of the welfare activity or on the benefits accrued to the people. Every human activity becomes acceptable in the name of the ideology of communism or socialism with no accountability for any thing. Thus ideology becomes more important than the well being of the people. It is this dichotomy between the concept and precept of communism and socialism that has caused their collapse. The "feudal lord centric" mental state is perpetuated under the guise or mask of "social welfare centric" concerns. One of the classic examples of this is the political initiative on the free or nearly free distribution of power for farmers. The reality is the power is given to a few rich farmers as the other farmers in the villages cannot even afford to have a pump. Further, the power is mostly stolen by the rich urban industrialists and is then put under the head of transmission & distribution loss. It is this process of stealing that becomes profitable for every one, from politicians, administrators of power corporations. This gives reasons for investing more by borrowing and at the same time winning elections on the social plank. But any attempt at plugging this heist of power would invariably create a revolt in the rank and file of the party in power. This rank and file of the party in power forms a very thin layer of society, as this would result in the blocking of revenue earning mechanism, which is actually a bleeding mechanism. This revolt would be given the respectability of the fight for the well being and elevation of the poor and the under privileged. Thus this becomes a part of the great democratic process. Though the power minister, Kumaramangalam, was honest to admit that the T & D losses do not stand for transmission and distribution losses but stand for Theft & Dacoity losses, the issue of solving this key power problem got mired in politics through what can be called shadow boxing. This is a case of perfectly organized rip off of the tax payer and the poor people, and the winners in this game are the politicians, the trade unions, the employees of the electricity boards.

Politicians are the bridge between the people and the constitution. Therefore they represent an extremely important segment of any society. It is unfair to call the fraternity of politicians dishonest. Because there are a fairly large number of politicians who are honest and have the desire to contribute to the well being of the people. There are dishonest doctors who trade in kidneys and spurious medicines. That does not make the entire medical fraternity suspect. It is necessary that we look at the politicians with respects they ensure the law of the rule and rule by constitution. Their survival and well being is as important as the survival of the constitution and the society. In many respects the job of the politician is a thankless job as he is pulled in all directions by the bested groups. In spite of this, the politician has been able to do well for the society and this is some thing that needs to be acknowledged in all sincerity.

The main pastime of a few politicians is to amass as much wealth as possible in as short a duration as possible and utilize the remaining time for addressing rallies creating an ambiance of social reformation. Who ever is good in performing this act of make believe is sure to succeed till some one else who is more crafty and articulate and ruthless and mean makes a grand entrance on the political scene. A new slogan is coined and a new alliance is announced with the sole intention of saving the nation. The suffering of the people is good news as without that there can be no way of saving the people. If the suffering of the people is eliminated then the politicians will loose their aim in life in as much as if there is no suffering the rich will not be able to give alms and therefore save their souls. Thus, the influential section of the society wants the majority of the society to be in a state of poverty, ignorance, fear and helplessness. Only then would the small influential section get a chance to retain their influence and lord over them, debate over the way the majority can be uplifted and brood over the way the majority can be salvaged. Thus, the influential can keep themselves busy worrying over the state of the majority of the people. This would give them a chance to dabble in social service. If the majority of the people are also well off, how on earth can the influential few spend their time and what on earth will they be able to talk about in the late night parties?

This explains the notices issued to Tarun Bharat Sangh of Rajendra Singh in Rajasthan seeking explanation as why they should not be prosecuted for the illegal acts of rain water harvesting that has benefited tens of thousands of people living in drought prone areas. These poor villagers are now living a better life solely due to the successful rain water harvesting and this is an unacceptable state as far as the few feudal lords are concerned. Therefore the very existence of the few influential and manipulating lords is threatened. Further, how will they be able to atone for the sins committed during the process of amassing of wealth if there is an improvement in the living conditions of the masses? There will be none to receive the alms. How then can the suffering soul of the rich and the powerful be saved? It would be unfair to ask them or expect them not to amass wealth rather than trying to atone for it later. This is another classic case of consolation of mind.

iv

Loss making companies bring good news. This gives a great opportunity to show the "social welfare centric" concerns and policies of those in power. In fact, whenever such opportunities present themselves the first thing that is done is to make sure that status quo is maintained. There is great stability in holding on to status quo. Then set up committees or commissions to find solutions. This helps to reward those who are loyal to the center of power and helps to keep the "hope" of the people alive.

Care must be taken to make sure that the "hope" is not fulfilled as any attempt to fulfill the "hope" would create "new hope" amongst the people that would undo those who fulfill the "hope". Therefore the best way to rule a society is to hold on to status quo and fulfill the "hope" at a very controlled and regulated manner that is at the discretion of the rulers. The "new hope" must necessarily have a new leader. Thus this is an opportune time to create a base for the "dynasty" to take on the mantle of serving the people and continue the great task of eradicating all the ills that were being eradicated by the illustrious members of the "dynasty". The good work can continue for many more generations, till a revolution wipes out the dynasty. This happened in Czar's Russia. The other case study can be the rise of Adolph Hitler who was ignored by Germans for a very long time before they started believing that he really had the answer to the ills of the German society.

The case of Adolph Hitler is very interesting. From the beginning, he and his friends were advocating the removal of democracy from the Fatherland and holding Jews responsible for the misery. Initially nobody bothered about his fiery statements. But with the passage of time, the economic hardship forced many, though not all, Germans to listen to him and his friends, the Nazis. Thus, the circumstances can make the mind rationalize the irrational. The few Germans who decided to listen to Adolph Hitler found in his words an honest assessment of the cause of the problem of the Fatherland:

(a) Removal of democracy and establishing dictatorship to enforce discipline

(b) Making the Jews the target as they had all the wealth

Were these assessments also not heard in every society whenever the society faced economic crisis? Whenever there is a crisis, either solutions are visible or scapegoats are visible. In many of the cases, the scapegoats are the preferred options as this helps the leaders to divert the attention of the followers and at the same time help in settling old scores. The scapegoats are of two types, the economically well off and the religiously different. The scapegoats in the form of those who were religiously different were targeted in Europe during the times of crusades. This is when the Christians with the active backing of the church put to stake the non-believers who were either Muslims or those who did not believe in the business of God. The Muslims did the same, all in the name of God. It is interesting to remember that in the history of man-kind, those who declared their intention of protecting the interests of "their" God or his followers were in reality not interested in either the God or the followers. Their main intention had been and will be the increase in the number of the followers. This in turn defines the clout, both financial and ability to control and influence the process of decision making. Therefore the influence of those who control the masses through religious means or in the name of God becomes frightening. God is not only an extremely good business proposition but also an entity that can be made into a frighteningly malicious thought.

The mind, being what it is, rationalizes every thing that is irrational. The mind justifies and glorifies every irrational act, and history is made. Often it is explained that economic backwardness & illiteracy are the basic root causes for the occurrence of such a human disaster. But the ground reality is that the people who are economically deprived and illiterate and the law abiding educated citizens are the ones who are at the receiving end. Further, a study of the background of those who are actively involved in such a human disaster indicates that the persons who actively participate are those who have either a political ambition or religious fervor and eager to harvest and save the souls by bringing them to their fold. Both the politician and the religious zealots have a lot to gain; one gains the votes and the other the believers. This happens to be the life giving elixir or potion for both the politician and the religious zealot. Therefore, it becomes important to make sure that illiteracy, bigotry and suspicion must be nursed at all costs as these provide a perfect cover for them. Thus the state of illiteracy, bigotry and suspicion is of great value in as much as the loss making public sector enterprises present a profitable venture. If this is not "consolation of mind", what else can be?

6

Governance

It was very nice on the part of Chidambaram, who was once the Commerce and then the Finance Minister, to have said that this country needs politicians who treat the country as their constituency and think and perform on those lines. The first few years of independent India were possibly the only years where we had politicians and leaders who considered the nation as their constituency. The reason for this was that the leaders of that time were the ones who had taken part in the freedom struggle and knew the value of the freedom and the struggle associated with it. However it is to be acknowledged that a large number of people who lost their every thing in the freedom struggle lived a life of penury while many who managed to stay close to the key persons reaped the harvest. With the slow exit of the key figures from the national scene what was left behind were these persons who had managed to stay close to them. Thus the transition to a creed of manipulators and pretenders was set into motion soon after the death of Jawaharlal Nehru. This was also the beginning of the system of feudalistic democracy. In the present day scenario, we have a few politicians have always looked upon this country as an extension of the village from where they come.

Jawaharlal Nehru was a romanticist and a dreamer. Unfortunately romance is never uninterrupted and dreams rarely come true. In spite of his noble efforts, he had problems with those who had successfully positioned themselves around the centers of power. The fire in him that every one saw when he thundered from the sands of Choupathy, Mumbai that every black marketer will be hanged from the lamp posts, was sadly missing. He soon realized that the Congress had changed beyond recognition. The value system, the dreams and the idealism of the Congress of pre-independent era and for that matter of fifties were slowly and surely eroding. Soon he realized the wisdom behind Mahatma Gandhi's advice. The Mahatma had advised both Nehru and Patel soon after India became independent to dissolve the Congress Party. His argument was that the Congress party was launched for the purpose of winning the freedom. Once this aim was achieved, there was no use of this party since the need of the hour was governance of the country. Therefore it is necessary to have parties based on political ideologies and not based on the single principle of fighting the British rulers. Unfortunately both Jawaharlal Nehru and Sardar Patel did not heed Gandhi's advice.

Nehru did roar once or twice when he threatened to leave Congress and form his own party. But the fat sharks that surrounded him had enough tricks in their bags to dissuade him from doing this. It is interesting to note that the Mahatma had refused to accept the advice of Annie Beseant who had launched the Home Rule Movement. Annie Beseant had advised the Mahatma not to launch his now famous non-cooperation movement in spite of it being non-violent. Her argument was that the best way to fight was to resort to the legal process rather than launching the non-cooperation movement. The non-violent non-cooperation movement is as bad as or for that matter worse than any violent movement. In both the cases, the people would show scant respect for law and order. However, if the movement is a violent one it becomes easier for the government to quell it. But if the movement becomes non-violent then the government in power would have extreme difficulty in restoring orderliness.

Today Annie Beseant's argument makes much sense as every day we have protests where shutters are pulled down and non-violent non-cooperation agitation has become the order of the day causing immense discomfort, damage and loss to both the people and the nation. Further, in the present days the threat of violence is always at the back of the non violent movement. In the end it is indeed ironical to find that both the apostles did not accept the advice of their peers. Today the non-cooperation movement, in the hands of the unscrupulous leaders, has become a curse for this country. It appears that the only way to salvage this country from the clutches of the unscrupulous leaders is to ban the non-violent and violent non-cooperation movements. This may appear to be extremely unfortunate as the potent weapon honed by our Mahatma for freeing this country from the British rule is now being damned. But the other way of looking at this is that the non-violent non-cooperation movement served the purpose during the time when this country was under a foreign rule. Now the call of the hour is that we need to build and not agitate. This does not in any way mean that acts of injustice must be tolerated. This only supports the view of Annie Beseant who said that the best way to fight is to take recourse to legal methods. The society must not become a party to taking the issues to the streets and indulge in destruction of public property or follow the non-cooperation movement by forcing the shutters down, *bandh*, in a few cities or all over the country.

But this would mean that legal system must be strengthened. Strengthening of the judiciary has different connotations for different people. Strengthening would refer to increasing the number of judges, and therefore benches, at all levels from the lowest level to the highest level. This helps in easy access to the judiciary. The access becomes easy only when the case filed by the common man comes up for hearing at an early date. This "early date" should in principle be not over a week! This may be a tall order but this alone will instill faith in judiciary for both the common man who is seeking justice and also for those who appear to have become habituated to committing frauds. This alone will put a hold on the mal-administration that has been the bane of this country. But even the attempt to strengthen judiciary will create tremendous uneasiness in some sections of the society. Here the phrase "attempt to strengthen judiciary" refers to the increasing the number of sitting judges and having mechanism to clear the pending cases. Once the pending cases are cleared then the mechanism created for clearing the pending cases would get absorbed in the judicial infrastructure. This alone would help the common man to get justice quickly, without delay. Dispensing of justice without delay is an essential condition for stopping of the scandals, scams, corruption, nepotism and such other feudalistic characteristics of the human beings either close to the center of power or in power. However, the strengthening of judiciary will affect those who are in power and also those who are close to the center of power. Justice M. N. Venkatachaliah, who was the Chairman of the National Human Rights Commission had indicated that sixty percent of all arrests made by the police in India are unnecessary and unjustified and this accounted for about forty three percent of the total expenditure incurred by the jails. The Commission suggests the adopting of the British Institution of recorders and assistant recorders for disposing of large number of minor offences, which hither to are being classified as criminal cases. The commission has advocated the need for a massive decriminalization of procedures. For example many of the offences that are now classified as crimes can be classified as compounded civil wrongs.

Any attempt at strengthening of judiciary would be looked upon as an attempt to make the legislature week. If the judiciary is strengthened then the elected members in the name of the mandate that they have received by the people, *janadesh*, would find it difficult to turn the law of the land upside down in the name of governance. Thus the politicians would be forced to govern the nation with in the frame work of the constitution and the purview of judiciary, which is definitely not very interesting. The recent court judgment with regard to the polluting vehicles, polluting industries and the relief work in earth quake hit areas in Gujarat provide a very interesting picture of the sense of loss of power felt by politicians. Therefore the thought of strengthening of judiciary will not be acceptable to the politicians. The policy decisions would automatically be made in the courts. This will not be acceptable to the bureaucrats and the politicians. This brings the conflict between the role of the executive and judiciary to a penultimate state. In fact this should not happen at all. The policy decisions must be made by the executive. The judiciary is only expected to provide a corrective mechanism with constitution as the frame wok. The executive is responsible for the governance of a nation. But when the executive does not function the way it is expected to function, with in the frame work of the constitution or the law of the land, the nation has the right to turn to the judiciary. Thus, if the judiciary ends up getting into the driver's seat, the fault lies solely with the failure of the executive to perform. Here the state (or is it status?) of the bureaucrats is the most interesting one as they stand between the politicians and the process of governance. These bureaucrats are picked from amongst the best of the students that this country can produce. They are then put in the framework of rules and regulations as devised by the British rulers in the 18th and 19th century and then given the task of governance of the country.

Thus the framework with in which they need to govern the country is represented on one hand by the constitution of India that is vibrant and that takes into account the aspirations of the people as projected by their elected leaders in the parliament. On the other hand the implementation rules are those devised by the British rulers that are typically aimed at keeping the society backward and treating the Indians as suspects. The bureaucracy is expected to help pave the way for effective governance and therefore keep in view the constitution of India and re-frame the laws framed during the British rule. But this never happened as the preservation of the British system helped to create a new breed of rulers. There never was any governance. Thus the Indian administrative machinery is saddled with the task of screening the good from the rest instead of screening the bad from the rest. The people are still treated as suspects till they prove their innocence. In the other countries, the common man is looked upon as an honest person and the energy, efforts and resources are spent to detect those who commit frauds. Here the entire society, except those in power and those who are close to the center of power, are looked upon as suspects. When India got independence one of the roles of the Indian Administrative Service, which was the erstwhile Indian Civil Service, was to carry on the administration from where the British rulers had left off. It was thought that an equally important role for the Indian Administrative Service was to transform the administrative mechanism to remove the all pervading overtly colonial flavor. The British rulers had framed the laws and the rules to keep an eye on all natives who were always looked upon with suspicion and to hold on to the status quo and ensure perpetual control over India, the Jewel in the Crown. Till today, even after celebrating fifty two years of independence, the laws remain feudalistic in nature as this gives a great sense of power to the administrators. Some may view this as a state of decadence. The pleasure of looking down upon others is some thing that cannot be forgone. In one of the shows presented by Bhaskar Ghosh on the Star Movies TV channel, he made a very interesting observation. The bureaucrat will never allow the power to say "NO" slip away from his/her hands. Also, the bureaucrat loves to see some one folding his/her hands and requesting for help even if what is being asked is within the rights of the individual and therefore folding of hands is not called for. The importance of a bureaucrat is believed to be directly proportional to the number of people waiting to meet him or her and the duration for which they are made to wait. This justifies redtapism. So much about governance. All this stems from the singular act of consoling the mind into believing that pre-serving the self is more important than the well being of the society.

Many people believe that the only way to feel the warmth of power is to have a long line of people waiting outside the office to meet them. If the administration becomes transparent and the decision making predictable then nobody in his/her right sense would bother to meet the bureaucrats or the per-sons who scan through the files. This would amount to a tremendous loss of importance and therefore there might be an epidemic of depression or a wide spread loss of sense of belonging amongst the bureaucrats and the politicians. But the advantage of making administration transparent is that this will strike at the roots of corruption and help in making the administration-people inter-action irrelevant. But the disadvantage is that this will not be acceptable to the bureaucrats and the politicians. Thus unfortunately the basic law of gover-nance that has been followed is not to work for the well being of the people but to ensure that the process of governance does not in any way diminish the need for bureaucratic intervention at regular intervals and different stages. This intervention at every stage of the public-government interaction is the cause of corruption, nepotism and arbitrariness and it is absolutely important that this is protected and preserved at all costs.

The problem has become compounded with the arrival of *bhai log*, the brotherhood, into politics. The process of criminalization of politics was initi-ated by Indira Gandhi during the days of emergency when the loyalty to the individual became more important than sane advice or loyalty to the well being of the nation or society. With this entry of the *bhai log*, brotherhood, into active politics in the seventies, the new working philosophy or the sumo motto became "every thing is fixable". With this started the widening of the chasm between activities that can be called "constitutionally correct" and the activities that can be called "politically correct". Those bureaucrats who were considered "constitutionally correct" were looked upon as anti development and therefore anti people. Thus a systematic process of politicizing of the administration started in the seventies. The principle was more or less the same as that followed by the US Government, viz., "if you are not with us then you are against us". Thus it became beneficial to be on the wrong side than on the right side of law. Any attempt to be on the right side would result in going over to the wrong side of those at and around the center of power. Thus the wrong side of law was acknowledged and accepted as the best side. All is well that ends well, at least for the bureaucrats.

It was around this time that a new theory was formulated and given social acceptance. The new thought process was that there is nothing great in being an honest man. Honesty shows two things. One is that the fellow is incapable of taking bribe and that weakness cannot be glorified into a virtue. And the other is that the person is not near or close to the center of power. If one happens to be honest in spite of being near or close to the center of power, then it only indicates one's inability/weakness in not utilizing or en-cashing the "feel powerful factor". After all, the saying "make hay when the sun shines" was not coined in the seventies. It is a very old saying. Thus such a person did not deserve to be at the center of power. With this another thought process was slowly getting legitimized. In a democracy, people elect representatives to the legislature. Therefore, if a set of people got elected to power, it only means that they have been empowered to rule the nation. Therefore, by corollary, they have the right to administer or govern the state/nation in a way that they think right. This is the current interpretation of the basic concept of democracy, *janadesh*. The conflict that one sees here is the eternal conflict between the principles of democracy and feudalism. Feudalism, in principle, is not governed by the constitutional frame work approved by the state. It is the lord, landlord or the feudal lord who, by virtue of the financial clout in the midst of abject poverty and failure of governance, lays down the framework. The attempt that is being made by every political party is to provide a legal sanctity to the feudalistic frame work through the *janadesh*, the election process. It is agreed that a political party gets elected or gets the *janadesh* based on the manifesto that the party presents just before the election. This election manifesto is a statement of the beliefs of the party, what it stands for, the action plan for the next five years covering the developmental issues and the foreign policy issues, defense issues and social welfare issues involving women, health, education, minorities etc. But the frame work for the implementation of these beliefs cannot be some thing out side of the constitution. Under no circumstances can the constitutional frame work be violated.

Many knowledgeable and discerning persons have advocated that the social welfare issues involving women development, primary education and health must become a part of the development program. That is, these should not be treated as social functions of the government but must be looked upon as important development activities, more important than building steel plants or power plants or dams or any other similar construction or asset creating activity.

Whichever way one looks at these issues, these are not to the liking of those in power! Be it the strengthening of judiciary resulting in clearing of all pending cases and dispensing of justice with in a short time so as to make justice a meaningful thing. Or the eradication of illiteracy and empowering of people at the lowest level so as to help them to decide for themselves the path of progress that the state needs to follow. Both these will undercut and hurt the interests of the leaders.

An excellent way of consoling one's mind is to talk to God and feel happy to have successfully offloaded one's burden that would result in a state of elation and to find one self on a flight to heavenly feeling. During my school days, my teacher used to advise me to talk to a wall. i never understood the implication of this advice. i had always considered this idea of standing in front of a wall and talking to it a very dumb advice. Now after all these years of experience, i find that this advice is really a profound one that provides one with peace of mind. When one starts talking to the wall, one is in effect talking to oneself. The process of consoling one's mind gets interrupted and reality dawns on oneself. Thus, at the end of this session of talking to the wall, one finds oneself getting a better understanding of the ground reality and thus helps in understanding and accepting the same. The inability to accept the reality or come to terms with reality is the root cause of the need to console the mind with irrational reasoning. The process of consolation of mind creates only confusion as the process of consolation is necessarily an event driven phenomenon.

ii

The entry of the *bhai log*, members of brotherhood, into the politics has made far reaching changes in the quality of administration in India. There appears to be a parallel law, parallel security, parallel judiciary and a parallel economy. These are based on a better footing than the main stream government activities. The *bhai log* have brought about an enormous change in the psyche of the people. This has led to people making profound observations like, "He is very honest and sincere. If you give him money (bribe) the work will be done" This means that there are people who take bribe and do not do any thing! The mention of the *bhai log* brings to one's mind the book titled "With No Regrets". This is written by Krishna Huthee Singh. The book "With No Regrets" was published some time in 1964 or 1965 after the death of Jawaharlal Nehru. Unfortunately, this book is out of print. This book is about the impressions of an young girl about the changes that overtake Anand Bhavan in Allahabad during the days of freedom struggle. Here the author recollects what ever she had witnessed in Anand Bhavan where she grew up and the book is a tribute to the person whom she fondly calls *bhai,* the brother. The name of the brother is Jawaharlal Nehru. Fortunately there is a great difference between that *bhai* who was a sentimental romanticist and these *bhai log* who are two timing opportunists taking the nation for a long ride.

She was the youngest child in Anand Bhavan. Her state was possibly unique in that she was a witness to the great happenings and also a witness to the great personalities who came to Anand Bhavan to meet her father, Motilal Nehru. Unlike Indira who in many ways loved to play the role of hostess during such meetings, Krishna, being the youngest, was left to herself and was content with watching the proceedings from a distance. Possibly, Krishna did not have the urge to be in the midst of the great personalities. She had the unique opportunity of being an observer. She recollects the day when Motilal Nehru was given the news of the arrest of his son Jawahar. By that time there had been a total transformation of both Anand Bhavan and the Nehru household. Motilal Nehru was sitting in a chair in his *khadi dhoti,* hand spun cloth wrapped round the waste, and was lost in his thoughts. There was silence all round. Suddenly Motilal got up and took a mat. He spread it on the floor on which the carpets had been removed. He without saying any thing slept on the mat on the floor. Possibly this marked the total and complete transformation of an aristocrat who used to get his clothes stitched in Paris and hired British governess for his children. There were tears in the eyes of Krishna. Motilal Nehru was trying to find out how his dear son Jawahar would be spending the night in the jail, sleeping on the floor. The grand old man was trying to get a feel of what Jawahar would be going through in the cell. The book is a recollection of many such episodes that took place in Anand Bhavan. Krishna felt that the transformation that took place in Anand Bhavan with reference to

(a) the state of rank aristocracy to the state of nationalism

(b) the use of finest of the clothes from France to the thick, rough/coarse khadi clothes

(c) the ambiance of European grandeur to a completely Indian ambiance

was "with no regrets" in view of India gaining independence on the 15th of August 1947. Krishna felt with hindsight that the sacrifice made was "With No Regrets". She does not mean that India became independent because of the transformations that took place in Anand Bhavan alone as there were thousands of other people and families who sacrificed every thing and then lived a life of penury and oblivion. Krishna's world centered around Anand Bhavan and the book is a record of the transformation that changed her world. She and her family members have not been in lime light or center stage unlike some of the members of Indira Gandhi family. Looking at the present scenario would Krishna still say that whatever sacrifices were made during the freedom struggle were "With No Regrets"? More so looking at the way the country is being governed, the way the men of straw have been governing the nation.

The subject of the governance of a country is fascinating because of the many pulls and pushes that are exerted on the government machinery and the balancing act performed by the government machinery. There have been a few biographies covering the experiences of administrators at various levels. These persons have served the nation in various capacities as Presidents, Prime ministers, Bureaucrats, etc. They have discussed their experiences in the decision making process and the issues involved in effecting the decision making process. A thought related to the need for making the process of decision making as transparent as possible always keeps recurring. The decision making can be classified into two categories:

(a) strategic nature involving internal security

(b) general nature involving development issues

The decision making related to strategic issues cannot become transparent for obvious reasons. Whereas the decision making related to development issues can be made transparent. Therefore when ever the issue of transparent administration or decision making is suggested this refers only to the development issues. The development issues can be subdivided into

(a) village development involving the water supply, housing, roads, electricity, communication, basic health, primary and adult education, child and women welfare, small irrigation, supply of seeds and fertilizers, poultry, live stock and live stock grazing, preserving and marketing of agricultural produce, housing, public distribution system, public grievance etc

(b) urban development involving public transport, water supply, electricity, roads, education, health, public distribution system, public grievance etc

(c) industrial development involving the setting up of industries, infrastructure like roads, railways, telecommunication, power, public grievance etc

Thus transparency would refer to making public the finer details about the project wise fund allocation and implementation strategies, and the outcome of the implementation process on a week to week or month to month basis. Any time scale that is larger than this would become meaningless as this would amount to the monkey eating the banana and going away leaving no trace of either the banana or the banana peal. One cannot go on spending one's energy and resources for finding and identifying the monkey and getting witnesses to corroborate the crime that the monkey had committed about an year back or a few years back. Therefore the information dissemination is necessary to reduce corruption, and the transparency of governance should aim at letting people know what they want to know and not what the bureaucracy wants the people to know.

Consider the program of digging wells or bore wells and other small irrigation projects like building tanks etc. A large amount of money is spent on this and invariably the projects start on paper and end on paper. The people do know that money is going down the drain. But should not the people know the exact location where the tank was to have been constructed or the wells/bore wells were to have been dug? Further should not the people know the exact amount of money that was spent on each one of these activities? Further, it would be necessary to make public the information on the implementation schedule with reference to the date or week or month during which the work would start. This information is always available in the records of the government that are extremely difficult to track and trace. Therefore the ready availability of this information can always help social activists to question and if necessary move the court for justice. The trouble is that the bureaucrats and the politicians do not think so. The *Sahibs*, bosses, derive their power from withholding the information justifying the belief that information is power. Thus, if every thing becomes transparent then people would not find it necessary to approach the Sahibs for information or favors.

It was interesting and amusing to hear the recent experiences of a social activist at the Facilitation (Computer) Counters that were recently inaugurated by various ministries. He, being a social activist, went to the Ministry of

Rural Development. What he got from the computer was the same old pamphlets and publicity brochures, and no meaningful information that can be used for checking the performance or progress or impact of the projects. Thus the meaningful information was hidden and the bureaucracy wasted tax payer's money on perpetuating this farce. The social activist was expecting the following information:

(a) Information of Project Details and the Associated Expenditure (planned or already spent) to be given in the hierarchical manner relating the various administrative units. For example information pertaining to any village in a *taluk, zilla parishad*, district and state relating to money spent and the projects completed must be available at the Facilitation Counter. Then any one can check the validity of the data.

(b) Further the data can be based on the on going projects in various villages with time frame so that any body interested in seeing the work being done can do so by going to the village. Is this not a valid ambition level of a taxpayer?

(c) Thus the data of the Planned Projects, On going Projects and the Completed Projects covering information on the exact location, money allocated/spent, duration of the project, implementing agency and status of the project must become an open domain information for easy access. This helps even the beneficiaries to monitor the projects and therefore is better than the usual audit process that takes place years after the projects are closed.

(d) This kind of data must not be limited only to the projects in rural areas. In fact there is a lot of money that goes into such projects as computerization, technology upgradation of public sector companies, infrastructure development projects related to roads, railways, airports, power, communication etc. In all these cases detailed information on the planned projects, exact location of the projects, duration of the projects, implementing agency, status of the projects, money to be spent or already spent on these projects etc must be made available on computers at the Facilitation Counters. This data must be accessible over the net.

(e) These data pertaining to the projects that are planned or in the process of implementation in Rural, Urban, Infrastructure and other areas must be updated at regular intervals of not greater than three months to provide current status of the projects. In fact the interval must have a relevance to the duration of the project and the expected amount of work that can be completed in a month.

He, the social activist, found it hard to believe that the bureaucracy could take the beneficiaries of the projects and the nation for a ride by starting the Facilitation Counters in a grand style that do not contain any meaningful information that can be used for independent project monitoring. Thus the facilitation counters were short on content. But then, was it not the original idea to prevent independent monitoring of all development projects? The anathema for monitoring is both from the politicians and the bureaucrats for different reasons. The politicians are more interested about making hay while the sun shines, and therefore any checks and balances and monitoring will not be to their liking. These checks, balances and monitoring will make the process of abuse of the economic system extremely difficult, if not impossible. Therefore, the attempt to become leaders and contest elections becomes no more an attractive proposition. Of what use is the power if they cannot bend the laws, manipulate the funding of projects and get not only rich but also make the near and dear ones also rich? Have they not got the support of the people in the form of *janadesh*? This appears to be perfectly logical. Politics is not similar to other professions as there is a fairly large risk involved. For example, a politician may not get elected in the next election. Further, when he gets elected he would have made promises to a large number of supporters who control votes. Many of the promises would obviously be impossible to fulfill with in the legal framework.

There is a need to ensure that the political parties must also mention about the constitutional and fiscal validity of the promises that are incorporated in the election manifesto. That is, the election manifesto that will be released by the political parties must not only contain promises but also contain the ways and means of implementing them with in the frame work of constitution and with in the ambit of fiscal discipline. In other words the parties should not be allowed to make wild promises to the people and then go about tampering the law of the land just because they think that they have the mandate to do so. The mandate that a party gets is always with in the framework of the constitution of India. Further, the promises in the election manifesto cannot be the basis for increasing the circulation of currency notes causing fiscal disaster. The party that is elected to power must not look at the governance of the nation as a limited exercise that is limited to the mandated five years. There is an urgent need to realize that the decisions that a party in power takes will have a long lasting influence on the society, much after the party in power is gone. Therefore there is a need to insulate the society from the indiscretions of the political parties in power.

On the other hand the bureaucrats are protected by constitution. The reason for this protection is that bureaucracy is the arm of the government that implements the political will and decision as might be approved by the parliament. This is the permanent entity in an uncertain and impermanent political environment. Whenever a political party comes to power, it can only indulge in transferring of the bureaucrats and get those bureaucrats with the right temperament in the right positions. Thus the bureaucracy needs to be insulated from the political uncertainties in order to make sure that a viable administrative mechanism is present at all times of peace and political unrest. Thus the founding fathers of the Indian Constitution have done India proud by establishing an administrative machinery that has served this country well. But in the recent past the criminalization of politics has resulted in the politicization of bureaucracy. The only thing that a politician can do to them is to transfer them to a remote location as a punishment for non-compliance. Non-compliance refers to not acceding to the wishes of the politicians. This does not refer to not adhering to the rule of law or constitution. Those who follow the laws of the land are considered to be people who do not have the urge to move up the ladder and become successful and may be termed anti development. The bureaucrats have a different set of value system that sometimes coincides with the value system of the politicians. They face a tremendous dichotomy and are torn between two opposing value systems. This is a tragedy because the best brains are selected after grueling and marathon written and aural tests. These are then trained to become bureaucrats. After a few years they find that they are buffeted between Politicians, some of whom are rank criminals or have extremely close links with criminals. Thus the cream of the country are left to deal with leaders some of whom have dubious background and links with the criminals. They invariably end up with a Shakespearean dilemma, "To be or Not to be". In this case it is, "To obey or Not to obey" or "To comply or Not to comply". Thus the bureaucracy is divided into two streams. One that can bend any thing including themselves and the other that sees only the rule book and nothing else is visible (highly short sighted or myopic state). The stream that is willing to bend succeeds as it believes in playing the game as it unfolds. They are very sensitive to the direction of the wind and are always adept at relocating themselves depending on the direction of the wind. These are the ones who display a tremendous capability to survive and climb the ladder, and can be looked upon as those who have a lot in common with the creepers. These are also called "great survivors". The others become the odd ones, often called the "Also Rans".

Is there a way of overcoming this lacuna in our administrative system? Consider some of the programs:

(a) Infrastructure Development

    (i)   Roads

    (ii) Railways including Public Transport in Metropolis

    (iii) Airlines and Airports

    (iv) Telecommunication

    (v) Broadcasting: Radio and Television

    (vi) Power

    (vii) Housing

    (viii) Water Supply

    (ix) Public Distribution

    (x) Garbage and Sewerage Disposal

(b) Storage and Transport Mechanism for Agricultural Produce

    (i)   Grains

    (ii) Fruits

    (iii) Vegetables

    (iv) Poultry

    (v) Milk

    (vi) etc

(c) Rural Development

    (i)   Wells, bore wells, tanks, rain water harvesting etc

    (ii) Basic health

    (iii) Primary and Adult education

    (iv) Roads

    (v) etc

These are some of the developmental activities that need to be implemented irrespective of the party in power. Therefore, the social activist, was wondering whether it is possible to evolve a mechanism where by the political party that comes to power will have no authority to change the priority given to the implementation of these activities. This appears to be an utopian idea. But, why should this be a utopian idea? Every political party does allocate fairly large sum of money to these social and development projects. After all the profession of politicians is to uplift people. They are always busy uplifting people. The problem starts after the allocation of large sums of money to these projects. The long conduit from either the national capital or the state capital to the recipient institution or organization or individual is ridden with a fairly large number of holes. These holes are in the form of middle men, power brokers, the rural rich, the head men etc who have links with the politicians. These holes keep changing in color and size depending on the political party in power. A change in the political party in power does not in any way change the system for better. One set of holes will be replaced by another set of holes. All these different sets of holes have the same characteristic. This is like a tree full of monkeys, all on different branches and at different levels. Some monkeys are climbing up and some are moving down. Monkeys on the top look down and see a tree full of smiling faces. Monkeys at the bottom look up and see nothing but assholes!

This combination makes it difficult to get the information on the details of the fund release and projects associated with the fund release, even though this information is available in files some where in the government. Some where in the middle some body in the respective ministries would have collected information on projects and their costing. This information gets translated into the budgetary allocation and therefore the information related to the mapping between the funds and the associated projects exist some where in each ministry. Thus the social activist was interested in having access to this information. The social activist found it hard to believe that every thing other than this vital information that relates to the well being of the people was made available at the facilitation counter. This vital information related to the specific projects from the details of work, duration of the work, start date of the work, contractor to whom the work is assigned, the amount of money to be released at different intervals of time, etc. This information, which would help in detecting any misuse of funds before it is too late, is considered to be a national secret, not fit to be made public. If this information is made public or open, then manipulation cannot take place. This will bring some sense of accountability in the governance of this country. Today, we have no option but to look to the Judiciary to intervene and direct the government to make public all information related to funds allocated, funds spent, work completed and work pending related to all projects. The access to judiciary and more so the access to justice must be easy for a common man. This is the only way to ensure accountability in the governance of a country.

There are two opinions about justice. One is, "Justice delayed is Justice denied". Another is "Justice delayed is better than justice denied". The second statement is an example of consolation of mind. What is needed is to have a judicial system that delivers justice without undue delay. There is also a strong belief that the process of delivering justice cannot be hurried as this affects the quality of judgment. There is an element of truth in this perception and therefore the need of the hour is to have more judges at all levels.

We should increase the number of judges in the Supreme Court and High Courts to at least three times the present strength. At the lowest level there will be three times the number of Magistrates in each place. Some may view this elaborate arrangement of judiciary as a waste of money and therefore not called for. What is often not realized is that the best check on governance comes from the ability of the citizen to challenge the government ruling rather than a debate on the subject in the parliament or legislature. There cannot be a debate on every issue that is of concern or interest to the citizen. The time available in the parliament or legislature is barely sufficient for discussing larger issues facing the country or state. Normally, the citizen has three options before him/her for getting a help from the government when ever he/she feels threatened. They are

(a) Go to the police station

(b) Go to the local politician

(c) Go to the court

The option of resorting to militancy is to be avoided at all costs as this does not help any one. It only brings about destruction. Therefore, with the three options left to the citizen, the need to have the option to go to the court for respite in the event of the first and second option failing becomes absolutely necessary in order to ensure democratic norms of establishing the rule of the law. This option also helps in checking mal-administration/governance. Generally the people expect the administration to indulge in self corrective or self cleaning processes and respond to the petitions, *faryad*, that they submit to government. Generally this does not always happen. As long as the decisions made are with in the framework of the rules and are transparent, one does not face any problem. Unfortunately, this ideal situation is hard to achieve. This difficulty in achieving an ideal condition forces the society to have a fall back option of an effective legal system. The mechanism of governance invariably follows the route of setting up of committees to arrive at convenient solutions/decisions. In many of the cases process of establishing of committees is more a case of consolation of mind than an act of just governance. In these cases the need for the legal system becomes necessary to prevent the distinct possibility of reducing the governance to a farce.

When the process of governance becomes a farce with no easy access to judiciary, the underworld sets up a parallel structure. The bureaucracy cannot handle this by increasing its own strength or the strength of the police or paramilitary forces. The answer is to increase the strength of judiciary and ensure that the citizen gets justice with in affordable cost and time of not greater than a month. That is, the first judgment in the lowest court is delivered in a month's time. After this, there will be appeals to higher courts. The time cycle for completing the judicial process, from the lowest to the highest courts, should not be so long as to defeat the very purpose of seeking justice. The total duration of time from filing of a case in the sessions court to the dispensing of the case in the supreme court, assuming that the litigant has gone up to the supreme court, must not be greater than twelve months. Only then will there be a fear of law and hopefully fear of God.

The problem with the present legal system is that it is overburdened. The number of judges at all levels, from lower court to the highest court, has not been enhanced to keep in line with the explosion in the cases being filed relating to criminal or civil issues. The criminalization of every activity in the society and the insensitization of the people have made a peaceful community living an impossible activity. Therefore there is a need for the expansion and strengthening of the judiciary to provide the necessary mechanism to prevent the misuse of power, to deliver justice with in acceptable limits of time and to prevent the under world from setting up a parallel judicial establishment where one can seek justice by paying ransom money. Any extension of the time needed to get justice would result in either people indulging in consolation of mind or resorting to unfair methods to settle scores or get even or get justice.

It is inhuman to see thousands of accused languishing in the jails without a trial. This is not only inhuman but also a gross misuse of power. Any one can be charged with any thing and thrown into jail. The accused will have to wait for his turn to appear before the court to prove his innocence and this may take years and in some cases decades. All through this period, the accused will have to be in jail. This is no justice and this cannot be the way of handing down justice. Therefore, what ever may be the arguments about the expenditure involved in having an elaborate judicial system, the existence of an elaborate judicial system alone can solve the problem of corruption, misuse of power and non-governance. Such an elaborate judicial system helps the people and therefore the society, but it puts those in power in great difficulty. Thus the opposition to such an elaborate judicial system comes from the vested interests whose existence, influence and power get threatened.

iii

Have the founding fathers of the Indian Constitution committed a blunder in choosing the model of the constitution/governance while framing the

Constitution? The blunder can be on two counts. The first one was that the Founding Fathers were not clever enough to imagine the kind of situation that the politicians would create in the long run. But then, this cannot be called a blunder as this refers to a case where the successors were smarter than the predecessors. Did the Founding Fathers make a wrong selection of mechanism of governance by choosing the British system? The Constituent Assembly did study different methods of governance, German, French, British & the American, and decided that the best way to govern India is by the modified British method of governance. The reason for arriving at this decision was that the modified system presents a mechanism of every segment of the society being represented in the parliament due to the reservations of constituencies. Further, these elected members will have the freedom to elect a leader who goes on to become the Prime Minister. In principle this is indeed the best way to govern a nation as complex as India. Therefore, the fault of the Founding Fathers was that they were not as clever as their successors and therefore did not anticipate the kind of mess the successors would create.

The other problem is the issue that is related to the relationship between the judiciary and the executive or the parliament. The question is who is superior to whom. Can judiciary dictate terms to the executive? The judiciary has every right to pass judgment on the constitutional issues pertaining to the passing of bills in the parliament. The problem is more in the area of perception of the two contending parties: politicians in power and the judiciary. The party in power believes that their job is to govern as per the mandate given to them by the people. Therefore they, in the process of governing the nation, feel the need to change certain parts of the framework without which they believe that governance would not be possible. The change in the framework would invariably result in the change in the constitution or in giving the executive certain powers to implement the solution to the problems. Constitution allows the amending of constitution as long as the party in power has two thirds majority. This process of finding and implementing solutions to the problems creates the conflict between executive and judiciary, if the solutions serve the partisan interests of the party in power. The difficulty relates not to the attempts made to resolve the problems the society faces but to the solutions that are expected to solve the problems. For example, clamping of emergency and suspending of fundamental rights was one of the solutions that was implemented that did not solve any of the basic problems of the people. But it solved the problems of the leaders!

The problems that the society is facing have been known for a long time, even before the end of the British rule. These problems have not changed. Irrespective of whichever politician or political party and bureaucrat are in power at any given time, the problems faced by the society and the various segments of the society remain the same. The only thing that happens is that the problems are given new color and new solutions are offered to the people as part of the election manifesto. The solutions as contained in the election manifesto and the solutions that might be offered to the people after coming to power are in many cases not related. In most of the cases, no solutions are offered. What normally happens is that the money gets disbursed and the process of finding solutions to the problems continues.

There are two reasons for this. The politician believes in making as much money as possible in as short a time as possible. This is the only insurance for the politician as he does not know his future in spite of keeping the company of God-men. The other reason is that the political process of contesting the elections involves in making weird promises not only to the people of the constituency but also to the middlemen who control and manipulate the vote banks. The promises made to the people are always of no consequence and this has been proven again and again in the past. However, the middlemen are not as meek as the people in whose name the elections have been fought. They will never let go their pound of flesh and blood. It is this process of fulfilling the weird promises made to the middlemen that creates the holes in the funding conduit. Thus, the programs for which money is released are as per the promises made to the people by the politicians. The holes in the funding conduit are placed or created to satisfy the promises made to the middlemen. Therefore whenever a new politician comes into power or a new political party comes into power the only change that takes place is replacing the old funding conduit with a new funding conduit with different types of holes that cater to different kinds of middle men. Thus, irrespective of the political party in power, the improvement in the living conditions in this society has always been minimal.

Can the solution to this be the presidential system? The proponents of the presidential system of governance believe that this system offers many advantages to the people. One of the major advantages is that people know who is going to govern the country as they will be voting and electing the president at the center or the governor at the state level. In fact the presidential system will block the possibility of the manipulation process for getting an undesirable politician elected to the prime-minister's or chief minister's position as a consensus candidate. This process of an undesirable politician becoming a consensus candidate for the top post is definitely a mockery of democracy. Further, the president and the governor will have the freedom to use the services of experts to advice and administer. They need not have to be the elected members of legislature or parliament. Thus, the process of direct election of the president and governor helps not only to overcome the uncertainty factor about the leader but also to get the right kind of people to administer the nation. But the presidential system also has problems. One of them is that posed by the demographic spread based on language and religion, and would pose a severe strain on the entire process of governance. The issue is what if the candidate gets elected on the votes of a few regions making the entire process of election partisan in nature. Different states have different population and therefore this is a distinct possibility. If this possibility occurs, then the already divided society will erupt into a state of civil war based on real or imaginary issues. The strife will definitely be more on the imaginary issues than on the real issues as no body is interested in solving or addressing real issues. One of the options for overcoming this difficulty may be to specify that the candidate must get a minimum percentage of votes in each state. This is also not a practical or feasible solution. There is a great difference between the American & Indian societies. US is a melting pot with a predominantly single language and a single culture or way of living. On the other hand, the Indian society has never been a melting pot. It had the courage and generosity of nurturing different cultures including the cultures of those who took shelter in India unable to bear the atrocities of the invaders of their land. The Indian society is a combination of composite sub cultures, each of which is as well developed and refined as any in the west. In addition these culturally different people have been living together in harmony for over a few thousand years, longer than the history of US. Therefore the presidential system has the potential to create problems in the Indian scenario. After all, the founding fathers of the Indian constitution were neither biased nor ignorant when they opted for the British system of governance. One cannot blindly pick something that might work under certain conditions out side India, transplant it in the Indian conditions and expect it to work. Unfortunately this appears to be the thought process of some of our intellectuals who are awed by the American system.

Thus the fundamental problem with the Indian governance is not the choice between the presidential form of US and the prime ministerial system of Britain, even though some have made it that. The real issue is how does one prevent the creation of holes in the funding conduit and plug the holes, when ever created, in the funding conduit, even though none is interested in acknowledging this issue. It is here that the social activist was surprised when he found that the bureaucracy had successfully performed the rope trick when they made public the Facilitation Counters at various ministries that do not contain any meaningful information. Here the question is not whether the bureaucracy is willing to give information or not. The argument will be that any one in need of information can approach the concerned officer and the request will be granted. Therefore there is no denying of the right to information. This is a classic example of the fact that no bureaucrat likes to loose the privilege of meeting people who come with folded hands for information that they have every right to access. The bureaucrat tells his subordinate to give the man with folded hands access to the required information and then a computer print out is taken and given to the man with folded hand. Does this not show the power of the bureaucrat? The question is why not allow the free access to this information without having to meet any bureaucrat at the Facilitation Counters? This avoids the trouble of going and seeking an appointment with the ever busy bureaucrat who invariably spends his/her time in attending meetings. The government/bureaucrats have every right to deny access to the information related to the terrorists, criminals, smugglers, antisocial elements, defense, external affairs related information and other information related to both internal and external security. These are sensitive and therefore must be protected. However, the information related development projects must be made transparent. There is a need for the opening up of the critical information pertaining to the progress of each of the development projects along with the fund status. This opening up must be in real terms. That is, the information must be available on a web site for every one to see and access. After all, whose nation is this and whose money is that? Further, the process of tendering and finalizing of the award of the work should also be made open and transparent. This will avoid the award of the contracts to organizations that have only political links and no technical ability.

Therefore the interesting question is "Who gains by refusing to open up the gates/windows to information that relate to the development projects?" The reason for asking this question is that in the past the audit process has helped only in conducting the postmortem study or analysis of a project that has been either completed or that has gone for a six. This kind of report does not help either the nation or the taxpayer, even though this might help those in power or those who were in power. This is similar to the difference between the biopsy report and autopsy report. Biopsy report helps us to identify the problem and therefore find a solution to it and save the patient and help the family. On the other hand, the autopsy report helps us to identify the cause of death and therefore does not help the patient or the family. It may help the police. The people who might benefit from not opening up the critical information that would help in plugging the holes in the funding conduit are:

(a) The bureaucrats who have the fear of loosing their power as nobody would go to them for any information

(b) The politicians who loose the power to manipulate and help those who had helped them to get elected

(c) The middlemen who specialize in fixing of deals

Thus, the people who get affected by the opening up of information are unfortunately those who will have to approve the opening up of information! So we have become witness to the great rope trick by the bureaucrats at the expense of the taxpayer. This rope trick satisfies the important persons by holding on to the status quo and succeeds in fooling the people who have no say in any thing. This is a classic example of feudalistic democracy. It is here that the judgment by the bench of Gujarat high court in the public interest case filed by Kartikeya Sarabhai after Gujarat was hit by the devastating earth quake brings hope to the Indian people.

After India became free, the ICS (Indian Civil Service) became IAS (Indian Administrative Service) and it was expected to keep the aspirations of the society and reframe the rules, clauses and sub-clauses to ensure that the citizens are looked upon as honest unlike during the British rule. This meant that the pedestals would be removed and method of conducting business would be more on partnership basis rather than feudalistic basis. This would have resulted in a loss of importance and power for the bureaucrats and politicians. Thus, the need to preserve the feeling of grandeur and power resulted in perpetuating the ills of the British rule. We are still being run as a colony where any body can be thrown into jail for years without a trial. Thus, feudalism has been perpetuated by carefully neglecting to take into account the need to strengthen the judiciary in terms of the number of judges, which would have curtailed the power of the bureaucrats and politicians. Today the accused is literally at the mercy of the lawyers and advocates who can seek new dates of hearing forcing the accused to spend a long time in the jail without a hearing. What ever may be one's views, it does give a great satisfaction for those in power to be in a position where every one else is more than eager to pay respects. This is a classic case of feudalism with a touch of democracy. We, as a nation, seem to have crashed into a state of despair. Having gone into that state, we seem to have lost the ability to reason and plan the way of coming out of this man made mess. This has resulted in every individual getting into a state of "consolation of mind", rationalizing the irrational. The thought that "things could have been worse" also happens to be a case of consolation of mind.

iv

Is it not strange and at the same time pathetic that we keep looking to God for help all the time? Do we have any other option? This society has been a feudal society for many centuries. The result of that has been devastating to the extent that we have been told not to question the elders or teachers or for that matter any one. We have become a generation of docile and subservient citizen who have lost the capacity to fight for our rights. The result is that a few unscrupulous politicians who manage to come to power hold the nation to ransom and take the nation for a long drive. Thus the action of a few of the unscrupulous elements has successfully paralyzed the entire nation. It is unfair to assume and conclude that there are no honest politicians or bureaucrats in this country. The question is how does one empower honest politicians and bureaucrats? Or still better, how does one make sure that the honest majority is not side-lined and paralyzed by the corrupt minority? The issue therefore boils down to having politicians who consider India as their constituency as suggested by Chidambaram. Today, most of our politicians try to map the village or district politics to the nation causing confusion and chaos. But the tragedy of this country is that there are no more national political parties even though every party calls itself a national party. The major political parties like the Congress, Bharatiya Janata Party and Janata Dal have been reduced to regional parties. Thus in the nineties India has witnessed a strange phenomenon of a few regional parties joining hands and forming a government at the center. This joining of hands by a few regional parties to form a coalition government at the center gets the ripple effect of the regional politics. In many cases, the ripple effect becomes a tidal wave and the government at the center is washed away without a trace.

Therefore the answer to this kind of problem that the nation is facing since nineties is definitely not the holding of another general election. The general election will always result in a hung parliament as the people have realized that there is nothing to choose and every political party does the same and looks the same after a few months in power. Power normalizes every political party to the same extent as to make it difficult to differentiate between them. The only way to differentiate is to look at their heads for the party head gear or listen to the words that they speak. The hung parliament results in the formation of an unstable coalition government that in due course of time gives way to another coalition government. The end result is that the people are taken for a ride, prices shoot up, law and order break down, living conditions deteriorate and the politicians either indulge in horse-trading or recommend another election that the nation can ill afford. Politicians are needed to articulate the ambition of the people, which is definitely needed in a plural society like the Indian society, where it is necessary for every community, regional, tribal and religious, to have a mechanism of projecting their concerns and ambitions. Thus the politicians and therefore the parliament/legislature are necessary to function as safety valves. Therefore the question is not, how can we marginalize the politicians? The question is, can the nation be insulated from the erring politicians?

The process of governance is dictated by the political thoughts of the party that is elected to power. In the case of the coalition government, the process of governance is dictated by the common set of the differing thought processes of the cooperating political parties. It is here that the small regional parties get into the act of projecting the regional bias on to the nation. The problem becomes compounded when a bigger share of the projects is demanded in return for the support. In many cases the demand is not just for the development projects. The expectation would be for the turning of Nelson's eye on corrupt practices of the regional leaders in return for support. The result is the frequent changes in the coalition government and changing of political partners at the center. The worst case scenario is the conducting of frequent general elections at exorbitant costs. Frequent general elections increase corruption, inflation and the cost of living. The attendant feature of this is the failure of the law and order with the underground elements having a field day. Therefore the prime concern is to protect the nation from the vagaries of the power brokers and fantasies of the few regional leaders.

The problem here is that any solution that one may find would definitely be not acceptable to all the political parties. The problem becomes more complex because of the fact that the judiciary cannot be pro-active but can only be reactive. One of the major difficulties is to define or quantify corruption. That is, when does an act of commission or omission become a corrupt act? For example there can be no confusion about whether fodder scam or petrol pump scam can be called a case of corruption or not. On the other hand can the act of getting some one an out of turn gas connection or a telephone connection be termed an act of corruption? If one keeps oneself to the book of rules, then any act that has been committed in exchange of money or a favor can be termed as a corrupt act. The same is true with the allotment of a government flat/accommodation. Therefore the necessary condition that needs to be enforced on the politicians is that they need to follow the book of rules. Is it feasible to expect the politicians, whose main job is to serve the people, to hold on to the book of rules? Are we justified in attempting to achieve the impossible?

The concept of extended family makes it difficult to define a corrupt act. Can the following acts be called corrupt?

(a) I have given him/her a television set from the profit that I made.

(b) I have given him/her a car from the profits that I made.

(c) I have given him/her a flat from the profits that I made.

(d) I have given him/her a farm house from the profits that I made.

This is essentially a method of induction that is taught as part of Mathematics! The philosophy is, "He/She is a member of my family. The profits that I got were after a lot of price negotiations. Therefore there is nothing wrong in helping a member of my extended family from my own funds" It is the concept of extended family that makes it hard to get witnesses who can stick to their statements. This makes it harder for the courts to convict any one accused of corruption as the long time needed to resolve a case provides enough time for the process of white washing of the witnesses.

Consider the case of hung parliament and legislature. People have lost faith in every party and therefore they have nothing to choose. The result is that the national parties have been reduced to regional parties. The other reason may be that Congress party that was once a national party was reduced to the state of regional party due to the controlled intra-party fights and maneuvers. These intra-party fights and maneuvers were actively encouraged by the powerful central leadership in order to keep the regional bosses at bay. Nevertheless the end result is the fragmented vote bank and hung parliament. The result of this is the birth of a new form of trading activity called horse-trading, where the value of the elected member becomes higher depending upon the fate of the ruling political party. That is, the value of such a member goes up as the fate of the party in power hinges on the whims and fancies of this lone member. This was some thing that the founding fathers of Indian Constitution had not foreseen. They expected that the elected members of the parliament or legislature would act in a responsible manner and conduct the business of the state in a serious manner. But the serious business of running the state has been converted to monkey business. The elected members of the parliament and legislature have violated every written code of conduct of the governance of the state. The problem is that these members have been given privileges. Therefore the question is how does one handle those with privileges and who do not understand their responsibilities?

Before considering another utopian idea, it worthwhile to recollect the present scenario. The elections are held. The result is a hung parliament. The option is a coalition government. There is a race for forming the government. The President of India calls the party with the largest number of seats that is still far below the required majority to form the government. The leader of that party gets into a huddle and after a good deal of arithmetic calculations, produces a coalition government. This government has inherent problems and contradictions as the election manifesto of these parties are at loggerheads. Still, for the sake of the people of India, they stand united with plastic smiles on their faces and clasping each other's hands for the fear of loosing their position. But then, clasping each other's hands at all times become very tiring. At some stage, one lets go the hands. The coalition government falls. The President of India repeats the process. Another coalition government is formed that also has no long guaranteed life because of the inherent contradictions. At the end the President of India dissolves the parliament on the advice of the Prime Minister and the Chief Election Commissioner announces the election schedule.

Now is the time to consider a utopian idea. Can't the elections be held only once in five years, come what may? Supposing the elections are held and no party gets a clear majority. Then a coalition government comes to power. After some time the coalition government falls due to the inherent contradictions. Another coalition government comes to power. This also falls due to inherent contradictions. At this stage, the President tries other options of allowing any other party to form a coalition government. When all these attempts fail and the mandatory five year term is not over, should the parliament become a dummy debating forum with no power to legislate? Should the President become the administrator and govern the country for the remaining period of the mandatory five year period? As the mandatory five year term come to an end, the Chief Election Commissioner announces the election schedule for the parliament. The same thing would happen at the state level. The Governor takes over the responsibilities of governance of the state and the legislature becomes a dummy forum for debates with no power to legislate. As the mandatory five year term comes to an end, the Chief Election Commissioner announces the election schedule for the legislature. Does this not solve all problems?

Second utopian solution is that the areas of development activities resulting in creation of wealth & assets for the country must always be funded with a certain fixed percentage of GNP. However, the constitutional bench of the judiciary can repeal this expenditure if contested by the people and proved in the court of law to be irrelevant at the given time and therefore malafide with no enduring benefits to the people. This would possibly avoid the occurrence of the many scams that have been the bane of our society. Also this will overcome the possibility of all like-minded politicians joining hands and taking this country for a ride. The development projects cannot take the form of a loan *mela* (festive gathering for disbursing loans) leading to the creation of large number of non performing assets. All development projects must result in creation of wealth and assets for the nation and not for the individual politician or the political party. However, there will be problems relating to the weaker sections who are in need of subsidy from the government. The projects that are aimed at overcoming the problems of the weaker sections must be implemented within the mandatory period of five years in such a way as to make the future need for such projects redundant. That is the political parties cannot go on eradicating poverty for fifty years and still put the poverty alleviation as one of the main planks in the election manifesto. After all, whose money is that and whose nation is this?

It would be unrealistic to expect the politicians to support these utopian solutions. The politicians may boycott elections. Isn't this good news? The President and Governors would rule the nation and the states with the help of the bureaucratic machinery. The election of the President would become impossible without the members of the parliament and legislature. Isn't this another good news? The Chief Justice of India would become and remain the Acting President of India for a predefined duration. The Chief Justice of High Court would become the Acting Governor of the state for a predefined duration. Can any nation expect any thing better than this? The politicians would threaten to agitate. This should not really be a problem. Release all criminals. Fill the jails with politicians. Has there been a better cleansing process than this in any other society? This would achieve an absolutely peaceful change of guard ever achieved in any part of the world. Let the President & Governors rule the nation for about five years. Was this not the gist of what Subhash Chandra Bose had said about the action plan to be followed for a free India? His vision was to educate the people in rural India the meaning and essence of freedom. He said this alone will prevent a second freedom struggle. He could easily see through the mask of all those people who surrounded the key persons who were involved in the freedom struggle. Thus his words have been proved to be right in that we are now in the process of launching a second freedom struggle. This time the struggle is against our own politicians who hold the key to effecting a change in the process of governance. The key is the constitutional route to a peaceful change of governance. The trouble with this country is that every one, with the exception of politicians, come with in the ambit of the law of the land.

The politicians who are involved in various corruption cases are enjoying their lives and are active in national politics. The concept of justice appears to be ineffective as far as the Indian politicians are concerned partly because of the inordinate delay in dispensing with justice. The longer the time it takes to dispense justice, the greater the possibility of the witnesses being either bought or traumatized. Our politicians have perfected the art of governance of the nation to such an extent as to make scams an integral part of the governance. The philosophy appears to be "What is governance without a few scams"? The scams have been made an integral part of national politics. Every party in power uses these scams to threaten and warn the tainted ones to keep off. At the same time the scams are never taken to their logical conclusion as the intention is never to take them to logical conclusion. If the political party in power takes these cases to logical conclusion, then they would have set precedence. Setting such precedence is definitely not in the interests of the politicians. There are two reasons for this:

(a) This would leave the party in power with no stick to beat the opposition

(b) This would leave the party in power in a very precarious position

Thus every politician who became the Prime Minister after Rajiv Gandhi has invoked the name of Bofors to keep the Congress on their toes and also to browbeat the nation. Nobody knows the truth and unfortunately Rajiv Gandhi is not there to defend his name. Time and again the nation has been told about the various scams and precious little has been done to punish the concerned politicians and to bring these cases to conclusion.

Even in the neighboring countries like Malaysia, attempts are being made to bring the erring politicians to book. Here in India we seem to have perfected the process of soft peddling the issue of corruption at high places and have successfully built an institution round corruption. However, one always finds people talk about corruption and fight against corruption. This is more for the rabble rousing and vote catching with the sole intention of painting a picture of a better alternative to occupy the seat of power. Thus the best job in the nation is the job of a politician. The best thing to do is to establish close links with a politician. It is precisely for this reason that the bureaucracy has been politicized. It is not that the bureaucracy was unwilling and was forcefully politicized by the circumstances. There is a great benefit in getting politicized. There is no great honor in remaining apolitical. It shows the weakness of the individuals in not being able to respond to the changing dynamic situation. If the aim is to break this kind of a thought process and activity, there appears to be only one option, that of stopping the process of the "consolation of mind". But this might appear to be utopian in nature in a society that has shown tremendous patience and perseverance in the face of all odds, which in itself is a classic case of consolation of mind.

V

The subject of governance and constitution bring us to two interesting books written by two persons with completely different background. The books are The History of American Constitution by Justice Earl Warren and The Governance of Britain by Sir Harold Wilson. Justice Earl Warren was an eminent jurist and judge and is an authority on the American constitution. Sir

Harold Wilson was the British Prime Minister. Both, one an eminent jurist and the other a politician, had different perspective of governance and constitution. It must be acknowledged that neither the American solutions nor the British solutions solve Indian problems. All solutions have to be found in such a way as to suit the local needs. The solutions cannot be transplanted from one region with a certain cultural setting to another region with a different cultural setting. The challenge is to adapt the solutions that may have been found for similar problems elsewhere to the local cultural ethos. An attempt is made to find such utopian solution by suggesting certain changes to the constitution.

The utopian solution, in italics below, comprises of the following changes to or inclusions in the Constitution of India. These are referred to as "Utopian Amendments".

1. **Utopian First Amendment:** *There shall be only one general election every five years.* If the parties elected to power cannot form the government then they shall sit as dummy members of the parliament/legislature with no power to legislate but can only debate. The cause for not being able to form the government may be either because they have no clear majority to rule or because the coalition partners do not like to look at each other's faces.

2. **Utopian Second Amendment:** *In the event of the parties not being able to form a government, then the President/Governor would take over the administration of the nation/state. The President/Governor would then exercise his/her powers to appoint minister(s) who can be elected member(s) from any party or from outside of the parliament to look after each ministry.*

3. *Utopian Third Amendment: The President/Governor would then nominate one of the elected representative, irrespective of seniority, as Prime Minister/Chief Minister. This make shift cabinet would consider the views expressed on the floor of the house to govern the nation/state. However, the actual governing will be done by the President/Governor through this make shift cabinet. The main reason for having a make shift cabinet (which could have been replaced by the secretaries directly reporting to the President) is that it gives access to the people to represent their views and thus keep a check on the government machinery. This arrangement will be in place for the remaining mandatory period at the end of which, the election schedule will be announced by the Chief Election Commissioner.*

4. *Utopian Fourth Amendment: All political leaders will get the normal security cover and there shall be no personal security ring comprising of Black Cats with AK47 or any other weapon, automatic, semi automatic or man-*

ual. The reason for this is having such a security ring has become a status symbol. Also, in most of the cases the on looker will have difficulty in comprehending about who is protected from whom. Further, every profession has its in built risks and therefore the person who chooses the profession must also learn to live with the risk. This is true with the professions of Firemen, Military, Police and other jobs. It is necessary to bring politics and politicians to the ground and make them live like other human beings. Further, all such personalized security ring for the non-sitting members of the legislature/parliament including the ex-prime ministers and other cabinet members will be with drawn. The politicians must live with the people and die in the midst of people. Politics must be declared as another profession and therefore the politicians must learn to live with the risks associated with their profession.

5. **Utopian Fifth Amendment:** *The oath and allegiance shall be with reference to the Constitution and not any religious book or text.*

6. **Utopian Sixth Amendment:** *All Tendering Procedures and the Evaluation of Tenders including the selection process and award of the contract must be made public on the web sites of each ministry/public sector ensuring transparency and shall be available at all facilitation counters attached each ministry. These shall pertain to the construction, procurement and service activities involving public money. The aim is to make public all data available on the selection and financial aspects of the project to avoid pilferage and scams and scandals.*

7. **Utopian Seventh Amendment:** *The process of making public all data must apply to the defense procurement also as these cannot be treated as secret. All the big powers and arms dealers know exactly the kind of weapons that every other country possesses. Information about deployment details must be kept secret and not the financial aspects of the procurement.*

8. **Utopian Eighth Amendment:** *There will be the institution of Lok Pal, in addition to the existing courts, in New Delhi and in all state capitals to probe the corruption cases and other charges, involving all public servants including all members of parliament and legislature with no exception. They shall have the power to direct the IB, CBI, Revenue Intelligence and other agencies of both central and state government to probe into the cases that they are dealing. The central/state government or the parliament/legislature cannot come in the way of functioning of Lok Pal. All the judges of these courts will be appointed by the Chief Justice of India in consultation with four senior judges of the Supreme Court and will be appointed by the President of India. Every one, from President, Prime Minister, Governor,*

Chief Minister, Ministers of State & Center, Bureaucrats, Members of the Parliament & Legislature, Officers of Public Sector companies, Clerks and Peons will come under the purview of these courts. Lok Pal will have the powers to order the dismissal of all those who come under his/her purview if found corrupt or found not discharging the duties as expected by the Executive with in the frame work of the constitution.

9. *Utopian Ninth Amendment: The government shall nominate more judges at all levels with the sole intention of making sure that no one will have to stay in the prison for more than fifteen days to get a hearing. If a person in the jail cannot get a hearing for over a month, and if the case is not discharged with in twelve months from the court, he/she shall be released and all charges against the person shall be withdrawn. It is a pity that there are thousands languishing in the jails for years without even getting a chance of a hearing, let alone getting to hear a judgment from the court. We are a nation where we keep recruiting bureaucrats and at the same time have great difficulty in nominating judges for clearing thousands of pending cases resulting in thousands languishing in the jails. The number of judges in Supreme Court and High Court will be increased to make sure that the back log of the pending cases is cleared as quickly as possible. This can be done by appointing the retired judges of the Supreme Court and High Court to fill special additional benches created for the purpose of clearing the pending cases. At the same time efforts should be made to appoint new judges in place of the retired judges so as to enhance the strength of the judiciary. Once the cases are cleared, the number of judges in various courts will be kept at the increased level in order to make sure that the appellants do not have to wait for justice.*

10. *Utopian Tenth Amendment: Issues related to insurgency will be dealt with by the courts, if referred to by either the government or public through public interest litigation, in a manner that will fall outside the purview of Human Rights Commission. Invariably, the media and the Human Rights Commission appear not to be bothered about the police, para-military and army personnel who lay down their lives fighting the criminals and terrorists. Instead the criminals and the terrorists are elevated to the status of heroes as this suits the interests of some of the parties who are known to have links with such outfits. A list of such known and proven terrorists must be published giving details of the crimes committed by them. All efforts must be made to ensure that a terrorist is not kept in jail for months together to avoid the occurrence of such cases as hijacking of planes or kidnapping of important persons. There shall be a separate tribunal/bench for*

trying the terrorists and the trial of a terrorist shall be completed with in thirty days. Each judge shall hear not more than ten cases each day and the judgment shall be delivered at the end of thirty working days. Any attempt by any of the contesting parties to get indefinite adjournment shall be awarded a very stiff penalty to ensure discipline and commitment to the resolution of disputes.

11. **Utopian Eleventh Amendment:** *A pay commission without any members from the bureaucracy, retired or in service, will be set up to redefine the salary structure. The assumption that no body can get a salary more than a bureaucrat must be dispensed with. Also, the practice that only an IAS officer must become a Cabinet Secretary must also be dispensed with. The teachers, nurses, policemen, ward boys in the hospital, postmen and other similar persons must be given better emoluments. They should not be expected to work in an altruistic environment, as people cannot live on patriotism. For example, the society must give financial benefits to teachers who are expected to groom the children. This alone will help in picking the persons with the right kind of attitude for teaching profession. In the same way the policeman must be respected by the society and given financial benefits. This alone will help in getting the persons with the right kind of attitude for the police force. If the teacher and the policeman were to stay in dilapidated houses or in places that resemble slums, it would be atrocious to expect these persons living in such despicable conditions to do their job in a fair manner. Can the society expect the policemen to maintain law and order, and not swayed by the bribe especially when the politicians have a price? Are we not fooling ourselves by suppressing those elements of the society that are to play a major and dominant role in character building? Are not these people more important to the society than the engineers, scientists and administrators? The policeman on the beat represents the government and therefore the attitude of the policeman is more important than that of even the Prime Minister or for that matter the President. This does not mean that the policeman, teacher, nurse etc must get the same salary as a bureaucrat or President or Prime Minister. This only means that these people who have a dominant role to play in a society must be recognized and must be given a mechanism to lead a decent and respectable life. If they live in slums and if we expect them to build and mold the character of the young ones then we definitely need psychiatric help. A society that does not recognize this has only one way to go, down, and no other way.*

12. **Utopian Twelfth Amendment:** *Every citizen must first be looked upon as honest and efforts must be spent to locate the dishonest. Today the practice*

is the other way round. This is related to the problem of attitude of the individual and this attitude is linked to the feudalistic approach of the person occupying a position of authority.

13. **Utopian Thirteenth Amendment:** President, Vice President, Governor, Prime Minister, Chief Minister, Ministers at Center & State, Members of Parliament and Legislature, President, Secretaries and other office bearers of Political Parties, Bureaucrats and other government officials and their families shall not get public money for their medical treatment abroad. If the specialized treatment does not exist in India, then they shall endure the pain peacefully with courage in India in the same way as the common man does. This shall make them realize the need to respect and support and encourage people with specialization and not indulge in manipulation by putting people with no merit in top positions just because they belong to certain caste or religion or related to some important person.

14. **Utopian Fourteenth Amendment:** President, Vice President, Governor, Prime Minister, Chief Minister, Ministers at Center & State, Members of Parliament and Legislature, Presidents, Secretaries and other office bearers of Political Parties, Bureaucrats and other government officials shall not go abroad for medical treatment, even if the medical expenses are met by personal funds, government funds, friends, enemies, supporters or relatives. Nor will they get foreign experts to India to treat them. If they do, they forfeit their positions. This will ensure the need to build facilities in India and acknowledge and respect the experts and not just play caste politics.

15. **Utopian Fifteenth Amendment:** Every effort must be made to provide avenues for the betterment of the socially and educationally backward people. Further, there shall be only one set of criteria for promotion for every one. There shall be no dilution in the criterion for the backward people. The dilution of the criterion must be limited to the initial encouragement by way of reservation in schools, colleges and initial recruitment alone. This should not be stretched to the ridiculous extent of allowing the student to climb the ladder and become chief surgeon or chief engineer or director. Merit alone must be the criterion for promotion and not caste or any other criterion.

16. **Utopian Sixteenth Amendment:** All the sitting members of the parliament and bureaucrats shall spend a minimum of thirty days near the Siachen Glacier in exactly the same way as a soldier with no extra facilities or special amenities. This will help the members of the parliament and the bureaucrats to remember the problems faced by the defense personnel whenever the subject of a cut in the defense budget is discussed. In the same

way all bureaucrats will spend a period of three months on the Himalayan front in addition to spending thirty days on the Siachen Glacier to get a better understanding of the conditions under which the troops fight. This will help them to take quick decisions in defense related issues. This will also help in establishing a meaningful civilian control over the defense services. This will help the decision makers to appreciate the ground realities.

17. *Utopian Eighteenth Amendment: When ever there is a shortage of power and water, every area, including the area of residence of very important persons including President, Vice President, Governor, Prime Minister, Chief Minister, Ministers at Center & State, Members of Parliament and Legislature, President, Secretaries and other office bearers of Political Parties Bureaucrats and other senior government officials, will face load shedding and cuts in water supply. They shall not get the facility of generator sets or other battery back up at the cost of the public money or party funds. This will make those who are in power to realize the importance of good governance.*

18. *Utopian Nineteenth Amendment: Every school from the kindergarten level to the higher secondary and the 10+2 must be affiliated to the Secondary Education Board. This rule shall apply to the regular and the open school irrespective of whether they are run by the government agencies or private institutions including religious organizations. In the case of schools that are aimed at teaching only religious texts like Veda, Bible, Koran, Guru Granth Sahib, etc it is mandatory for the children to learn other basic subjects like Social Studies, Geography, Environment Sciences, History, the national language (Hindi) and the state language as compulsory subjects. It is all the more important to make them realize the rights of the people belonging to other faiths rather than talking about their own God with no reverence to others including those who may not believe in any God. It is necessary to inculcate in the mind of the children at a very young age a sense of belonging to the nation. They should not be insulated from the rest of the society by making them study their own religion and made to grow up as insensitive human beings. Being sensitive to one's own needs and beliefs is definitely not the way to grow up in a multi cultural society.*

19. *Utopian Twentieth Amendment: In the case of riots, communal or otherwise, where children are the only survivors having lost their elders in the rioting, the victims need not have to go to the police station to file First Information Report. The magistrate with the police must go to them, wherever they are housed and record their statements and register the First Information Report. The traumatized children should not be forced to go to*

a police station to lodge a complaint or a First Information Report. Every effort must be made to heal the wounds rather than aggravate suffering by the process of interrogation in a police station. Further, the leaders, religious or political or otherwise, shall be forced to pay for all the damages caused during the rioting. If the leaders, religious or political or otherwise, do not have assets then the assets of the religious group or parties or associates shall be seized and these persons responsible for initiating the riots shall be made to work for the community.

20. ***Utopian Twenty-first Amendment:*** *In the case of riots, communal or otherwise, where girls or women have been sexually abused, the victims need not have to go to the police station to file First Information Report. The magistrate with the police must go to them, wherever they are housed and record their statements and register the First Information Report. The traumatized girls or women should not be forced to go to a police station to lodge a complaint or a First Information Report. Every effort must be made to heal the wounds rather than aggravate suffering by the process of interrogation in a police station.*

One of the Utopian though related to "*a sitting member of the legislature or parliament cannot change the political party. He/she must resign from the legislature/parliament, resign from the political party and then contest the elections that will be held once in five years under a new party symbol or as an independent*" has been transformed in to a reality by the parliament. Further the number of ministers/cabinet posts that can be created in any state has been linked to the strength of the legislature. This will help in the curbing of the natural tendency of some of the politicized who specialize in horse trading an the eve of the swearing ceremony and cabinet formation. The Indian politicians have showed great courage to clean up the political processes by staying with in the system and this augurs well for the future of the nation.

Can these be called utopian thoughts? Can we not expect accountability from our leaders? Can we not expect these from our own government? These are the normal things that bring every citizen, including the politicians who are enjoying unchecked privileges, with in the framework of the laws of the land. The fact is that any thing that creates hurdles or obstruction to the phenomenal elbow space that the leaders have created for themselves over the years will be resisted. The laws are only for those who have a natural flair to obey the laws and not for those who have a natural flair for disobeying the laws. The bureaucracy and the politicians believe that they need to be treated in a different way, different from the rest of the people and therefore are above law. The section of the society that contributes to the wealth and well being of

the entire society, is always given a step motherly treatment. This is very similar to the story of a beggar. A beggar used to go to a particular house every day
as he was sure that the kind lady would give alms. One day, it so happened that
there was nothing left in the house and therefore the kind lady apologized to
the beggar for not being in a position to give him alms. The beggar, in return,
abused her for not giving him alms! Similar things happen in offices where the
sincere and hard working persons are abused and given stringent targets to
achieve while manipulators become the eyes and ears of the bosses! The
rationale behind this is that since that particular section of the society is contributing to the wealth and well being of the entire society, why not use them
for a piggyback ride? Unfortunately, it is not realized that penalizing efficiency
would bring the society and therefore the nation down.

Mr. Shyamal Mukherjee of Indian Civil Service who was the Cabinet
Secretary during the time of Jawaharlal Nehru has suggested that the time has
come to abolish IAS. In an interview published in India Today, he has indicated that the service has outlived its utility. The management of Orissa super
cyclone, Gujarat earthquake, starvation of people in many districts of Orissa,
Madhya Pradeash and Rajasthan in the midst of huge food grain stock, and
many more such cases have shown the failure of the administrative machinery.
The concept of civilian control that was enforced during the British rule has
been extended to ridiculous levels by having bureaucrats overseeing the work
of specialized man power. One finds them in public sector undertakings that
specialize in as diverse areas as banking to manufacturing to service. Nothing
can be more counter productive than this. Today, the bureaucracy is unfortunately known more for their arrogance and manipulation capabilities than for
their administrative or governance capabilities.

But the assumption that abolishing bureaucracy will solve the ills of the
society is also a far fetched idea! There are cases where the institutions managed by scientific man power are more mis managed than scientifically managed! Therefore, the issue is not whether to abolish bureaucracy or not, but to
ensure that bureaucracy does not become a stumbling block. There is no reason to doubt the efficacy of the bureaucracy. A nation does need bureaucracy
as otherwise, there will be rank anarchy. What needs to be achieved is to ensure
that bureaucracy does not get into the habit of cornering all positions including the ones that need scientific and technological expertise in the name or
garb of administration. Therefore, what is needed in a society is to bring in
experts and put them in positions of authority where ever required with out
threatening the very fabric of the society as bureaucracy is needed in as much
a the politicians are needed to hold the society together.

The sad state of governance in India can be presented by the following classic case studies:

Acceptance of the fact that even after fifty years of independence, the polity and the bureaucracy has not put in place a proper distribution and overseeing mechanism to implement rural development projects in spite of huge funds being made available by every political party in every budget is in itself a sad state of affairs. The result is non utilization of funds and therefore the rural population do not get water to drink, food to eat, basic medical care, schooling for children. The bureaucracy has the constitutional protection and the bureaucrats keep jumping from one chair to another with the sole aim of reaching the top of the bureau.

George Fernandes, the politician, had to step in to ensure that the defense personnel get the necessary equipment and personal gear to fight the battle on Siachen glacier.

The bureaucracy had no expertise to handle the relief operations either after the Orissa super cyclone or Gujarat earthquake. Even after one week of the occurrence of the disaster, the administration had no plan or strategy to provide relief to the victims.

A large population in a number of districts in Orissa, Madhya Pradesh, Rajasthan face famine with no food to eat. At the same time, the warehouses are flooded with food grains and are left to rot.

It is hard to believe that even after fifty years of independent governance, the administrative machinery has not succeeded in creating a structure to address this kind of human suffering by providing relief to the people irrespective whether they are the victims of floods, famine, earthquake or cyclone. When ever a crisis strikes the people, the state and central administrative machinery indulge in the blame game making it look as if the well being of the people is no body's concern. The bureaucrats in spite of being generalists end up cornering all the benefits. Further, they get constitutional protection and therefore are not accountable for any thing. The democratic system makes it easy to remove the political party in power and not the members of bureaucracy who are more generalists than specialists. Thus Shyamal Mukherjee's suggestion to abolish the bureaucratic cadre and replace it with hired professionals with requisite expertise from industry deserves to be looked at from the point of view of giving the views of the experts the sanctity and respect that they deserve. Therefore, if a suggestion comes from an expert then there is a need for the bureaucracy to take a serious view of it and accept it. The acceptance can come after a debate. But the debate should not be for the purpose of transforming the bureaucrat into a specialist, which would then be used to put down the expert. This is the typical mind set that puts brakes on every administrative issue and bring the bureaucracy and the expert community into a conflict state. The proposed changes in labor laws, if approved and passed in the parliament, should make the process of hiring of experts on contract/short term basis with adequate compensation a feasible option.

Therefore, it is necessary to make the administrative machinery that includes the politicians accountable. There cannot be a stage where the politicians assume that when they are elected to power the people have given them the mandate to manage the affairs of the nation as they feel fit! The need to fill the vacant positions of judges in the lower courts has become urgent. At the same time, the need to increase the number of judges at all levels merits serious consideration and action. Further, there is a need to put a stop to the end less adjournments by levying stiff penalties on the litigant who seeks adjournment. This becomes necessary as this alone provides a means for the people to get justice without delay. The increase in the number of judges should not be looked upon as redundant and therefore a waste of public money. Increasing the number of judges resulting in a quicker hearing of the cases is the only way of safeguarding the interests of the people and therefore strengthening of the democracy. An early hearing of petitions/cases in the courts is a sure way of enforcing the respect for the rule of the law in those who are either in power or not in power. This will put an end to the "consolation of mind" as there will be no excuses and every thing becoming transparent will make the society all the more aware of the ground realities.

vi

A society can progress and reach great heights of cultural, technological and political evolution when different sections of a society share the same or similar dream in respect of the complete society or nation. This alone avoids fragmentation of the society. Thus the state must lend its support to all sections that contribute to the furthering of the well being of the society as a whole and this must be the principal job of the administration. The administration must keep a check on what is taught in the schools. What is taught in schools becomes more important than any thing else, as the children at an impressionable age must be protected from being subjected to religious fanaticism or fundamentalism. Teaching religious fanaticism or fundamentalism should not be looked upon as a derivative of the fundamental right of the freedom of worship! This would amount to stretching the freedom to an extent where it is bound to create all round misery. The administration and the political leadership must work towards avoidance of such a scenario. The onus will have to be on the local community leaders and not on the central or state leadership as this would help inculcate the thoughts of putting the larger interests of the society or country above the short term gains based on narrow thought processes. The people must be made to realize their responsibilities towards the society at large irrespective of the level and extent of this responsibility. The aim must be to make people to contribute to the well being of society and share the fruits of such an activity rather than put a demand on the society and become a burden or a drag. Those who are weak irrespective of their religious beliefs must be provided support to improve their lot.

There is a need to evolve some parameters to guide the allocation of help. This parameter cannot be based on the population as this would then lead to a number game and a demographic catastrophe. Some of the parameters that must be considered are

(a) Literacy rate taken as average of male & female literacy rates

(b) Birth rate

(c) Contribution to the setting up of institutions like schools, colleges, hospitals that are used by people belonging to other sections as well. These should not become places meant only for that particular section of the society and therefore should not be religious schools or colleges teaching theology

Thus the parameters chosen must help to quantify the extent to which the section of the society has integrated its ambitions with the ambitions of the entire society.

There is a need to specify parameters that are important from the point of view of having impact or influence on the living conditions of the society. Further, it is proposed to provide weighting factors to these parameters in order to indicate the importance or influence that these parameters would have on the living conditions of the people. These parameters can be

(a) Basic Education Level (up to 10th standard): P_{BEL}

(b) Literacy Rate: P_L

(c) Birth Rate: P_{BR}

(d) Service to Society (institutions that have been set up for the benefit of society and not for the benefit of any particular community, sect, caste or religion): P_{SS}

The basic education level and basic literacy refer to the ability of the people to understand the forces in the society and to fend for themselves. Here the basic education does not refer to the students going through the rigors of conventional science and mathematics courses. Here, the education is more vocational in the sense that the studies/curriculum are integrated with the environment in which the student is living. That is the syllabus is integrated with the work he is expected to do in the village and therefore the student feels motivated to attend classes as he/she sees the advantages of such an education in improving his/her life. These also help the people in making them understand the documents that they are made to sign. There is no second opinion about the fact that the ability to read and write, and the basic education up to 10th standard will bring about a revolutionary change in the process of governance and parliamentary democracy. The other parameter is the birth rate, which is in the hands of the people. But this parameter is influenced by the community, political leaders and the level of awareness of people. This must be made a politically sensitive issue. Otherwise the motto might become,

"Producing children is our birth right,

Providing for us is your constitutional obligation"!

This marks the birth of a vote bank. Once this is achieved, the number game starts and the society gets into the fast track of demographic disaster. The last parameter refers to the contribution made by the community to well being of the society by creating assets in the areas of education, health, libraries etc. This parameter serves to acknowledge the vision of the leaders of the community that helped in building harmony in the society and creating such assets that helped in building bridges between various communities. This would lead to the progress and prosperity of the society taking all the elements of the society in its fold. Thus these parameters present the various initiatives that the community leaders can take for the betterment of society as a whole. The stress should not be on putting conflicting demands on the government or political parties in power or bureaucracy but to join hands to build a better society that would be inherited by the children. Thus the stress is on cooperative peaceful living. These parameters apply not only to individual communities but also to *taluks, zilla parishads,* non governmental organizations involved in social work, districts and state governments. Thus any grant that is to be given to any of these units must be decided only after evaluating these parameters. These parameters give a better picture or information about the well being of the people as the parameters relate to the achievements rather than money allocated or money spent. Thus, these can be looked upon as deliverables that can be measured or quantified, and not some thing abstract or philosophical and therefore immeasurable.

The weighting functions are decided by what is achievable and also on the possible impact or influence of the parameters on the well being of the entire society. The general literacy level, referred to as literacy rate, would to a certain extent help to empower the people. This will help them to understand the documents that they are asked to sign. These documents may relate to their property or the daily wage they earn or the decisions that they make as part of empowerment. Thus a segment of society that is capable of reading and writing presents an excellent level from where further steps leading to betterment of quality of life are easy to take. Thus the weighting function for the P_{LR} is given a value of 1. 0.

The basic education level is easier to achieve once the general literacy level is achieved. It must be borne in mind that the basic education level of 10th standard must help in creating a knowledge base for entrepreneurs and not end up creating a population that looks to government for jobs. Therefore the basic education level must be such as to provide the necessary understanding about the ways of life and the ability to manage one's life. This would also imply a need to bring about a change in the very education system. The education must not comprise of just mathematics, science and theories with no knowledge about managing one's own life. There is a need to weave, as it were, the daily occupation of the child or the adult into the curriculum that would enhance the value of education. This alone can bring about reasonable and recognizable changes in the living condition of the poorest of the poor. The weighting function for basic education level is given a value of 0. 25.

The birth rate is always related to the literacy rate. If the literacy rate is high, the birth rate will be low as the birth rate is a function of awareness about family planning and the ways of improving or bettering the quality of life both for the individuals and for the family. Thus, the weighting function for birth rate is given the same value as that of literacy rate, 1. 0.

The last parameter on service to society is not easy to account for due to the different affluent levels of the different communities. However, it should be easy to account for it if it is looked upon as part of the overall religious activity as the demands made on the government for different concessions are normally based on religion, caste and sub caste. In the first place, this kind of concessions based on religion or caste must be discouraged. The concessions should be based on economic backwardness of the individual or community rather than on the religion that is practiced by the beneficiary. Even though this may be an utopian thought, there is nothing wrong in dreaming about it. It is extremely difficult to change the ground reality. But the concept of service to society has no meaning or relevance to the section of the society that is at the bottom of the social ladder. However, there are some communities like

Lingayat, Vokkaliga etc in Karnataka who have been listed as OBC, other backward classes, but have built medical, engineering and other colleges that are providing service to the society. The need of the hour is that when certain communities have started building assets that are providing service to the society, these communities must take pride in coming out of the backward classification even if it amounts loosing out the many concessions provided by the government. This is the basic tenet of enhancing the self worth of an individual or a community. There is nothing great in parading one self as belonging to backward community. There is no great honor in being called backward. Thus, discarding the backward tag helps in giving the community a sense of belonging and a sense of contributing to the good of the society as they would have built bridges of harmony between different communities. The weighting function for service to society is given a value of 1.0.

In all these cases, these factors present a picture of the role played by the leaders, either of the political parties or of community, in improving the quality of life of the community or society without making rabble rousing speeches or blaming other communities or the party in power. The Feel Good Factor can be evaluated to find the level of the well being of the people of a nation, state or region or community during any given duration of time. There is a need to arrive at a mechanism of putting a number for the factor "service to the society". This service can be focused on to a part of a state and not necessarily on the entire state or nation. In case the contribution is not considerable, then a value of 0 is used. Giving a value to the factor "service to society" is subjective in nature and therefore presents a great opportunity for fudging the facts!

The objective of using these factors and parameters is to identify areas where proper usage of money is not made. These factors can also be used to evaluate the effectiveness of governance of political party in power to address the problems of the society. This gives an opportunity to take corrective action, which is the basis of good governance. The bottom line must be to ensure that the beneficiaries must receive the proposed or planned benefits with minimal loss or diversion of funds. This is the challenge before the bureaucracy and it is this that differentiates good governance from bad governance. It is also here that the Indian bureaucracy has failed to serve the needy and the poor even after fifty three years of independent governance.

Thus the Feel Good Factor that is a combination of all these can be represented as

Feel Good Factor =

$$(1 \times P_{LR}/100) \times (0.25 \times P_{BEL}/100) \times (1 + 1 \times P_{SS}/100)/(1 \times P_{BR}/100)$$
$$= \{P_{LR} \times P_{BEL} \times (1 + 0.01 \times P_{SS})/(400 \times P_{BR})\}$$

Some optimistic numbers for the various parameters can be:

Literacy Rate	P_{LR}	100%
Basic Education Level	P_{BEL}	60%
Service to Society	P_{SS}	75%
Birth Rate	P_{BR}	0. 25%

With the above numbers, the Feel good Factor becomes

Feel Good Factor = 100x60x(1 + 0.01x75)/(400x0.25)

$$= 105$$

There may be cases where a section of the society or even state government like Bihar has not been able to build adequate number of schools and hospitals. This is also valid in the case of states. Some states have schools but no teachers, hospitals but no doctors and nurses.

With the revised numbers, that may represent extreme cases,

Literacy Rate	P_{LR}	20%
Basic Education Level	P_{BEL}	20%
Service to Society	P_{SS}	1%
Birth Rate	P_{BR}	2%

the Feel Good Factor now becomes

Feel Good Factor = 20x20x(1 + 0.01x1)/(400x2)

$$= 0. 505$$

For a vibrant society the "Feel Good Factor must be between 30 to 60. When this becomes greater than 60 and approaches a value of around 100 there will be a distinct possibility of a demographic inversion whereby the population of the old starts becoming more than the population of the young and therefore the society faces the danger of becoming sick, unstable and weak. This has been the tragedy of the Parsi community. The community that had created wealth for the country even when the country was under colonial rule has, unfortunately, come to a state where the population of the elderly is more than that of the young. Thus, sooner than later the Parsi community would become a part of history and the day that happens, God forbid, would be a black day for the anthropologists and sociologists as India would have lost one of the most versatile and gifted community the world has ever seen. A study of the living conditions in the Leh district of Ladhak Hill Council of Jammu and Kashmir State shows that the human development factor in this region is very high, as good as in Kerala state in the south of India. The achievement of the administrative machinery in Leh district is commendable as that district has a fairly large population of nomads who migrate from one region to another depending on the climatic conditions (winter and summer) taking the sheep/goats for rearing. The migration of the nomads along with the sheep and goats from upper to lower (or vice versa) depending on the climatic conditions is accompanied by the migration of the school, black board, teacher and the students. Thus, the school also moves along with the nomads and the sheep/goats. Thus, the teaching goes on without a break even as the process of migration is on and it is this that makes the human development in Leh district commendable.

The states like Rajasthan, Uttar Pradesh, Bihar, Orissa etc have the value for "Feel Good Factor" less than 5! While some other states like Kerala have a value as 80. The national average is around 20! This speaks volumes about the progress and the planning that has been achieved in the last fifty years. The reason for this is the very low literacy rate and the basic education level in addition to a very high birth rate. We need to increase literacy rate and basic education level as these will bring the birth rate down automatically. The politicians at all levels have let these states and therefore the entire nation down. The tragedy is that their concern for furthering their existence and supremacy is so profound that they are not even aware of the fact that they have destroyed this nation. The tragedy becomes unfathomable because of the fact that those who are destroying the fabric of the society are those with a foot in the grave and another on the banana peel. Further each and every action of these grand old men and women, who are still wedded to their village politics and look upon the country as an extension of their village, is damaging the fabric of the composite society and therefore the future of the younger generation.

The "Feel Good Factor" is as important as creation of material wealth. A planned approach to

(a) boost the literacy rate and basic education level,

(b) curb the birth rate

will enhance the wealth creation process. This was the solution given by J. R. D. Tata in the fifties and sixties when he pleaded with the government that birth control and literacy must be looked upon as part of development plan. All his pleas fell on the deaf ears of the bureaucrats, politicians and planners confirming once again the saying of Sir C. V. Raman: "Those in power have no brains and those with brains have no power!" Thus the decisions were taken giving low priority to programs related to literacy drive and family planning. This helped in the process of dragging India into a state of confusion and darkness. Confusion was due to unabated birth rate and darkness was due to ever increasing illiteracy amongst the people. Thus the confusion and darkness that got created were of great help to the bureaucrats and politicians as these two states of human deprivation helped them to manipulate and hold on to the state of status-quo. Thus every thing was well planned and every piece of sound and good advice was ignored.

The "Feel Good Factor" decides whether a section of the society has some thing to loose or not in the event of law and order breaking down. The feel Good Factor can be calculated for different sections of a society belonging to the same region. If the value of the "Feel Good Factor" is very low for a section of a society, say less than 10, then it becomes evident that the majority of the population have nothing to gain or loose from the society. The people of that section of the society would be living in such a state that the very concept of law, order, judiciary, rule of law and other wonderful civilized concepts of living will loose all sense and meaning. The greed and avarice of a segment of affluent and influential section of the society steps in to exploit this situation and therefore the under privileged people become the exploited and abused part of the society. Thus, unwillingly, these under privileged sections of the society become the breeding ground for anti-social and anti-national activities. When this happens, the knee jerk reaction of the administrative machinery is to send in the police, paramilitary forces and in the end the army. The society appears to be racing towards the state of a black hole on earth with no light either entering or coming out. The state starts spending more money on the police and less and less on the betterment of the living conditions. This also happens to be an ideal situation for rationalizing the irrational.

The history tells us that for a long time Germans ignored the thoughts of Adolph Hitler. But, when the conditions all round were showing no signs of improvement, Germans tried to see a glimmer of hope in the thoughts of Adolph Hitler. Even at that stage, the majority of the Germans were not in favor of Adolph Hitler's ideology. But the circumstances were such that the Chancellor of Germany invited him to take over. The same is true with Mussolini in Italy. These happen to be the classic examples of the "Consolation of Mind". If our bureaucracy and political leaders do not change their actions and thought processes, we, in India, may be coming closer to the days of rationalizing the irrational and sink into the depths of despair and "Consolation of Mind".

vii

In life one comes across two kinds of people:

(a) Those who are normal and have an inclination to obey the rules and regulations

(b) Those who honestly believe that they are above rules and regulations

Those who believe that they are above the rules and regulations behave in more or less the same way as the early Anglo-Saxon settlers in Australia or America where the Native Aborigines and Native Red Indians were systematically killed or driven to a corner. One possibly cannot attribute this to the cruelty of Anglo-Saxons. It can be attributed to the fact that in the frame of mind of the early Anglo-Saxon settlers, the Native Aborigines and Native Red Indian had no place. The concept of peaceful coexistence of different cultural entities was not known to these early settlers, about two hundred years back. Contrast this to the Indian psyche that allowed the coexistence of Hindus, Buddhists, St. Thomas Christians, Jains, Jews, Armenians for nearly 1,900 years. Around 7th to 8th century the Muslim traders who settled down in some areas of Tamil nadu and Kerala coexisted peacefully with other communities with no communal riots for nearly 1,300 years. India also welcomed the people following the Zoroastrian faith who fled from Parsa in Persia, the present day Iran, unable to stand the tyranny of the riders on the horseback who came from the middle-east. One of the most architecturally beautiful Synagogues, the worshipping place of Jews, in the world is in India, near Kochi. In the recent times, the Bahai sect of Islam built a beautiful Lotus temple in India rather than building it in any of the many staunch Islamic countries. We have in India aborigines living in Andaman Nicobar Island, who have not yet been touched by the changes that have swept the main land. We also have a race that claims to have its origin in Africa living near coastal Gujarat. Nobody seems to be sure of the circumstances under which their ancestors came to India. A report in the science magazine, Nature, says that the DNA tests have shown that the Marathi speaking Jews in Konkan area, Maharashtra, India are the descendents of Moses. All the four sects of Buddhism, who fled Tibet, are thriving in India and in turn have contributed to the Indian society by making available the knowledge of Tibetan Medicine. Thus, the Indian psyche had no difficulty in absorbing people with different religious practices and different philosophies with in its fold and allowed to co-exist peacefully. Pluralism had always been the hall mark of the Indian psyche. Thus, much before the constitution was written and much before the democratic and secular principles dawned on the western civilizations, India had been practicing these principles for hundreds of years. Is not India, God's own Ark? The Indian ethos that had the ability to assimilate different heritages and allowing them to flourish was in for a violent shock when the nomad/tribes from the Central Asia and Middle East invaded the present day Afghanistan, Pakistan and India. These men on the horse back had no great cultural background and no great heritage to fall back upon for guidance for interaction with the other cultures. The situation was identical to what happened with Incas civilization when the Spanish crusaders landed there. In the same way as the Spanish crusaders had no frame of mind to accept any thing other than Spanish tradition, the men on the horse back also did not have any frame of mind to accept any thing other than what they thought their religious leaders had preached.

When Alexander invaded Persia and the present day Afghanistan there was no influx of refugees belonging to Zoroastrian or Buddhist or Hindu religion. The driving force behind Alexander's conquest was to avenge the burning of Athens by King Darius. Therefore the influence of God or religion was missing. Further Alexander encouraged inter religion marriages between Greeks and local gentry. But things were different in the case of the invasions by the Arab and Central Asian tribesmen. They were carrying with them the message of their God, as they had understood it, in the same way as the Spanish missionaries carried with them the message of their God, as they understood it, when then set their foot on South America. The only difference was that these acts were being enacted in different times, different geographical locations and with what they considered to be the messages from their respective Gods, who were thought to be different. The message of God had always been to fight the evil thoughts/forces with in to realize the kingdom of God with in. This was a call to the people to purify themselves and walk the path to salvation, union with God. But, this simple message got transformed into crusades with one single aim of eliminating those who did not believe in the message of their God. Thus, the process of eliminating the evil was either by forcing them to embrace their religion or killing them. As the horse riding tribesmen approached Persian Empire, there was an exodus of people of Zoroastrians to India and China. There had been a number of Buddhist Viharas that had been built in present day Afghanistan, Kazakistan, Tajikistan etc, some along the famous silk route. After Adi Sankara spread the Advaita philosophy, most of the Buddhist population, if not all, embraced Hinduism. When the Arab Tribesmen came riding the horses, the present day Afghanistan was still under the rule of the Shivite Shahi Kings Jayapala and Anandapala. Around 10th century AD, with the defeat of the Shivite Shahi Kings Jayapala and Anandapala the destruction of the Buddhist Viharas and the Hindu Temples was initiated. An exodus of Hindus, Zoroastrians and Buddhists started from these regions. Those who could not escape were either killed or converted to Islam. Thus, the absence of pluralism leading to the inability of the followers of Islam to respect those religions that existed and flourished before the birth of Prophet was responsible for destruction of the ancient Buddhist, Hindu and Zoroastrian heritage in these regions. This was in spite of the Prophet's teaching that other religions must be respected. The root cause for this kind of unwanted destruction was the misunderstanding of the term "Jihad". The word "jihad" means the destruction of evil with in oneself to realize the Kingdom of God that exists in oneself. It never meant killing of some one who does not share the same thoughts or practices as the man on the horse back! The flourishing Buddhist and Hindu cultural centers in these regions and the destruction of the Incas civilization in South America were more due to the inability of the followers to understand the teachings of the Prophet and the Savior. It is often said that the religion is the opium of the masses and also that the saints, saviors and the like die twice, once when they leave their bodies for the heavenly abode and the second time at the hands of their ardent followers. The question that these zealots did not ask was, "How many Gods and Kingdoms of Heaven can there be?"

The magnificent Buddhist and Hindu heritage that existed in Afghanistan and other places as late as 10th century AD that were built by Emperor Asoka and the Kushan Dynasty was the target of attacks by the Ghasnavids, Mahmud and even Aurangzeb of the Mughal dynasty that ruled India. Therefore the *fatwa,* the verdict with religious authority, which was issued by Mulla Mohammad Omar to destroy all the idols in Afghanistan was not surprising or shocking. Further the article by Sakina Yusuf Khan published in Times of India presents interesting facts. Maulana Abdul Khaliq, the Vice Chancellor of Darul Uloom, still holds the century old fatwa declaring India a Darul Hard, a country of war or conflict, valid even today! In addition, Safdar Nagori of SIMI, Students of Islamic Movement of India, an organization that appears to nurse the agenda of an Islamic India, claims to be bitter about being an Indian and has great respect for Osmana Bin Laden who has shown great character. It is sad that the secularism and the inexhaustible Indian tolerance are being used fully by such people to nurture and propagate hatred. These people should read the history and learn to respect the fact that many Islamic states have persecuted Muslims not to speak of people belonging to other communities. What is strange and even amusing is that S. A. Bukhari, the Imam of Jama Masjid of Delhi has thought it fit to support Taliban citing the demolition of Babri Masjid as the reason.

The most unfortunate part of all this is that these people have used the freedom that is available in a society to destroy the same society, especially because there is nothing in Koran that talks of any such hatred towards any one following any other religion or for that matter hatred towards any religion. The view of S. A. Bukhari is amusing and strange for the following reasons:

(a) None of the invaders or kings had no business to build a *masjid,* mosque, at the sites of any of the temples either at Ayodhya or Varanasi or Mathura or for that matter any at any other place as is evident even in Israel. These are acts of bigotry and cannot be attributed to any religion or a holy book. These were the acts normally practiced by all invaders for subjugating the natives. But unfortunately an act committed hundreds of years ago has become a burning issue tearing apart the lives of millions of innocent Jews, Hindus and Muslims. At the same time, this has become a means of manipulating the emotions of different communities and therefore has become a problem that no body wants to be resolved as this would help in furthering the political ambitions of a few ruthless manipulators on both sides.

(b) A religion that came into existence in the 7th century appears to have gotten into a state where "*jihad*" is interpreted in such a way as to make them declare war and create battle fields against all ancient cultures, religions and heritages. This is happening world wide in spite of the fact that neither Prophet nor Koran advocate such an attitude towards other cultures, religions and ways of life.

(c) The Buddhist centers in present day Afghanistan were destroyed and people were either massacred or converted to Islam by Ghaznavids, Mahmud, and others. A few could succeed in fleeing Afghanistan. Thus in the frame of mind of Ghaznavids, Mahmud, Taimur, Ghori, Chengiz Khan, Mulla Mohammad Omar and Bukhari the Imam of Jama Masjid, "If you are not a Muslim, you must be better dead than alive". The *fatwas* that are so frequently handed out with great elan speaks of scant respect for any thing and every thing other than their own concept of religion and God. These men seem to believe in only one principle, "Either your head or mine, it does not make any difference". This betrays scant respect for life, let alone God. This also represents extreme case of consolation of mind, a kind of mental state that was not seen even in the Nazis who did weird experiments on Jews.

(d) The most respected and historic Islamic Institute, Dar-Ul-Uloom, that still believes in the hundred year old decree that India is a nation of conflict is not in any of the self acclaimed and proclaimed Islamic State but in India.

(e) The Bahai sect of Islam, thought it fit to build their temple in Hindu India and not in any of the self acclaimed or proclaimed Islamic States.

Therefore Bukhari and other *mullas*, Imams in India must learn to stop complaining. Instead, they should join hands with other people professing different faiths and build a wonderful society where every religion and culture can thrive and share the wealth with others.

The early settlers in USA and Australia had no frame of mind to accept any body other than themselves. Pluralism was anathema to the domino theory. Domination and therefore aggression were looked upon as necessary ingredients for the well being of a society. This was aptly described by Adlai Stevenson who declared, "Either you are with us or you are against us". "If you are with us, then you need to think like us!" Therefore the one who did not think, much less dress or look like them, had no option but to die. A recent report in the Australian media about aggression being a part of certain societies and therefore the show of aggression by members of those societies should not be looked upon as a case of defiance or bad conduct on the field makes interesting reading. The Indian psyche has been the champion of pluralism. Pluralism had always been the strength of India. In the recent times, there has been a cause for rethinking about the efficacy of pluralism. Is pluralism a strength or is it a weakness?

The tragedy of the Indian society lies in the fact that in the recorded history, India had never plundered any other society and brought back wealth and riches. This should have been, under normal circumstances, the strength of a society. But the flip side of this is that our psyche or the mind set is such that we have difficulties in understanding the kinks in the thought process of not only our neighbors but also of the other nations. There is no validity in the argument that if we are just, our neighbors, friends and enemies also will be just. We cannot mirror our intentions, however just, reasonable and rational they might me, on others. On the other hand, the state of being reasonable is definitely a reason for others to be unreasonable. The recorded history shows that most of the civilized and rich and powerful societies of the world had plundered and destroyed other civilizations, societies and others' ways of living. Having achieved this, they brought back riches to their country and established their ways of living in the new land that they had conquered.

The other face of the Indian psyche is that any talk about money making or wealth or wealth creation becomes embarrassing. There is a rider on this. The feudalism and the associated ills are so deeply ingrained in the Indian way of thinking as to have made even the democratic process an exercise in feudalism. Thus, in spite of all the talk on empowerment and decentralization, the power is still vested in the hands of an individual or a few individuals. This has the blessings of the bureaucracy as they have every thing to loose once the empowerment and decentralization are put into effect. The result of this is the people have no information about their rights and the government has no intention of educating the people about their rights and how to get what they should be getting as a right, being a citizen of this country. Every bit is made to look as a favor from the boss or top, in the true tradition of feudalism.

viii

The God's creation is essentially an expression of pluralism, with every entity having the right to live in harmony with nature and share the bounty of the nature. Man, in his eagerness to show his supremacy, had been indulging in creating a monolithic control in the society. The history of mankind is replete with cases of the attempts to build and establish monolith control, either as ab-initio attempt or as a part of replacing an existing monolith control in a society by destroying the earlier one. A different kind of catastrophe is unfolding in terms of the World Trade Organization forcing through the concept of open trade of all commodities including the food products. The basic requirement of human beings of any society or culture is food. Then comes the industrial products or the white goods. The view of the World Trade Organization and a few of the member countries who have the necessary clout is that the opening of trade barrier will help in making available of the best quality commodities at the least price due to global competition. The Nobel Laureate and the renowned agricultural scientist Norman Borlaug has a different opinion. He has warned that the developing countries can never compete with the developed countries in the areas of food or agricultural subsidies. This is true in the area of not only the agricultural produce but also in the case of poultry, meat, fisheries, dairy products etc. Thus, if the import of these highly subsidized agricultural products is allowed, this will surely create instability in the agricultural sector resulting in the killing of the indigenous agriculture, poultry, meat and dairy industries. Borlaug says, "Agriculture is the first building block of a society. The peace and stability it brings is essential to investment and industrialization". Therefore when the local agriculture and food related industry gets derailed due to the cheaper imported food products, the following would be the scenario:

(a) Indigenous food production by the farmers would become economically not viable and therefore would lead to the death of agriculture

(b) Millions will become unemployed in rural India

(c) Mounting food import bill and total dependence on food imports

(d) Manufacturing industry that is already under attack would face bigger challenges

(e) The economy would fail on all fronts

(f) Food rioting would start and a large section of the population would reach a state of not gaining or not loosing any thing, which is an ideal state for an all round chaos

(g) The society becomes dependent on the dictates of the developed society

(h) A new form of colonization will be put in place

This appears to be the pre-view of the dooms day. As far as India is concerned, the food rioting would take place only in the urban India as the rural India, even today has the experience of living without the help of the public distribution system that is supposed to give the rural people food grains at affordable prices.

It is necessary that for the general well being of all sections of the society in all nations, the food as an item of trade must be taken off from the purview of World Trade Organization regime. Food as a commodity of trade should be a bilateral issue and therefore depending on the ground reality it can be imported based on bilateral import/export agreements. If this is not done, food riots would become the order of the day and as 11th September 2001 has shown the consequences would be more horrifying than

(a) the senseless destruction of the Bamiyan Buddhas by *Mulla* Mohammad Omar or

(b) the massacre of Buddhists by Ghanznavids or

(c) the massacre of Hindus by Taimur or Ghazni or

(d) the burning of Athens by King Darius or

(e) the burning of Persepolis by King Alexander or

(f) the experiments on and the killing of Jews by the Nazis.

All the above are the classic examples of the worst kind of consolation of mind. We, the mankind, knowingly or unknowingly are heading towards a state of chaos that is going to be more violent and cataclysmic than any event witnessed so far. We have all become a set of toads or cats that think that the best way to wish away a problem is to close ones eyes. This is yet another case of consolation of mind. History has been a never ending case of consolation of mind.

ix

A joke has been posted on internet. A world survey recently conducted by the UN posed the following question: "Can you please give us your opinion about the food shortage in the rest of the world". The survey was a huge failure because:

- In Africa, no one knows what "food" is
- In western Europe no one knows what "shortage" is
- In eastern Europe no one knows what "opinion" is
- In South America no one knows what "please" is
- In the US no one knows what "rest of the world" is

We are all the victims of consolation of mind of different kind.

The most unfortunate thing is that these actions of establishing monolith control in a society have been done mostly in the name of God or in the name of nationalism. Those who do not believe in my God become the heathens. This gives me the right to start crusades or *jihad* against those who do not believe in my God. Or for that matter start a crusade against any one who is different from me or us!

The thought process is, "My attempt to spread the teachings of my religion becomes God's work while your attempt to do so becomes fundamentalism. Therefore, you shall not come in the way of my work of God that shall liberate your people. My God gives you salvation while your God does not give you any thing and therefore not good enough! Come and embrace my God who is the only God, and my way is the only way of living."

The result of the inability to comprehend the principle of pluralism was the destruction of the Incas civilization, destruction and killing of native Red Indians in America and aborigines in Australia. The destruction of temples by the tribals on the horse back left a permanent scar on the Indian ethos. In the recent times, the number games played by the politicians is once again transforming the scar into an un-healable wound. This God's own Ark is now being threatened again by unscrupulous politicians, who after dividing the society in the name of religion and caste, are now in the process of tearing apart the very cultural fabric of this country in the name of democracy and secularism.

This is reflected in the oft-repeated demand for proving the patriotism of individuals belonging to a certain community or asking people of one state living in another state to prove their loyalty to the state where they are living. Fortunately this has not yet come to the level of asking persons belonging to different caste or sub-caste to prove their patriotism. This is very similar to the hysterical state in America in the sixties when there was a great anti communist movement. McCarthy unleashed the attack on the immigrants asking them to prove their patriotism towards America. The onus of proving one's innocence in addition to, not being a communist sympathizer rested with the individual. The people who were targeted for this kind of humiliating attack and slander were the immigrants from the east European countries. This not only caused the ruin of many innocent and honest people but also resulted in leaving a permanent scar, stigma culminating in ruin of many families. Many were forced to change their name to avoid becoming the victims of a witch-hunt. Goldie Hawn and Charles Bronson are a few of those who changed their names to escape the attention of rabble-rousing patriots. This phenomenon came to be called McCarthyism.

Are our politicians following the process of starting the movement of McCarthyism in India? It is very easy to ask an individual or a group of individuals to prove their patriotism or loyalty. This does give a sense of power to those who ask others to prove their loyalties. This is often referred to as speaking with a poker face, which is often considered the hall mark of leadership. In the long run this would prove to be counter productive and would become the main cause of the collapse of the composite society like ours. The tragic case of the trumped up spy scandal that dogged the two eminent space scientists of Indian Space Research Organization till the entire case was dismissed by the Supreme Court is a pointer to the rot that has set in the administrative machinery. The Supreme Court judgment made interesting reading as it projected very clearly the flimsiness of the evidence on which the entire case was built. The question that comes up is that when two of the very important, senior and brilliant scientists were implicated in a spy scandal,

(a) Is it not the responsibility of the senior men/women in the intelligence set up to oversee the kind of evidences that were being made the basis of such allegations?

(b) Is it not the responsibility of the bureaucracy that exercises the civilian control over the intelligence set up to make sure that no injustice is being done to the individuals?

The Supreme Court judgment does not present a favorable picture of the entire episode.

The more frightening question that comes up is that if this was the fate of well-known, senior and eminent scientists, what would be the fate of ordinary citizens thousands of whom are languishing in the jails even without a trial? Is there not a mechanism in the governance of a nation where there is an effective mechanism of checks and balances at every stage? Getting legal help is so expensive and time consuming that the common man can only think of it and not opt for it. The code of conduct for the leaders/politicians/bureaucrats, and the checks and balances for governance assume great importance in a composite society like India. This is especially true when the tendency to follow the principle of McCarthyism, that ruined many innocent lives/families in America in the sixties, appears to be on the rise. The other reason is that there are large number of families in India who have their roots in the present day Bangladesh and Pakistan, in addition to the large population belonging to other religions. Thus any attempt at unleashing McCarthyism as a means of curbing/controlling people belonging to one religion or caste or sub-caste, or speaking different language would cause irreparable damage to the national psyche and ethos.

An interaction with the common man gives one the distinct feeling that the Indian psyche, though in tact to a large extent, is being subjected to tremendous pressure to change for the worse by a few manipulators who seem to have paralyzed the society. An interaction with people from Bihar, the most maligned state in India, is an eye opener. Bihar, which was once called Magadh, was the cradle of a great heritage both in terms of learning and statecraft. The greatest Buddhist centers of learning were in Bihar. The ruins of these centers, especially the Nalanda University, that were excavated by the Archeological Department funded to a large extent by late Sir Ratan Tata, can be seen even today in Bihar. One of the greatest treatises on Governance and Financial Management was written by Vishnu Gupta, Chanakya, of Magadh Empire (350BC-350AD). Even now the people of Bihar, with the exception of the top thin layer that appears to be in control, are highly refined, cultured and proud. It is remarkable that this region has always been in a state of turmoil with no semblance of governance. No ticket collector on a train to Patna has the courage to ask for tickets for the fear of being thrown out of the running train. Bihar has one of the highest figures for illiteracy and birth rate making the state ideally suited for exploitation. The financial mismanagement is the order of the day. This is a classic example of a handful successfully paralyzing the entire society.

The worst part of the Indian democracy has been the ease with which a set of corrupt politicians meet and discuss seat adjustment for the general elections both at the center and the state, and become united to fight for saving democracy and secularism. This justifies the profound statement of the Adlai Stevenson "There are No Permanent Enemies or Friends. There are Only Permanent Interests". Was not this profound statement made to represent international ties and diplomacy? We seem to have perfected this to suit the bloated ambitions of the bureaucrats and politicians whose concern for their own interests is far greater than that for the interests of the nation. The entire process of administration is an extension of village feudalism. Every action is an act of favor either to the people or to the nation! The age old wisdom on the

(a) King being a Representative of the People;

(b) King is there only because there is the Nation and not vice versa

have been conveniently forgotten or discarded. In its place has come the new slogan, *hum hain to sub kuch hai, hum nahi hain to kuch bhi nahi hain!*, which translates to, "If I am there then every thing is there, If I am not there then nothing is there!"

An interesting message came across on the inter net: "Indians succeed, India fails" It is reproduced below.

"In this new millennium, I would like to sum up our performance in the 20th century in one sentence. Indians have succeeded in countries ruled by whites, but failed in their own. This outcome would have astonished leaders of our independence movement. They declared Indians were kept down by white rule and could flourish only under self-rule. This seemed self-evident. The harsh reality today is that the Indians are succeeding brilliantly in countries ruled by whites, but failing in India. They are flourishing in the USA and Britain. But those that stay in India are pulled down by an outrageous system that fails to reward merit or talent, fails to allow people and businesses to grow, and the real power lies with *netas, babus,* and assorted manipulators. Once Indians go to white-ruled countries, they soar and conquer summits once occupied only by whites. While Indians have soared, India has stagnated. At independence India was the most advanced of all colonies, with the best prospects. Today with a GNP per head of $ 370, it occupies a lowly 177th position among 209 countries of the world. But poverty is by no means the only or main problem. India ranks near the bottom in the UNDP's Human Development Index, but high up in Transparency International's Corruption Index. The *neta-babu raj* brought in by socialist policies is only one reason for India's failure. Money, muscle and influence matter most. At independence we were justly proud of our politicians. Today we regard them as scoundrels and criminals. They have created a jungle of laws in the holy name of socialism, and used these to line their pockets and create patronage networks. No influential crook suffers. The mafia flourish unhindered because they have political links. Talent cannot take you far amidst such rank non governance. We are still in our ancient feudal system where no rules applied to the powerful. After fifty years, citizens wail that India is a lawless land where no rules are obeyed. The lack of transparent rules is a major reason why the talented Indians cannot rise in India. A second reason is the *neta-babu raj* remains intact despite supposed liberalization. But once the talented Indians go to rule-based societies in the west, they take off. In those societies all people play by the same rules, all have freedom to innovate without being strangled by regulations. This, then, is why

Indians succeed in countries ruled by whites, and fail in their own. It is the saddest story of the century."

There are bureaucrats like Bishnupada Sethi, the District Collector of Nuapada District in Orissa, who in less than an year succeeded in making the administration work like it is supposed to. He made sure that the village *panchayats* were entrusted the task of running the public distribution system. Today, the villagers get the ration and there is no hungry person in the entire district of Nuapada. In order to achieve this, he had to sack thirteen defiant *sarpanchs,* the village head men, making him the target of the vested interests, from the president of *Zilla Parishad* to the politicians, private retailers to the clique of officials and contractors. But the question that is on every one's mind is, "Will Bishnupada Sethi survive the wrath of the officialdom that believes more in pomp and words and less in good work?" Bishnupada's tenure as the collector of Nuapada district appears uncertain. Further, his future in the officialdom may not be bright as the system rejects the efficient and the honest men and women!

Would Krishna Hutheesingh still be able to look around and then declare that the metamorphosis that overtook Anand Bhavan in Allahabad during the freedom struggle was "With No Regret"? Or would she feel depressed at the prevailing state of affairs and regret the sacrifices made by the society during the freedom struggle?

Can we have a system in place that helps in making "Nice Guys Finish First" instead of the present system where, in the words of B. K. Nehru, "Nice Guys Finish Second"?

These two books make very interesting reading. They are set in two different times. The book "With No Regrets", though written in 1963–1964, is set in the pre-independent India when there were leaders of the stature of Mahatma Gandhi, Sardar Patel, Jawaharlal Nehru, Maulana Azad, Rajaji and others. There was an air of idealism to build a modern independent India. Therefore, the sacrifices that were made was "With No Regrets" as the goal of an independent India had been achieved.

The second book by B. K. Nehru is more a biographical record of his tenure in the Independent India and therefore refers to post independent India. After about fifty years of independence, we seem to be in a state of despair and we find that a thin layer of dubious men and women are steering the future of this country. The system that has been put in place is capable of nurturing only the dubious ones with the "Nice Guys Finishing Second".

The most interesting thing about these two books is that they are written by two cousins with the same family roots. The journey from Krishna Hutheesingh's "With No Regrets" to B. K. Nehru's "Nice Guys Finish Second" tells the story of the state of the Indian Mind: a classic case of "consolation of mind"

A man dies and goes to hell. There he finds that there is a different hell for each country. He goes first to the German hell and asks, "What do they do here?" He is told "First they put you in an electric chair for an hour. Then they lay you on a bed of nails for another hour. Then the German devil comes in and whips you for the rest of the day" The man does not like the sound of that at all, so he moves on. He checks out the USA hell as well as the Russian hell and many more. He discovers that they are all more or less the same as the German hell. Then he comes to the Indian hell and finds that there is a very long line of people waiting to get in. Amazed he asks, "What do they do here?"

He is told "First they put you in an electric chair for an hour. Then they lay you on a bed of nails for another hour. Then the Indian devil comes in and whips you for the rest of the day" "But that is exactly the same as all the other hells. Why are there so many people waiting to get in?

"Because there is never any electricity, so the electric chair does not work. Someone stole all the nails. And the devil used to be a government employee, so he comes in, signs the register and then goes back home..."

Is there a possibility of changing the governance in India so that at least the surplus food grains are used for food for work? The work that can be assigned to the people in remote villages can be for harnessing rainwater and recovering fallow land that can be used for either cultivation or forestation or creation of pasture lands. For the people, a generous ration of food grains is as precious as life itself and therefore the food grains would be well looked after. On the other hand the bureaucracy treats food stocks as a statistical figure that has no other significance. This explains the coexistence of rotting food grains and hungry people, a combination that only Indian polity and bureaucracy can produce.

7

Community Living

Kalidasa, a 4th AD poet, in his play, Shakuntalam, narrates a scene that is possibly a superb representation of the Indian ethos and the value system of the Indian society of the bygone days. When King Dushyanta tries to shoot an arrow at a deer, he is commanded by a hermit boy not to shoot the arrow as the deer belongs to the hermitage. The king obeys the command of the hermit boy. In the present age, the hermit boy might have been man handled by the security. Thus, the society of the bygone years had practiced such an openness as to ensure that even the kings and other administrators were approachable inspite of the security ring. Also even the king and the administrators were held accountable. The king was always considered a representative of the people. King Bharata even went to the extent of disowning his nine sons who had no competence to govern the nation and instead nominated his guard as his successor because of his courage, and understanding of *dharma* and the obligations of a king. In those days the king was looked upon as a *pratinidhi*, the representative of the people. Therefore, there was a kind of a democratic monarchy. That is, the people could go to him and demand justice without having to go through the long, never ending officialdom that is popularly called bureaucracy. The king was not expected to look upon the kingdom as his personal fiefdom. His advisers were *rishis, kul guru,* who were well versed in *dharma.* They not only had a thorough understanding of the right and the wrong, but also always acted in favor of the right irrespective of the persons involved in an issue of concern. The king always used to consult his advisers, ministers and the members of the court before taking a decision. There was no show off by the king or his ministers. The kingdom was looked upon as something that belonged to the people and was given to the king for the purpose of nurturing. Thus the king was only a care taker with the necessary powers to take care of the interests of the people and the kingdom. Because of these reasons the king was also looked upon as an entity representing God; a person whose deeds are based on *dharma,* justice and the teachings of the scriptures. All this changed with the advent of *Kali Yug.* The era of *Kali Yug* is said to have commenced during the rule of King Parikshit, the descendent of Pandavas. An interesting question that comes to mind is, "What caused the shift from a democratic monarchy based on the rule of *dharma* to the self perpetuating and gratifying rule of the kings?" There is a flaw in this question because even during the period of *Krit Yug, Treta Yug, Dwapara Yug,* with the exception of possibly *Sat Yug,* the God had to come down for a total of eight times. This proves that all those exciting things that are said to be proprietary to *Kali Yug* was present even during these other *Yug*as too. The only difference between that state and the present state may be that the level of deceit, injustice, exploitation, suppression is more wide spread and deep rooted in the present day society. These possibly have become a way of life; a part of the daily routine that does not affect our sensibilities any more. Possibly this is due to the change of *samay,* time, from *Sat Yug* to *Krit Yug* to *Treta Yug* to *Dwapar Yug* to *Kali Yug.* We are not to be blamed. It is *samay,* time, that needs to be blamed for all the mess. We are fine and nothing is wrong with us.

In the present day, after about five thousand years since the advent of the era of *Kali Yug,* the administrators practice management by abuse and manipulation. The dynastic ascent, irrespective of whether the incumbent is capable or not, is a law that is taken for granted, and eagerly and heartily endorsed as the only way to salvation of not only an individual but also of a society and therefore a nation. In fact questions and apprehensions will be raised on the very definition of the word "capable or capability". The advisers to the king or the dictator or the elected leader are mostly cronies who cannot differentiate between bajra and wheat, let alone differentiating between right and wrong. Prof. Minhas, the famous economist resigned from the Planning Commission stating that the Indian Agrarian economy is being planned/managed by those who cannot differentiate between wheat and bajra. This reminds one of a joke on the economists. "A man walking along a road in the country side comes across a shepherd with a huge flock of sheep." He tells the shepherd, "I will bet you $ 100 against one of your sheep that I can tell you the exact number in this flock". The shepherd thinks it over; it is a large flock so he takes the bet. "937" says the man. The shepherd is astonished, because the answer is absolutely right. He says, "OK, I am a man of my words. Take a sheep." The man picks one up and begins to walk away. "Wait", cries the shepherd, "Let me have a chance to get even. Double or nothing that I can guess your exact occupation." The man says sure. "You are an economist for a government think-tank", says the shepherd. "Amazing", responds the man, "You are exactly right. But tell me how did you deduce that?" "Well", says the shepherd, "put down my dog and I will tell you."

The rural development programs are planned by those who have no idea about the ground reality in the villages. These have resulted in the starting of a large number of projects on paper and ending them on paper with no perceptible change in the living conditions of the people living in the rural areas. At the same time the migration of people to a few metropolis has increased to an extent that we now have a few mega-metros with a large population living in slums, living in unlivable conditions. But they manage to earn their livelihood and therefore the conditions in the slums in the cities are better than the conditions in the villages, which are any way unlivable. The problem with India is not that the country is poor. This is a rich country with poor people and manipulated by a group of a few educated people, politicians and criminals. This is true of every developing society.

A large amount of money has been spent on "socially uplifting" or "poverty alleviation" projects, which appear to have helped the middlemen to alleviate their own poverty rather than alleviating the poverty of the intended beneficiaries. The plans have failed to address the problems of the rural India either because of the mismatch between the plans churned out in the well furnished offices of the experts and the ground reality in the villages, or because the government administrative machinery is incapable of implementing projects as it is trained to hold on to status quo in the true British style or the reasons can be both. The reasons for the failure to make a success of the various well meaning projects that have been launched again and again by many different governments are:

(a) The administrative machinery is trained to hold on to status quo and we are still holding on to the antiquated rules and regulations and acts of more than a century old which were framed with the sole purpose of holding on to the supremacy of the British rule. Holding on to the antiquated rules, regulations and acts helps to maintain the supremacy of the new ruling class which has taken over from the British rulers.

(b) The development, over a period of time, of a fine blend of cooperation between the administrative machinery, politicians and the criminals as reported in the print media covering the report by the Vohra Commission. But, it would be unfair to damn the entire administrative machinery and every politician. It is no God's commandment that all crooks belong to one religion or speak one language or belong to one profession or belong to one region or belong to one nation or have one particular color of skin or hair or belong to one political party.

But the nexus of the small segment of the politicians, the small segment of the administrative machinery and the entire brotherhood of crooks and criminals have successfully stalled every attempt that is made to improve the living conditions of the vast under privileged masses of this country.

This has been aggravated by the phenomenal increase in population making the issues of poverty eradication, criminalization of politics, failure of law and order, providing better infrastructure facilities like transport, power, health, etc irrelevant. The reason is that with the inherent deficiency in the implementation of development projects, there is no way of addressing these issues, as with each passing day the issue becomes more and more complex. Further, this puts a strain on the kind of resources that the nation has or can muster through aid or borrowings from capital market. No political party has included or wants to include in the manifesto the necessity for control of population as an issue that needs to be addressed on a war footing. The prime reason for this is the fear of losing votes. One way of controlling the population is by educating the people on the need to have a small family. The other way is by a method of rewarding those who limit their families that may be termed a method of carrot and stick, and therefore a coercive activity. The nation is in a hopeless situation and the leadership, both political and the administrative, are blissfully unconcerned about these and are worried only about their own survival and prosperity. However we do hear, now and then as an icing on top of a cake, about the need to improve the living conditions of the people. Of course the cake belongs to the affluent and powerful section of the society that is in minority. This minority has got nothing to do with the majority in whose name the nation is being uplifted. The easiest way to address the problems of population, health, and managing the other important issues in rural India is to spread education. The spread of education would result in the people in the rural areas demanding certain types of projects that would bring prosperity to the area. This would take away from the political parties the power to decide on behalf of the people and therefore plan and work on grand projects that help only those who are either in power or close to power. Here lies the story of the absence of governance.

ii

Therefore "Is there a way out of this sad state of affairs?" In light of the failure to spread literacy to make the people capable of looking after themselves, the solution to the problems need to be found and implemented outside the ambit of the government that is controlled by the political and administrative machinery. Here again there is a problem. Any development activity that is aimed at improving the economic level of the deprived masses would go against all the calculations of those in power or those who aspire to be in power. That is, there is always a resistance to cooperative living as this does not give any leverage to a few individuals to upstage the rest of the society. The reason for the dichotomous situation is that, any improvement in the living conditions of the masses will result in the devolution of the vote banks that will not be tolerated by those in power as this will shake their base. Therefore the rate and extent of development and the areas of development are decided by the politicians alone keeping their own well being in view. This has been caricatured in a brilliant way by R. K. Laxman in his cartoon strip, You Said It. The scene is a village. A leader is talking to his manager/close confidant. He says, "I am told that this village has water, electricity, schools, hospitals etc. Then how do I get my vote?" Thus, whenever there is a disturbance in the equilibrium between the state of the people and the well being of politicians, there is bound to be violence, and the extent of violence is dependent on the threat perception of the politicians. The administrative machinery rushes police and paramilitary forces to control the violence resulting in the holding on to the status-quo that brings happiness to the politicians. The administration then sets up a commission of inquiry and all is well that ends well.

One of the rare acts of providing help to the needy to make them self reliant, by an individual who has worked outside the domain of religion, has been performed by Sally or Shalini Devi Holkar. She is an American by birth, married to Richard Holkar the scion of the Indore royal family. She had a passion for touring rural India, a strange passion indeed, and therefore was aware of all the problems of the rural India. She started the organization called "REHWA", a womens' income generation project aimed at popularizing the Maheshwari sarees and fabric. Maheshwari was the capital of Indore state in 18th century. She provided the designs and marketing inputs, imposing strict quality control and the rest was done by the crafts men/women. Today these Maheshwari Sarees and fabrics are widely used both within and without India helping about 200 weaver families. Cannot this be replicated elsewhere rather than giving alms and charity to the needy, thus crippling them and the children born to them for all the years to come? Charity kills the desire to earn their livelihood and therefore is more damaging than leaving them to their fate, which may be death due to starvation. If at all one wants to help the people, one must try to emulate what Shalini Holkar did in Maheshwari. She helped in giving key inputs like designs, marketing and quality control, to the weavers so that the marketability of the handloom fabrics that they produce improves and they succeed in becoming economically self reliant. The problem is not the lack of funds but the reluctance of the vested interests to improve the economic condition of the poor for the fear of loss of influence. For example, if the people become literate and learn to look after their interests and therefore start asserting their rights, most of the politicians and the Godheads would loose their influence, power and in all probability their seats in parliament/assembly. Thus the practice of the hour is to glorify poverty as a God given gift and hold on to the status-quo so that those in power retain their power and those with influence retain their influence. The rich retain their riches and poor retain their glory. That is both the middle men and the deprived retain their hegemony and glory respectively. This sounds more like the propaganda statement of Naxal group that is fighting against the land lords in the villages. But on second thoughts, this is definitely not a propaganda statement but a realistic representation of the ground reality.

iii

The sight of a large number of beggars and lepers who throng the places of worship is an eyesore. But those devotees who come to the place of worship with the intention of distributing food to these, would consider this as a mechanism of achieving salvation. This is also looked upon as an act of compassion and concern for the poor. But, the problem is unfortunately much more complicated from more than one view point. From the point of view of demography or population studies, the health of a nation or the future of a nation depends on which of the segments of the population is growing or which of the population segment is not growing. Therefore, from this point of view the future of India is absolutely bleak irrespective of which party comes to power. A study of the growth pattern of the population clearly indicates that the increase of population of the segment that cannot support itself is much more than the increase of population of the segment that can create wealth and prosperity for the society and therefore the nation. Thus the demographic imbalance that one sees in India is unfortunately a self consuming state which is becoming an irreversible process taking the nation closer to disaster, every minute, hour, day, week, month and year, with no signs of respite. This is so inspite of the perceptible fall in the overall birth rate in India. The reason for this sad state of affairs is that the segment of the population that cannot support itself supports the political parties as they happen to be the vote banks. Thus, the politicians, criminals and the guardians of the gates of God's own kingdom are all united and working for one goal: to have influence over the masses and not to loose the hold over the masses, come what may.

Long long ago, Mr. J. R. D. Tata had forecast that India will have this kind of problem unless otherwise some serious steps are taken to reverse the trend. He had even suggested that generous financial rewards may be given to those who restrict the size of the family to three or four. This would mean restricting the number of children to one or two. His contention was that it is advisable even to cut the plan size to allow for generous funding for controlling the population and spread of literacy, and look upon family planning and literacy drive as development activities. The reasoning was that the spread of literacy and controlling of the population would automatically get reflected in the rise of per capita income and therefore generous funding for such an activity should be looked upon as a plan outlay even though no material assets are being created. Further, he amplified his appeal by stating that the government must give importance to the creation of wealth and not to the distribution of wealth. If there is no creation of wealth, how can there be a distribution of wealth. On the contrary, there will be only a distribution of poverty and that is precisely what is happening in this country. He could easily visualize a demographic disaster in the making and raised alarm. He laid the foundation stone of the International Institution of Population Studies as far back as in 1956. Even the staunch communist, Deng Xiaoping, urged the comrades to create wealth first and worry about the consequences later. But the all knowing mandarins in the government and the all ignorant politicians found this unacceptable proposition and continued with the Stalin's concept of planning the economy of the nation without worrying too much about the population growth. However, Stalin's Russia gave great importance to education and health. Thus, India copied the ills of the two systems, communism and capitalism, and created and perpetuated a system called socialism. In fact, at one time, the policy was, "More the people, More the hands that can propel the nation forward". This was very similar to the Stalin's concept of calling a Russian woman giving birth to more number of children, the Mother Russia. It was only much later in 1992, that J. R. D. Tata's contribution was recognized by both UN and India. The UN bestowed on him the UN Population Award in 1992. After this award was given the all knowing mandarins in Delhi, possibly woke up, and acknowledged his contribution to the creation of wealth, talent, exacting standards, work culture, the list is endless, by conferring on him the highest honor, Bharat Ratna in 1992.

The first serious attempt to control the population was made when Dr. Chandrashekhar, a well known demographer who passed away recently, joined Mrs. Indira Gandhi's cabinet as Minister of State, Health and Family Welfare.

He introduced the use of condoms and a gift of a transistor radio for every man who underwent the vasectomy operation and adopted the family planning measure. He had not anticipated the problems that would be thrown up due to the need to educate the people and to break the cultural barriers. In one of the promotional camps, in Andhra Pradesh, the health worker, who happened to be lady, showed to a well built, healthy young man how to use the condom. She explained the use of the condom by putting the condom on her thumb and advised him to have a healthy relationship with his wife. The young man took two boxes of condom and came back within a few weeks complaining that his wife had become pregnant. On being asked to explain what happened, he narrated that he had followed the steps indicated by the sister (the lady health worker) and inspite of it, his wife ended up becoming pregnant. Still the health workers could not understand the reasons for this mishap. He was then requested to elaborate every action, leaving the most obvious one that he undertook. He then said that he had put the condom on to his left thumb in the same way as the sister had demonstrated and then went to bed with his wife. This made the sister blush and realized that the use of condom was going to be a failure in India. The problem was, how should a health worker, much less a lady health worker, explain to a man the way the condom is to be used. Thus what was feasible in a western society became infeasible in the Indian society. The man had capped the wrong object. What a country! Even today, the politicians do not consider illiteracy and the control of population as problems that need to be addressed on a war footing. The only reason for this is the fear of loosing the vote banks. Therefore it would be a futile exercise to expect the government machinery to create awareness in the people that might result in the erosion of the political support.

iv

Therefore the only way to come out of this eternal loop is to appeal to the rich to do what the TATAs have done in and around Jamshedpur, and also to do what Sally, nee Shalini Devi Holkar, has done in Maheshwari. Others who have brought a smile on the weary faces of the under privileged are Dr. Kurien, Ila Bhatt, Anna Hazare, Care of India Today, Tulsi Munda, Rajendra Singh and many others. There are many more who have done a great job of making the poor self reliant and my sincere apologies to those great men and women for not being able to know them and their names and therefore for not being able to record their names here. The one thing that is common to all these is that they never indulged in charity. Instead they succeeded in educating the people about the advantages of community work and the need for fending for themselves instead of waiting for someone else to come and uplift them. This did wonders and is a reassurance that people are willing to listen and follow the words of advice if they see for themselves a future, and they are convinced of their well being in following the advice. The first and foremost rule of the game is "Never Indulge in Charity". Charity kills the initiative and the will to live on one's own efforts. The need is to emulate Shalini Devi Holkar who gave the necessary inputs and used the existing skills and crafts to turn them around and make them economically independent and today the Maheshwari sarees are exported to other countries.

We have people like Tulsi Munda, who is an illiterate but has brought about revolution in the seventeen odd villages in the Adivasi area of Orissa. She is responsible for starting a number of schools where the children of poor mining labor not only study but are also looked after. Recently Government of India honored her with Padma Shri. Even the bureaucrats would find it difficult to match Tulsi Munda's track record inspite of all the power, privileges, clout and the authority that they enjoy.

Keeping this in view it is proposed to make an appeal to the "Emerging Presidents Group". The Emerging Presidents Group comprises of all the young, energetic, educated and young scions/heirs to the vast industrial empires who, in their own way, are associated with charitable activities. This group comprises of young people who

(a) Are not spoiled

(b) Are not arrogant about their heirloom

(c) Are highly educated and cultured

(d) Have a vision of what they want to achieve

(e) Are hardworking

(f) Do not believe in throwing their weight around

(g) Take themselves and their work seriously

(h) Have professional approach to management

(i) Are focussed and professional in their approach

The list of the young scions is long and impressive. All the scions are in some way or the other, in some form or the other involved in some charitable work and some have even formed or founded charitable trusts.

This appeal is more in the form of request to the Emerging Presidents. The first request to the Emerging Presidents is, as suggested earlier, not to indulge in charity. Those who receive charity will become and remain indebted for the rest of their life with no desire to live on their own. We have today a whole generation living on charity which, helps only the politicians and criminals. Charity is something which must be reserved only for the old and the sick and not for anyone and every one. Therefore the need is to emulate the deeds of the people like Dr. Kurien, Shalini Devi Holkar, Rajendra Singh who nurtured the talent, crafts and the skills that already existed in the villages by providing the necessary inputs to harness these assets of the villagers into a successful development or business proposition. The Emerging Presidents are ideally suited to do this job as each one of them is educated in management and is highly skilled and talented having seen both worlds, and therefore can think differently to provide working solutions to the varied problems of the people in the rural India. It is recognized that this is easier written than done. The one common area of activity to be used as start point is rain water harnessing, making attempts to raise the water table and campaigning against the use of deep bore wells. The other areas of activity can be as varied as poultry, mushroom farming, vegetable farming, fruits farming, flower farming, milk diary, weaving, marine farming etc depending on the ground reality and the skills that exist in the region. In all these the thrust will have to be for meeting the needs of metropolis and the export market and therefore the inputs that would be needed are in the areas of preservation of goods/produce at the place of farming and during transportation, quality of the product and packaging. Planning any venture exclusively for the Indian market keeping in view the swadeshi spirit would make the venture commercially not viable. The reason is that the Indian market, as on date, cannot pay for a quality product and anything that is done that does not fetch good returns cannot become a meaningful business proposition. The urban society is a pampered one and it is accustomed to getting every thing at subsidized rates. However, the produce can be targeted to the small upper segment of the market, which then would demand quality.

Consider the water supply, food grains and other essential commodities, health services, transportation, electricity/fuel for cooking food etc. In respect of all these, the rural society remains as backward as it was in spite of massive outlays made for rural development and the government sanctioning Rupees ten million to each member of the parliament for addressing the needs of the people of his/her constituency at the micro level. Irrespective of whether it is at micro or macro level, very rarely do the elected members of the parliament get time to study and understand the problems of the rural society. In all probability, the reason for sanctioning Rupees ten million was not to implement meaningful projects in rural areas at all that would result in the disturbing of the vote banks and the status quo that prevails. The disturbance in the status quo would create survival problems for the politicians. Therefore the problem is that every meaningful assumption postulated while formulating a project and every thought provoking act of the administration are systematically curtailed and derailed to an extent that the beneficiaries are left where they were. This in no way means that development has not taken place in rural India. It only means that there is a large gap between what has been achieved and what could have been achieved. This process of thwarting of implementation of meaningful projects helps in the creation of a new class of the rural rich who are out side the tax net. The politicians are busy wheeling, dealing and politicking. They have no intention to cause an erosion of their vote base by treating the rural and urban rich alike and make sure that the rural rich also pay tax to the exchequer. The politicians and the rural rich are a part of the same game. This makes them the two faces of the same coin. Thus money for rural projects is cornered by the rural rich that helps to hold on to status quo as far as the rest of the villagers are concerned. Thus the vote banks are kept in tact and are ready to be manipulated by the rural rich. The rural society has been consciously left in a state of negligence and disarray while the urban society has perfected the art of holding the society and administration to ransom by resorting to strikes and agitation. Consciously or unconsciously, we have cultivated a tendency to look heavenwards for solutions. The recent report on the misuse of the huge funds allocated to the rural development projects is an eye opener.

Thus, this small group of rural rich with their affiliation to political parties or close links with the politicians provide a very effective filter between the beneficiaries and the vast sums of money that are being spent to improve their living conditions. It is unfair to expect the politicians to look into the administrative aspects of governance as this is the responsibility of bureaucrats. Therefore it is unfair to attribute the cause of failure of governance to the politicians alone. In many cases, the vast sums of money allocated for development projects are unspent due to the absence of infrastructure for implementing them. Thus, the bureaucracy even after about fifty years of independence has not been able to put the basic infrastructure for governing the nation. This is indeed a strange case of a rich nation with poor people. Thus, any attempt to address the problems of the lower strata of the population will always elicit opposition from the small section of politicians, the middle men, bureaucrats and rural rich, which at times becomes very violent. The Emerging Presidents must keep this in mind before they even think of starting their projects. From this point of view, starting meaningful projects in rural India is more difficult than setting up of an industry. This was put in a very interesting manner by Prabhudas Patwari, the well-known Gandhian from Gujarat who was the Governor of

Tamil Nadu, in one of the extra mural lectures organized at Indian Institute of Technology Madras, Chennai. He, in the course of the lecture, said, "Today I feel like talking. I want to tell you people that what you are studying and what you plan to do after completing your studies has little relevance to vast population of India. Please understand that it is easy to look after a computer but very difficult to look after a cow." This was greeted with an all round applause and laughter from both the faculty and the students in the auditorium. But isn't this the truth, the only truth and the whole unadulterated truth? Even after fifty years of independence the government, politicians and the administrators have been promising to eradicate poverty, provide basic necessities like potable water, meaningful levels of nourishment to people etc. In the new millenium, 2001, a few districts in Orissa & Rajasthan are facing drought. The people are starving and are forced to eat poisonous roots. The ware houses of Food Corporation of India in Orissa and Rajasthan are overflowing with food grains. The government has not been able to take the surplus food grains and distribute them to the starving millions. The victims of the Gujarat earth quake of January 2001 wrote a letter to the President of India in May 2001 in their blood to impress upon the government on the deplorable state of governance. If this had happened in any of the Anglo-Saxon societies of Australia, Europe, Britain, USA or Canada blood of those in power would have flown. The insensitivity of the bureaucratic machinery is mind boggling and the media is going crazy over the Maha Kumbh at Prayag and the Ram Temple at the disputed site in Ayodhya. Can the mind sink to greater depths than this? It is amazing to see the extent to which the mind can be consoled. R. K. Laxman, the cartoonist par excellence, has portrayed this aspect of Indian life in one of his cartoons. Here, a politician is screaming over the microphone and exhorting people not to listen to others and vote only for his party. The reason being that only his party has experience in eradicating poverty as his party has been doing this job of eradicating poverty from the last fifty years.

V

Therefore the Emerging Presidents of India's Corporate Sector, who are definitely interested in doing their bit to wipe the tears from a few eyes of the rural poor as Mahatma Gandhi had put it, would need the guidance, help, advice and support of people like Dr. Kurien, Ila Bhatt, Anna Hazare, (Sally) Shalini Devi Holkar, Care of India Today, Rajendra Singh, Tulsi Munda and the like. They can also derive inspiration from what J. R. D. Tata had said. "Every company has a special continuing responsibility towards the people of the area in which it is located. The company should spare its engineers, doctors, managers and advise the people of the villages and supervise new development undertaken as a cooperative effort by them and the company". TATA STEEL is possibly the first organization/industry to have the position of Divisional Manager: Rural and Tribal Service. The person who is holding this post is a highly qualified and foreign educated person, Viraf Mehta, a postgraduate from University College, London. He is associated with the TATA Council for Community Initiative which again is the first of its kind in India which has been set up by the TATA Group. The good news is that there are well qualified people who are willing to work in altruistic conditions and in such areas as community development of rural and tribal areas.

The excellent work carried out by Rajendra Singh and his friends of Tarun Bharat Sangh is an example that is worth emulating by the corporate sector. Their work has transformed the life in about 650 villages in Rajasthan and is an example of what can be achieved by a few dedicated, honest and sincere persons even without the help from either the bureaucracy or the politicians. The basic principle on which Tarun Bharat Sangh works is that there is no charity or aid. The beneficiaries either contribute labor or money, and therefore the assumption that some body else will come and solve their problems is punctured from the beginning. Rajendra Singh has shown that the best way to get the desired results is to train them to take decisions, and never ever take decisions on their behalf. This is the antithesis of feudalistic approach to providing assistance or the working of the planning commission where unconnected and unrelated people decide the way a village life is to be improved. But even here the mechanism of governance, instead of supporting such a people oriented program, thought it wise to issue a legal notice asking Tarun Bharat to explain the construction of wells and other small water storing/harvesting projects that had been started or completed. The mechanism of governance has always been supportive to the process of digging deep bore wells that are known to cause irreparable damage to the water table leading to draughts/famine. These are known to cause ecological disaster causing water famine. But the reason for the political and bureaucratic machinery supporting the digging of deep bore wells is that these benefit the rural rich. At the same time, the politicians find it easy and convenient to sanction these projects and retain their influence over the rural rich. Thus, in all areas of mismanagement, the mechanism of governance has always supported the instruments that encourage and initiate disaster.

Feudalism brings with it the necessary arrogance, either of power or wealth, which defeats the very purpose of making the people independent. The associated arrogance will make sure that the help to the people is always limited to suit the conveniences of the feudal lord and not to suit the conveniences of the intended beneficiaries. The Indian Administrative Service was expected to reorient the administrative practices to suit the new climate that was to be ushered into India after independence. None of this happened. The rules and laws are obsolete to the extent that when villagers dig a well by contributing their labor and money, the administration declares the well to be illegal and a police constable is stationed near it so that the villagers do not draw water from it. Why not empower people like Rajendra Singh and give them a free and supporting hand instead of helping either the demolition of a mosque or building a temple? The demolition of mosque or building of temple guarantees the role of politicians.

The project chosen for implementation must be in accordance with the local needs, expertise, skills, crafts that are available for further development or honing. That is, if the proposal is for mushroom farming, then the local population must know at least how a mushroom looks like and what inputs are involved in mushroom farming. The projects aimed at improving the life of the people should not include an element of retraining and making them experts in a new trade or craft. The projects aimed at improving the life of the people must aim at building on the existing strength of the people. The issue of retraining or opening new avenues shall be taken up only after the inherent strength are tapped and the people become confident of taking the next step. Otherwise, the money will be spent on attempt to retrain the illiterate masses resulting in yet another scam! An example of such a scam in the making is the literacy drive where

- Teachers are not getting their salaries
- Majority of the schools in rural India do not even have the mechanism of getting pieces of chalk to write on black boards
- Government is planning to put computers in schools and palm tops to the children to open the window to the world!

Further a necessary element of the project must be to build an infrastructure for ensuring that the produce is preserved till it reaches its destination so that it is protected from the vagaries of the weather or climatic conditions. The produce must be of such a quality as to sell in foreign market so that the farmers get higher and quicker benefits. The government must lift restrictions on the movement of essential commodities with in the state, with in the nation and out of the nation. The restrictions are in place to ensure that the rich and the organized urban population get the essential commodities at the right prices and not to ensure that the starving and under nourished millions in rural India get food. The rural population that is poor does not in any way get any thing from the public distribution system. Thus, the policies are enforced for the well being of the organized, influential and feudal lords. The costs of inputs with or without a small interest must be recovered from the project or business. The small or no interest then becomes an act of charity and the recovery of the investment gives a signal to the people to become self reliant and to become capable of managing and safeguarding their interests. Thus, the initial funding for a project is recovered and this becomes a rolling fund that can be augmented by adding fresh funds every year and identifying new projects to benefit more people. This is an achievable target as shown by the TATA Group (the TATA Council for Community Initiatives), Dr. Kurien, Ila Bhatt, Care of India Today, Tulsi Munda, Shalini Devi Holkar, Rajendra Singh and Anna Hazare.

In all these cases, the responsibility of formulating the project including the path that needs to be taken by the intended beneficiaries must not only rest with the intended beneficiaries but also facilitated by the recruitment of persons with the right temperament or deputed from the industry as part of the societal commitment as done by the TATA Group. That is, it must be made clear to the intended beneficiaries that there is no charity in this activity of improving the living conditions of the people. There are costs involved in carrying out the tasks and these must be recognized and must be borne by the intended beneficiaries. Therefore, only an initial funding is being provided as a seed money or help, which may be in terms of specialized man power (technical and management), or money or equipment, for the purpose of nucleating the project and to get started with the activity of improving the living conditions. Thus the funding, which is recoverable over a period of a few years, may be three years, is for bringing about the necessary changes in the thought processes and also possibly for sustaining the project during the initial period when it cannot sustain itself. Since it is assumed that the project would return its costs within three years, it becomes necessary that the produce that is produced must be of a quality that will address the requirements of either the export market or the top segment of the market with in India. It is only these segments that can appreciate the quality product and pay a higher price for the product that would be of great help to the rural poor. But this strategy of addressing the export market and the top segment of the Indian market, depending on the circumstances and threat perceptions, may come under attack by the elements with vested interests through their friends in the political and administrative set up. The line of attack would be a declaration to the effect that the need of the hour is to serve Indians and India, and not foreigners or foreign countries or the super rich with in the country.

Therefore, the view point that would be articulated might be that the export of every thing that is produced and that is edible must be stopped lest the prices of these commodities rise in urban India making life difficult for them. The philosophy behind this argument is that it is acceptable to have starving and under nourished people in villages but it is unacceptable to allow a rise in the prices of the basic commodities in urban areas. The problem is that none of these urban based policy makers believe in a fair play. They would like to remain pampered by getting the good things of life at throw away prices. Those in power are very particular about getting the best postings, best houses in the best location and best of every thing. Nobody bothers about the hardships of the farmer or his family and the conditions in which they live. On the other hand they are expected to produce wealth for the country so that the affluent, the influential and the organized people in the urban society can enjoy the life. The migrant laborers from villages live in slums in the metropolis; but these people are definitely better off than their village counterparts. It is this relative state that makes conditions ripe for violence waiting to be exploited by some party, political or otherwise. Therefore there is no rationale behind any of the political jargons that are raised in the name of patriotism for the stopping of movement of food commodities to market centers to meet the demand. The only rationale, if it can be called rationale at all, is the perpetuation of the self or the organized section of the urban society or the survival of a class of people who believe in easy life. The need is to improve the living conditions in the villages at all costs and force a reverse migration of people from metropolis to cities to towns and back to the villages.

The projects that are aimed at the betterment of the living conditions of a majority of the people always run into trouble and get stalled because of the vested interests of a few influential persons whose main aim is to rule by hook or crook. They believe like some of the politicians and bureaucrats who believe that they are born to rule. Most of the projects start and end on paper with the disbursal of money being the key to the success of the project. The motto is to ensure that all money is disbursed and the kitty is empty. This qualifies the project to be declared as successful. Any other parameter for measuring the success of the project would create more problems for the bureaucracy. The implementation mechanism at the ground level is nonexistent; even if it is existent, it is shoddy. Thus large amount of money is spent on exotic projects which are based on lofty ideals which unfortunately fail to provide relief to the needy and the under privileged. Whenever and wherever some of the social workers belonging to the non government organizations try to start and implement socially relevant projects in rural, tribal and remote areas, they end up getting caught in the local politics and cross fire making life difficult for the social workers. Some like Sanjay Ghose lose their lives. Any activity that results in the economic betterment of the poor disturbs the equilibrium in the society. The reason is that the poor are needed to serve the rich and the words poor and rich are relative. Some need the poor to do their jobs in the fields, houses etc and thus become the *mai bap,* the benefactor. While some others want to work for the poor to save their own souls. Therefore, there must be poor, come what may, in a society to satisfy the needs of the rich and the religious and pious, and every effort will be made to prevent the economic emancipation of the poor. Therefore, there is an element of truth in what the veteran Gandhian, Prabhudas Patwari, had said, "It is very easy to look after a computer but very difficult to look after a cow". The cow that yields milk serves as a vehicle of emancipation of the poor as it helps by giving not only the milk to drink or sell but also the dung cake to cook food.

vi

The first task before the emerging presidents would be to put an end to charity. The second task would be to associate themselves with those who have a proven record in rural development. They must take care to be patient and considerate. The progress in the implementation of the projects will never be as quick as they would like it to be. It is mandatory to think small which may not be to the liking of the emerging presidents. There is an absolute necessity to have abundant patience. The amount of patience that is needed here is much more than the patience that one needs when one is teaching one's child. Here, at every step, it must be borne in mind that one is dealing with people who have been taken for a long ride for decades and have been consistently sold a dream of seeing the light at the end of the tunnel. But all through their life, they have lived a life of darkness with no light, not even a speck of light, visible at the end of the tunnel. Theirs is a life that has been exploited for generations. Added to this will be the social forces that believe in holding on to the status quo that have the backing and active support of the politicians and administration machinery. In view of this, the rate at which they can absorb and assimilate changes in their lives is also going to be minimal in the initial years and gradually increase to the current level of the urban population. The greatest achievement would be to make them aware of their rights; how to exercise those rights and to take decisions to create changes in their lives. The input they would want during this process is a backing up in terms of infrastructure support either in the form of technical or management services and small finances. Thus the financial resources needed to make a perceptible change in their life is also minimal. This perceptible change would lead to a state where they would start looking for more inputs and therefore the progress would become a self sustaining one. In this process they will also learn to manage their own life and think of projects that they should be starting. The learning process will be quick. The need of the hour is to create an environment where they can learn and an environment that is devoid of vested interests, which is going to be the most difficult task. Thus the creation of an environment for growth can be looked upon as a charitable act and from the beginning the people who are the beneficiaries must be made to realize that every service costs money and they cannot get anything free. The first step will have to be education and to inculcate a feeling of self-esteem that had been crushed by the feudal system. The absence of charity will go a long way in creating a feeling of self-esteem and more important help in eliminating the feeling of remaining indebted for life.

Thus the role of the Emerging Presidents must be to create this environment. The recovery of the money that they have spent in an year can be made over a period of, say, three to five years. Thus the project comprises of the following aspects:

(a) Identifying the geographical area where the project is planned to be executed in addition to identifying the strengths and weaknesses of the people in that area. Knowing the weaknesses is more important than the strengths. Start the interaction with education of the rural masses. This in itself will be a formidable task as this will be opposed by the rural rich. An equitable society will never support a feudal system.

(b) Identifying the kind of project that would be started in that geographical area: poultry, vegetable farming, mushroom farming, weaving, bamboo work, carpentry, embroidery, fishery, sheep rearing, milk diary etc

(c) Work out a detailed project report on the infrastructure support that already exists (which is doubtful) and which needs to be made available in order to make sure that the project succeeds in giving expected returns to the intended beneficiaries.

(d) Work out the marketing outlets for the product under consideration in order to ensure that the intended beneficiaries get an assured return round the year. The stress will have to be on the elimination of the governing principle, "The middle man takes it all."

(e) Work out the kind of minimum help that would be needed from the government machinery without which the project would fail. Better to avoid taking up a project that would be tied to the performance of the government machinery as this may mean the death of the project even before it gets started.

(f) Identify the Non Government Organizations and the people who would be given the responsibility to implement this project. A few of the emerging presidents may join hands, pool the resources and start a group similar to TATA Council for Community Initiatives. Here it would be advisable to consult organizations/people like TATA Group (the TATA Council for Community Initiatives), Infosys Foundation, Dr. Kurien, Ila Bhatt, Shalini Devi Holkar, Anna Hazare, Viraf Mehta, Tulsi Minda, Care of India Today, Rajendra Singh and others. It is necessary to associate such people with the projects; discuss the details of the project with these people and incorporate the suggestions of these people to take into account the ground realities. That is the same kind of a project, say vegetable farming or poultry or any other, located in geographically and culturally different locations would need different packaging of solutions.

The detailed and careful planning of the items above is absolutely important. It is these factors that make the project a success or a failure. The commitment of the Emerging Presidents from the point of view of providing quality inputs and also the necessary infrastructure support will be of great help in these two key areas. One important and inevitable question that would arise from this is, "Why should the Emerging Presidents bother about these problems when they are already loaded with the other important projects, which happen to be their main activity?" There can be only one reason for this. The empires that are going to be built by these Emerging Presidents or the dreams that they have will not become a reality if their dream projects are to be islands of prosperity. It would be very unfortunate to have these islands of prosperity to be surrounded by people who have nothing to lose or gain. If this happens, then the educated unemployed youth would be sucked into the extortion business as is the case in some of the states of India. Therefore, these Emerging presidents have, in the words of J. R. D. Tata, a role to play or an obligation to fulfill in keeping the surroundings in a livable condition. This will make sure that their dream projects will thrive and prosper. Also, the betterment of the surroundings will provide a sort of natural insurance or a safety net for their dream projects. There is no reason to accept the prevailing state as a fait accompli. This would be giving in to consolation of mind, which is under the circumstances the greatest crime that can ever be committed.

8

Past Future

The title of this chapter "Past Future" is strange. But so is the working of the mind. The mythology, be it the Greek Mythology or the Indian Mythology or mythology of any other origin, has a number of stories that are hard to believe as they look very weird. They look weird because our conditioning of the mind and the present age of science make us to believe what can be verified. This is the age of rationalism and the stories that we read in the mythologies appear to be born more out of superstition than out of reason.

For example, the Hindu mythology portrays the God as comprising of three God Heads, the Trinity, who are bestowed with specific qualities and activities. The three specific qualities are:

(a) Creation: Lord Brahma

(b) Preservation: Lord Vishnu

(c) Dissolution: Lord Shiva

The Trinity is represented as an entity with three heads. The three characteristics represented by the three God Heads are also resident in each one of the living organisms. Different living organisms have the three characteristics in different proportions. Some have more of creativity and less of destructive attitude. While some have only destructive characteristics and the creativity is more tuned to destruction rather than harmonious living. Some are good in preserving the things that are created for harmonious living. Thus, the three elements of the divine characteristics are present in each of the living organisms in different proportions. This is so irrespective of whether one is a Hindu or a Muslim or a Christian or a Buddhist or Jain or Jew or any other religion.

The story of Bhsmasura, who got this name because of the power he got from Lord Shiva to turn any thing to ash by putting his palm over it, is interesting. Lord was very pleased with the penance performed by the *asura,* and in a moment of exuberance and kindness granted the boon. This *asura* was thrilled at having got hold of the powerful weapon and being able to turn any thing and every thing to ashes by keeping his palm over it. In Sanskrit, *Bhasma* refers to ash and hence the name Bhasmasura. Bhsmasura was thrilled beyond imagination at having received the boon from none other than lord Shiva. He went out testing his new prowess and found to his delight that every thing over which he put his palm turned into ash. Then, he thought of an ultimate test of his prowess. He wanted to put his palm over Lord Shiva's head. Lord Shiva having granted the boon had not thought of his devotee's possible ambition to test the boon by putting his palm over the Lord himself. But, having granted the boon, the Lord did not know how to save himself. This started a chase, the devotee chasing the Lord. Finally, Lord Shiva appealed to Lord Vishnu, the preserver of order in the universe, to save him. At this stage, Lord Vishnu, the preserver of the order in the universe, dons the form of a beautiful woman, Mohini, and stands before Bhasmasura. Bhasmasura, seeing the beautiful maiden in front of him forgets Lord Shiva and runs after her. She then starts dancing in front of him and encourages Bhasmasura to join her in the dance. As the duet proceeds, Bhasmasura, smitten by Mohini's beauty, looses his sense of reasoning. Mohini, weaves her movements in a sensuous way and puts her palm over her head. Bhasmasura, intoxicated by those sensuous movements imitates Mohini by putting his palm over his head and is reduced to ashes.

Don't we see similarities between this and the present situation? In fact, don't we see similarities between this and many of the situations that have plagued our society in our march towards great progress and in the conducting of the foreign affairs?

ii

The story of Raktabeeja is also interesting. The name Raktabeeja is a composite name comprising of two sub names. "*Rakta*" means blood and "*beeja*" means seed. The name implies that this demon or *asura* had been given a boon that when ever a drop of his blood falls on the ground, many more of his clones would be born ready to fight. That is, the falling of the drop of blood does not result in the birth of a baby albeit a clone of Raktabeeja, but would result in the rising of thousands of fully grown up warrior clones of Raktabeeja. Having been blessed by this boon, he went out conquering every thing in the universe. It became difficult to vanquish Raktabeeja as wounding him would create thousands of his clones for every drop of blood falling on the ground. Again, the Gods had no answer to the terror that was unleashed due to their own folly of granting all kinds of esoteric boons! Then the creator Lord Brahma suggested that the Goddess Shakti must be prevailed upon to save the universe from sure destruction. At this stage, The Goddess Shakti assimilated all the powers to take the role of the fierce looking blood drinking Goddess Kali. Her role was to ensure that not even a single drop of blood of Raktabeeja falls on the ground. This helped to mount the final attack on Raktabeeja and was killed with not even a single drop of blood falling on the ground, thanks to Goddess Kali.

The fall of one person would create thousands of such persons with the same terrible psyche. Don't we see similar things around us? Who can say, that mythology is all hogwash? There is a repetition of what ever has been happening for aeons. The difference is only in the extent to which we find such occurrences. The situation is nothing new. History and events keep repeating again and again, and every time we feel that things are changing for worse. A close look at the evolution or history of mankind tells us that things never ever changed. We only succeeded in consoling our minds to such an extent as to lull it to believe that all has become wonderful. This blissful state of self created hallucination that makes us believe that every thing is under control and perfect order continues till we stumble upon another ugly event. And life goes on.

Mythology is full of such stories that always look strange and unbelievable. The Greek Mythology talks of Hercules fighting the seven hooded snake. The seven hooded snake is depicted in Bhagavata, where Krishna dances on the seven hoods and vanquishes it. Here again, we refuse to believe the presence of seven hooded snake. The existence or non-existence of the seven hooded snake is not of any consequence. What is of consequence is that the evil that Hercules and Krishna fought and vanquished in Greece and India were of the same kind. Thus, neither the distance provides security nor does the policy "your enemy is my friend". When a Buddhist turns the wheel, the point which is turned away comes back again. We, in our ego centric state, do not realize this simple fact of life till we are hit directly. Have we not witnessed these thoughts in the recent times?

In the life of mankind, unfortunately, Violence has become God Centric! A brief record of the way God had been used to unleash misery and terrorize humanity is given below:

(a) Moses and his people who were treated as slaves by Remises were driven out of Egypt because Moses did not believe Remises to be the true King and God.

(b) The Roman Empire crucified Jesus Christ because he did not consider Julius Ceaser to be the true King or God.

(c) The Roman Empire unleashed terror on the non-believers. Many Jews and Armenians fled their countries and some took shelter in India.

(d) From the 8th & 11th Century, the Arab and Central Asian tribesmen went about spreading the revelation that they thought they had received resulting in the destruction of the Buddhist and Hindu heritage in the present day Afghanistan, Pakistan and India. The Buddhists and the Hindus in these regions were either killed or plundered and converted to Islam. The people of the Zoroastrian faith fled the present day Iran and some of them settled in India.

(e) In the 15th century, Vasco da Gama of Portugal landed at Kochi in Kerala, India and was greeted by people who were Christians for over thousand years. Yet, when the Anglo-Saxon missionaries landed in Goa, they went around breaking the one of the oldest Christian community, often called St. Thomas Christians because they had been practicing the Christian faith as taught by St. Thomas and held on to the Indian heritage.

(f) The destruction of the AZTEC and INCAS Civilization by the Spanish Missionaries in South America

(g) In the 20th Century,

(i) Adolph Hitler found the ultimate solution by practicing ethnic cleansing and killed hundreds and thousands of Jews.

(ii) The generals in Pakistan found a different kind of a solution by evicting more than ten million people belonging to minority communities from East Pakistan that ultimately resulted in the birth of Bangladesh. Unfortunately, USA had sent the 7th Fleet to Bay of Bengal in support of the Generals in Pakistan and become a party to the ethnic cleansing!

(iii) The government in Pakistan perfected the process of ethnic cleansing by bringing in mercenaries into Jammu and Kashmir in the name of jihad and drove tens of thousands of Hindus from the Kashmir Valley. They called it freedom struggle giving the honor of the greatest freedom fighter to Adolph Hitler. What is more unfortunate is that the groups like Hurriyat Conference in Jammu and

Kashmir that were a party to this ethnic cleansing of Jammu and Kashmir were entertained by the embassies of United Kingdom, United States of America and other developed nations. This reception and entertainment process stopped after 11th September 2001! Even today, mostly the Hindus and Sikhs are being killed in Jammu and Kashmir in the name of freedom struggle and this is supported by the Hurriyat Conference and of course the government of Pakistan! It is often forgotten that the state of Jammu and Kashmir is, in the same way as the other states in India, populated by more than two ethnic communities.

The defense that is put up by the Government of Pakistan and the Hurriyat Conference is that the terrorists not under their control. If this is the truth, then why cannot the Pakistan Government kill the terrorists? Or may be the Indian government may be helped to kill the terrorists in Pakistan?! This is precisely the area of cooperation between the Governments of Pakistan and United States of America, and for which Government of Pakistan is getting lot of money. The fight against terrorism has been transformed into a very good business proposition. The United States of America is rewarding the Government of Pakistan to help them fight the terrorists who were nurtured by Pakistan and who are hiding in the mountains. God help America.

(iv) Milosevic of Balkans region also practiced ethnic cleansing by putting to death thousands of Muslims, the case of "horse shoe". This is sub-judice. However, there existed a much bigger "horse shoe" that had one of its ends in Columbia, the backyard of Unites States of America, and the other end some where in Europe, in Netherlands. This was an intercontinental "horse shoe" that went through Africa, Asia and Europe through Central Asia. This "horse shoe" was nurtured by the drug and arms Mafia. The King's Institute in London was aware of this and so was the intelligence agency in Washington. But, this "horse shoe" did not threaten the interests of United States of America and Britain and therefore was allowed to be nurtured and every one turned a Nelson's eye on it till 11th September! A classic example of the wise biblical saying, "Never do to others what you do not want others to do to you"

(v) In the beginning of the 21st Century Osama bin Laden set up the Al Quaeda network and declared *Jihad* against United States of America by destroying the World Trade Center. Jihad has also been declared against Israel and India indicating very clearly that only Islam has the right to prevail on the earth and nothing else. This definitely cannot be a part of any kind of revelation. Al Quaeda was definitely not the first net work of sleepers. Such a net work had been put in place by the Sri Lankan Tamil Tigers, LTTE, much before Al Quaeda was discovered. In fact, King's Institute had the information about the links between LTTE Tamil Tigers and Al Quaeda. But, this band of sleepers did not threaten the interests of United States of America and Britain and therefore was allowed to be nurtured and every one turned a Nelson's eye on it till 11th September! A classic example of the wise biblical saying, "Never do to others what you do not want others to do to you"

(vi) The communal violence that is often seen in different parts of the world between Protestants & Catholics, Jews and Muslims, Sunni Muslims and Shia Muslims, Ahmadiyas and Sunni Muslims, Hindus and Muslims etc and the systematic approach that is followed in the killing of innocent civilians including women and children shows our barbaric nature. Also, this behavior of the human being irrespective of the religion to which one might belong disproves the Darwinian theory of evolution. These killings are engineered and manipulated in the name of God by a handful of manipulators with an eye on the seat of power. There has always been a perfect understanding between the ruthless manipulators of both sides of the feuding factions to keep the pot boiling. One set of ruthless manipulators cannot exist without the help and support of the other set of ruthless manipulators. Both happen to be the two faces of the same coin and therefore cannot face each other. The problems are never allowed to be resolved and this is the sure way of establishing one's importance and one's rein as the leader of the community. It is necessary to keep the God Centric disputes alive and well so as to prevent the flock from deserting the leaders. This is only the beginning and God alone knows what is in store for the human race.

The Indian case is a very special one as it is a wounded civilization. India that once took pride in encouraging people of different beliefs and faiths to coexist and thrive for over one thousand years has now become a victim of sectarian intolerance. The problem is not with the people of different faiths. The problem is with the leaders and the politicians who are more than eager to capture power in the name of religion, caste and God. This is achieved by keeping the pot boiling by not allowing the old wounds to heal. Every activity in India has a historical reference. These historical references are:

(a) The invading tribal people from the Central Asia killed, plundered and destroyed Hindus and their places of worship.

(b) Many of the Mosques were built by destroying the Hindu temples and many mosques have been built using the building materials used in the construction of temples.

(c) United States of America sent the seventh fleet to the Bay of Bengal in 1971 in support of the generals in Pakistan when more than ten million refugees poured into India. India was asked to show restraint!

(d) Since 1980 onwards Pakistan practiced the politics of *jihad* in the states of Punjab, and Jammu and Kashmir. This resulted in the killing of thousand of Sikhs and Hindus, and the western powers, especially United States of America, advised India to show restraint!

(e) The politics of *jihad* resulted in thousands of Hindus leaving Jammu and Kashmir and become refugees in their own country. This process of ethnic cleansing involved in nearly a million Hindu families leaving Kashmir Valley. This number of refugees is greater than the number of refugees created by Milosevic, who is being tried by the International Court at Hague. The western powers, especially United States of America and United Kingdom, advised India to show restraint making them party to the ethnic cleansing!

(f) The Hurriyat Conference, the separatist group in the state of Jammu and Kashmir, actively advocated the freedom movement that killed Sikhs and Hindus and drove thousands of Hindus out of Jammu and Kashmir. The Embassies of United States of America, Germany and the High Commission of United Kingdom hosted tea parties to the members of the Hurriyat Conference whenever the leaders of Hurriyat Conference were in New Delhi. The hosting of tea parties stopped after 11th September 2001! Hurriyat Conference, United States of America and United Kingdom became parties to ethnic cleansing by calling it freedom struggle and this changed after 11th September 2001!

(g) Thus, for over twenty years, India had been a victim of terrorism and the Hindus in the state of Jammu and Kashmir had been subjected to ethnic attacks and cleansing due to the politics of *jihad*.

(h) On the fateful day of 11th September 2001, the value system practiced and assiduously cultivated by the western powers turned upside down when United States of America became a victim of terrorist attack. This attack was, in some ways, a turning point in the history of the world! There was no talk of restraint either from United States of America or England! The United States of America set about bombing Afghanistan with the sole intention and purpose of putting an end to the politics of *jihad*. An international front for fight against terrorism was announced with all the fan fare.

The above facts give the distinct impression that the Hindu blood can be spilt with no fear of retribution. It is uncivilized and obnoxious to talk in terms of Christian blood, Muslim blood, Jewish blood and Hindu blood. But the acts of the leaders like

(a) Henry Kissinger, Madeline Albright who supported the leadership in Pakistan and asked Indian government to show restraint when ever the Hindus and Sikhs were killed,

(b) Leaders of Hurriyat Conference who have given the name of the freedom struggle to the process of ethnic cleansing in Kashmir involving the killing of Hindus and Sikhs,

(c) The secular politicians of India who have not bothered about the plight and suffering of the Kashmiri Pundits who fled from Kashmir and have been living in squalid conditions in New Delhi,

(d) The secular politicians of India who do not miss any opportunity to come to the defense of Muslims when ever they are targeted

make the obnoxious distinction between Hindu blood and Muslim blood a reality. This reinforces the belief that the Hindus can be asked to show restraint as had been happening all along. This kind of a recurring phenomenon becomes responsible for the break down of the psychological barrier that in turn is used by the political leadership to score points in their dream to capture power. When this goes on for a long time, an event like the Godhra carnage gets turned into a perfectly organized attack against an entire community. In the process innocent people are killed and property destroyed. The most unfortunate thing to have happened was that the Bohra Muslim community that is known for its liberal thoughts and love for peaceful living became the target for some thing that they would not even dream about. The Gujarat carnage was a success story for the manipulators belonging to both communities. The manipulators from both communities survive and thrive, and manage to get projected as leaders in this hour of great human tragedy. The ideal thing to achieve was the elimination of the manipulators of both communities and protection of the innocent people of both communities. There is always a difference between "What Is" and "What Should Be".

This is in many respects very similar to the impression that got generated soon after partition of India when Mahatma Gandhi was perceived to be appeasing Pakistan at the cost of India. This led to the tragic assassination of Mahatma Gandhi. Therefore, the actions that the leaders take and ideas that they project become the key to the process of manipulation of the society by the forces that call themselves either secular or nonsecular, nationalist or anti-nationalist. Every political party pitches in to exploit the inflamed passions and the seemingly end less misery with the sole intention of capturing the seat of power. Every act of omission or commission is given a religious twist. The political parties are more interested in either damning the entire community or defending the entire community than bringing the few culprits to justice. The modus operandi is to capitalize on the misery of the society and indulge in the blame game with an eye on the seat of power. At this stage, the politicians and the religious preachers who have no respect either for human life or God, unleash the principle of nationalism on those who practice a different faith than the one practiced by either the politician or religious preacher. Thus every political party and every religious preacher are guilty of being directly or indirectly responsible for the communal carnage that takes place. The tragedy is caused by the images that are flashed by the media that relate to

(a) Killing of innocent Hindu women, children and men in Jammu and Kashmir in the name of freedom struggle. No sane human being can endorse this act of killing people belonging to one religion as apart of freedom struggle. But this has been endorsed and rationalized by the Governments like Britain, United States of America, Australia etc in addition to the Islamic nations.

(b) The Pakistan leadership consistently negating the involvement of their citizens in such attacks on the Indian soil even when the identity cards and other details of the persons involved in such attacks are presented.

(c) The Pakistani leadership consistently telling lies, with the backing of the responsible western governments, about the criminals that it has sheltered and asking for proof of their crimes even when INTERPOL has issued Red Corner Notices against them.

(d) The ability of Pakistan to export mercinaries in the name of Islam who kill, rape, plunder women and children belonging to any religion including Islam.

(e) The ability of the Pakistani mercineries to cut the throat of Wall Street Journalist, Daniel Pearl, and making the video film of the same with great detail shows the kind of mental frame work and the motivation that Islam(?) has been able to inculcate into these men.

But in all these cases, the role of Islam is indeed debatable. Unfortunately, the vast majority of Muslims who also practice the religion of Islam have been put on the defensive by the dastardly acts of these zealots who have been doing every inconceivable act in the name of Islam. The actions of the zealots gives credibility to the belief that Islam, as a religion, has great difficulty in coexisting with other religions and therefore Muslims in general have great difficulty in coexisting with the rest of the society. This impression is becoming the cause of the division in the society. When an activity, by a few Muslim zealots, like the burning of Hindu pilgrims in a train takes place in Godhra in Gujarat state, this triggers a series of rationalized convoluted thought processes. This becomes a good enough reason to declare "enough is enough". The Hindu zealots set into motion a well planned carnage that results in hunting down the innocent Muslims and destroying their properties. No attempt is made to catch the Muslim zealots who committed the act of the burning of the pilgrims alive. Every one, other than the zealots, is hunted down. This is looked upon as a case of poetic justice little realizing that this very act of well planned and orchestrated attack on innocent Muslims fits into the game plan of the Muslim zealots. This, therefore, becomes the victory for the zealots of both communities and the losers are the innocent Hindus and the Muslims who have become the pawns in the hands of the zealots. This leaves the society more divided than ever before giving a great opportunity for the politicians to step in and serve the society in a way only politicians can do. Strife and division in a society are Godsend opportunities for the politicians, without which the politician will have no aim in life and thererfore these become the life giving elixir for the politicians. Without this life giving potion of strife and division, the very survival of the politician would be threatened.

The reasons behind the occurrence of communal violence can in many ways be looked upon as the enactment of McCarthyism that was practiced in United States of America during the days of cold war. McCarthyism, though appeared to be a nationalistic movement aimed at protecting the interests of United States of America, resulted in the ruining of the lives of thousands of honest, patriotic and sincere Americans. Their only fault was that they did not fit into the straight jacket definition of the Patriotic American as defined by Mc Carthy. The Indian society is in exactly the same situation with a few politicians and religious leaders asking the people of different faiths to prove their allegiance to the nation. The problem of the Indian society is far greater and bigger than the problem of American society at the time of Mc Carthy or for that matter the present day post 11th September American society. Similar state can be found in other communally sensitive areas like Ireland and the Middle East, which are historical in nature. The problem is that the Hindu religion itself is not a straight jacket religion unlike Islam or Christianity or Buddhism or Jainism. Therefore, in the words of the poet Javed Akhtar, this concept of proving one's allegiance to the nation can be turned upside down and this can set different segments of the Indian society at loggerheads with each other resulting in the destruction of the entire composite social fabric.

The urge to make others prove their loyalty or allegiance to the nation or an individual is immense as this gives a sense of importance and power. This has been used time and again to favor friends or punish those who are different and whose views are different from those in power. History has recorded that every society gets into this kind of a state when the mechanism of governance fails to address issues related to the well being of the people. The Germans never took Adolph Hitler and his few supporters seriously till the German economy failed to take off and the people were pushed in to a state of despair and misery. The same was true with the Roman Empire, which was ruined on account of the few individuals becoming more important than the community well being. In India, the politicians having let the nation down on the economic front have started to play with the emotions of the segments of the society. The tragedy that one sees in Jammu and Kashmir is a classic example of the failure of governance resulting in unprecedented corruption and human misery. The religious leaders and the politicians have joined hands with one purpose of keeping the different segments of the society divided and thus successfully hijack the key issues of development and prosperity. This helps them to impose feudalistic methods of governance where protection of the honor of the God and religion become all the more important than alleviating poverty, hunger and suffering of the people.

Thus, philosophizing the misery of the people as long as it does not affect one's own life is definitely not the best policy. On the other hand, the best policy is "never do to others what you do not want others to do to you". But this does not provide a sense of dynamism, authority, dominance and supremacy, and therefore a feeling of success. Thus the act of perpetuating the sense of dynamism, authority, dominance and supremacy is always laced with aggression and violence. Life always creates conflicting demands as none of us are in control of any thing, even though we believe to the contrary. The irony of modern life is

We spend all our time chasing money and loosing health,
When we make enough money, we loose it to regain health!
We spend all our time imposing our ideas on others believing
that we are doing a great job,
Towards the end of our career, we yearn for a few more years of
active life to undo all the wrongs!
We spend all our time believing that every thing must be kept
under control for better performance,
Towards the end of our career, we realize how wrong we were in
understanding nature!
We spend all our time believing that we are in complete control
of every thing,
Towards the end of our career, we realize that we were after all not
in control of any thing!
We spend all our time believing that we are doing a great job,
Towards the end of our career we yearn for another chance to
redo every thing!
We spend all our time questioning the existence or non existence
of God
When we come to the end of our life, we realize that God was
waiting for a call all along!
We mourn the death of our near and dear ones
Never believing that we too would one day be mourned!
The mind rationalizes the irrational
If this not consolation of mind, what else is?

We neither know how to live nor know how to die. One of the famous saying attributed to Red Indians of United States of America is "Never be afraid to die". This has been the basic tenet of teaching of all the saints and the saviors. Further, the well being of humanity has been the basis of all religions. The tragedy of modern man and modern times is that the concept of the well being of humanity conflicts with the furthering of one's own well being. Mahatma Gandhi had aptly described the state of the society when he said, "There is enough to meet every one's need but not every one's greed".

iii

Today, contrary to all beliefs, the greatest threat to the civilization and peace is the World Trade Organization. Inspite of the lofty ideals of opening of all markets to every other society/nation thus paving the way for growth of economies of all societies, the fact remains that the Nigerian sugar cane/sugar industry and South African poultry industry are in ruins. These are solely due to the cartel policy in fixing and manipulation of international prices of these commodities, and also the ability of the developed countries to provide hefty agricultural subsidies to their farmers. The developed economies need ready markets for their goods and therefore what better market can there be than the hungry societies that cannot fend for themselves.

There is a need to change the way the societies are governed. There is a need to ensure that the institutions that are to function as the corner stones of a democratic society are allowed to function and not end up getting diluted. The need of the hour is not to disburse aid but to help in the setting of institutions in every developing society that will help in effective project implementation and therefore improve governance. The ability of every society to be in a position to feed itself and provide the basic necessities of life to its people is the only way to establish a safer and better world. This is an achievable target.

As long as a large section of any society is disadvantaged, it would be difficult to feel secure even for the most powerful society. A better world is a safer world to live. There is a need to enhance the role of United Nations to wage a war against not only terrorism but also to bring about good and efficient governance. Further the World Trade Organization regime must not be allowed to create imperialism of a different kind. The developed nations must not make an issue of the labor standards as a means of creating trade barriers. The WTO Regime should not be a reflection of the desire of the developed economies to rule the world by dividing the continents in the same way as the imperialism in the 19th century resulted in the geographic division of South Americas, Africa & Asia amongst the developed countries. It is also necessary to recognize the influence of the subsidy regime as practiced by the developed nations with in the WTO Regime and allow the developing countries to impose tariff barriers to enforce a level playing ground. There is a need to remove the food and agriculture trade from the WTO Regime as it must be made the global action plan to make every society self reliant in food. Any attempt to make food as a trading commodity in the same way as steel or television will surely be the beginning of the end. The world bodies must at all costs avoid the start of food riots in any part of the global society. In the post 11th September scenario a food riot even in the farthest remote corner of the world will create disturbances even in the powerful developed societies. A safer world is an easily achievable goal that requires hard and sincere work. The only hindrance to achieving this goal is the desire to dominate over the weak and the greed to amass wealth at any cost.

There cannot be any reason for accepting the unreasonable actions of a few powerful societies who are in the habit of preserving their habitat at the cost of others. The human being has the unfortunate habit of not following the spirit of the teachings of wise men, irrespective of the religion to which they belong. Every one believes that he has received a revelation from his God that has authorized him to wage war against another nation or another religion or another society or impose conditions on women and children belonging to his own society. There are others who believe that they are above law, be it the man made law or the cosmic law. Therefore, it is unfortunate that the United States of America and Britain had to wait for the destruction of WTC towers to realize the fallacy of the foreign policies that they had been pursuing.

This does not in any way mean that the cause of terrorism is WTO. However, it must be acknowledged that WTO provides the one and the only chance to bridge the gap between the rich and the poor. There is a need to keep remembering Prof. Norman Borlaug's statement that the new order will bring in chaos unless otherwise the distribution mechanism and agriculture in every society are not nurtured with great care. Food cannot be looked upon as a trading commodity. The stability of society, east or west, north or south, would depend on the availability of adequate food for the people at affordable prices. The rest of the commodities are of no consequence. Food has the ability to become a single highly potent cause of creating strife, violence, despots, dictators, lost cause and finally international terrorism. The war against terrorism must be looked and understood keeping this new scenario of opening of markets and the sheer incapacity of the developing economies to reorient their economies, industries, agriculture, poultry and the most important issues of distribution system and health.

If only we had asked a simple question, much before the 11th of September 2001, pertaining to violence and terrorism we could have avoided the many ugly turns that the modern history has taken. The simple question is, "How do the Tamil Tigers get all the arms to take on the Sri Lankan army in a sea locked country?" The most interesting fact is that the faculty of the King's Institute in London had all the answers and no body bothered to ask that simple question. The one and only reason for this apathy is that the violent incidents were unfolding in a far away land, far away from civilized and developed societies. The answers to this simple question are frightening because of the long trail and foot prints that one gets to see. The trail and foot prints span the globe and is not a local phenomenon as the violence in these parts was linked to the drug lords in Columbia, Nigeria, Al Quaeda in Afghanistan, ISI in Pakistan and the mafia in Central Asia & Russia. Thus, the Tamil Tigers had access to the latest of the weapons funded by the drug money. This critical and crucial information was known to every one who mattered in every developed country including United States of America and England. All these persons had perfected the act of a toad till 11th of September 2001 and the reason for the restoration of the sight of the toad was that a very important society had become the victim of attack.

This track record of the developed societies makes the tall claims of the benefits and goodies that the Open Market regime under WTO would bring to all the societies including the developing societies suspect. The developed societies are never known for cooperative living. The business models followed by the powerful corporate business houses are all monolith in nature based on the principle "winner takes it all". The international corporate houses do not believe in cooperative living. Thus, externally the terrorists and the multi national corporate houses look different. Internally they seem to think alike and therefore the much touted clash of civilizations is a farce. Yet, we console our minds into believing that we are different and that we represent radically different ways of living and are given to radically different cultural values. If one has the time and inclination to get down to basics, one finds that under any given set of conditions there is hardly any difference in the behavioral patterns of people inspite of their being conditioned in different ways due to cultural differences.

The relationship between developed and developing countries on one hand and the relationship between the rich and poor in a developing society on the other hand are in many respects very similar. Any attempt by the poor to get an equitable distribution of resources is always looked upon as a destabilizing event and therefore is wished away. But the ills that one sees in the developing countries are not necessarily the making of the developed countries. The classic case of abundant, should one say rotting, food grains and a fairly large population that is under nourished in India is a glaring example of the failure on the part of the governance mechanism to use the food stocks to create permanent wealth in rural India. The rural India requires rain water harnessing, proper roads, facilities for marketing the agricultural, dairy, poultry products that they produce. At the same time, the abundant food grains could have been used effectively to take the schools to the children by giving them wholesome mid day meals thus eradicating both illiteracy and mal nourishment. But unfortunately, none of this happened and food stocks have remained a matter of statistics as far as the government of India is concerned. The tragedy is compounded by the fact that even the parliament does not debate the issue of rotting food grains.

Under these circumstances, it is always easy for the interested, biased, under world and the mercenary elements to thrive and try to carve out a niche area of influence with in the sovereign country. This has been the main problem of every developing society and after a certain stage, the effects spill over and the economy would start thriving on the illegal narcotics-arms trade. This becomes the common factor that would fuel the growth of parallel governments that would be the anti-thesis of democratic form of governments. This narco-arms trade factor would be the common base on which links to regimes in different geographical locations would be established creating one big happy family working on a totally different value system. The activities of these groups would then be linked to various social issues that would give a semblance or facade of respectability. These regimes hijack the social issues and convert them to socio-religious issues making them very appealing to the minds of oppressed population who would be eager to accept any solution in the hope of overcoming their misery. But soon, the people realize that the aim of the revised agenda is not to provide relief or succor to the suffering masses. In fact the aim is never intended to be deliverance from misery. The aim is always to perpetuate a new form of oppression in the name of religion and God that promises heaven after death. The solution is always projected as a total solution backed by a divine revelation.

This was witnessed during 800 AD to about 1300 AD when the tribesmen on the horse back went about ransacking and destroying every known symbol of civilization, culture, religion and heritage. The same was witnessed during the infamous crusades during the middle of the last millenium. Adolph Hitler perfected it by inventing new and novel methods of ethnic cleansing during the 1930s. Similar ethnic cleansing was witnessed in East Pakistan in 1970-1971 leading to the birth of Bangladesh. The process of ethnic cleansing was repeated in Kashmir when the Hindus, Sikhs and Gujars were systematically driven out or massacred by the mercenaries from other countries, who had been referred to as freedom fighters by Pakistan making Adolph Hitler the greatest of the freedom fighters. The Pol Pot regime specialized in mass graves that produced more human skulls than ever discovered before. Then came Osama bin Laden and his Al Quaeda, who tried to propagate their own concept of Islam and *jihad* and hijacked all the issues by recruiting mercenaries. Each one of these had invoked the revelations that they claim to have received from the God and put forth their ultimate solution that would take away all the miseries including the cause and source of such miseries. In addition to the recorded history, the mythology also cites many such instances where different revelations have been pitted against each other causing misery and bloodshed. Peace returns after a lot of bloodshed and suffering. The manipulators always like to keep the pot boiling and therefore peace will, sooner than later, be disturbed by another series of events involving similar claims but in a different place and a different setting. The root cause of all this misery is the attempt to make religion and the relationship between God and the man/woman a well oiled organized business like structure. There cannot be any business better and more profitable than the business of God. This business brings with it not only money but also phenomenal amount of following, influence and power that no democratic or autocratic rule can bestow. The man who claims to have had a divine revelation has the ability to become more dangerous than the most ruthless dictator. Any attempt to move religion away from the state of an organized movement that it is today, and make the relationship between God and the man/woman a personal belief would be resisted tooth and nail. The misery that one sees in the name of God or in the name of a spiritual leader is attributable only to the ruthless process of organized religion that believes in holding on to the followers without giving them the freedom to question. Thus, the pre-requisites for such a state to thrive in a society are:

(a) Poverty

(b) Ignorance. This does not necessarily translate to illiteracy as ignorance and illiteracy refer to two different states of mind.

When these two ingredients are mixed with religious fundamentalism, one gets a deadly potion that not only destroys every thing that it comes in contact with but also destroys itself in the end.

iv

The first act that needs to be put in place is to ensure that the entire population is given the basic necessities starting from food. Every society must become self sufficient in food if not in any thing else. A healthy society is the best bet against such a drift towards creation of a society that has difficulty in tolerating a plural society. Hunger fuels, helps and abets such a drift and therefore availability of food at the grass root level and not in the ware houses is important. A well nourished society is the best bet for long term peace and prosperity. Therefore, the plan of providing mid day meals to children attending schools was the best possible way of creating a healthy society even though this was planned and implemented keeping an eye on the vote bank. This was also the best way to get the children to the schools and take the burden off the parents. But for some strange reasons, a profound decision was taken to discontinue this and allow the food grains to rot.

A number of Non Government Organizations (NGO) have conducted a number of field studies in Uttar Pradesh on the problem of child education. The experiment that they did was to take the school to the children rather than try to bring the children to school. The concept of bringing children to school is an out come of conventional wisdom practiced both in ancient India of the *gurukula* fame and the western education system. The present scenario is unfortunately not suited for either of these two systems. The reasons are:

(a) Large population

(b) Economic backwardness making it necessary for the child to contribute to the income of the family

(c) Manipulation in the wages given to the daily wage laborers by the middlemen, the adults getting less than what they ought to be getting, resulting in the vicious circle of forced child labor

(d) The need for the child to become an earning member of the family defeats the attempt to take the child to the school.

It must also be stated here that no parent would like his/her children to remain illiterate or work or under nourished or remain economically backward. Therefore the work carried out by the NGO in Uttar Pradesh, a populous state in India, where they took the school to the children was novel and worth emulating every where. The school that is taken to the place of work of the child and the school that identifies itself with the work the child is doing is more beneficial than the lofty ideal of attempting to take the children to the school. The child may be involved in any kind of work in the form of grazing the cattle or working in the workshop or working in the restaurant. The need for the child to work is a necessity of life, and not an act of pleasure. The taking of the school to the child helped in achieving the unachievable, viz.,

(a) Helped in educating the child

(b) Helped in allowing the child to supplement the income of the family

(c) Helped in reducing the drop out level to near zero

This exercise would have been far more effective, if a nutritious mid day mean had been served to the children helping in the growth of the child and reducing the burden of the parents to feed the child. The food stock that is allowed to rot could have been used to give nourishing meal to the children.

The issue of child labor is, unfortunately, not a case of exploitation but a case of necessity due to the harsh living conditions. The manipulation of the daily wage given to the laborers, which in many cases force the parents to look to their children to augment the meager daily earnings, is a definite case of exploitation by the middle men. The laws that are meant to protect the vulnerable section of the society are ineffective as the people who are to be protected neither know the laws nor know their rights much less the ways of exercising their rights and get justice. The long years that require to get justice through the judicial process helps only those who have a staying power for years to approach the judiciary for justice. The rest have no option but to make tolerating injustice a way of life. This goes on till some one out of sheer frustration picks up a stone and throws it at the land lord. This either becomes a law and order problem or becomes the start of a revolution. Violence never solves any problem. Judiciary has become out of reach of the common man even though the judiciary is empowered to protect the interests of the citizen. We seem to have pushed ourselves into a messy situation. The best option of effecting corrective measures through peaceful community movement through legal means has become ineffective.

In this context, the World Trade Organization that has ushered in the new WTO Regime can become a blessing in disguise and help to change the ways of wealth distribution with in a society and between societies ensuring a fair level of well being. But, the problem with the WTO Regime is that it has emanated from the affluent and the powerful west. Therefore the societies that make up the majority of the south or the developing nations will have difficulty in adapting their practices and policies to be able to make the best use of the WTO Regime. The problem here is not only due to the developed societies but also due to the feudal nature of the developing societies. This would result in the ushering in of a different kind of dominance of one section over the other, as the battle now is for the control of the markets. We have a situation where the child labor is a consequence of the ineffective laws that stipulate minimum daily wage to the laborers, ineffective from implementation point of view. At the same time, we have the WTO regime, which bars the trade with those organizations and societies that allow child labor. Therefore, we need to have a universally accepted method of education for majority of the children who for no reason of theirs have become the victims of exploitation and the target of WTO regime.

It is here that the path breaking work of taking the school to the children that resulted in achieving zero drop out needs to be acknowledged as the only solution to the spread of literacy. This was achieved by a Non Government Organization (NGO) in the state of Uttar Pradesh, India. The child learns in the school and works to augment the meager earnings of his/her parents. There is a need to accept and acknowledge the ground reality of the child 's need to learn and earn, and it cannot be wished away and replaced by the romantic ideas of the west or the early tradition of India where

(a) the child goes to the school where the child studies and does no work

(b) or the child goes to the teacher's place and studies and serves the teacher by working in the master's house

The above options may indeed by ideal situations, which millions of Indian children will never be able to achieve even after a few decades. Therefore the first step of taking school to the child, providing the child with a nutritous mid day meal and then allowing the child to augment the parents' earnings is a necessity. Therefore the frame work with in which the rural and deprived society are to be rejuvinated cannot be the ideal situation of a child going to school for learning as desired by WTO. If an attempt is made to enforce the WTO model of child's education, there will be a human disaster, which may benefit the developed nations as the disaster will wipe out what ever has been painstakingly built over the years in the developing societies. A disaster in one remote corner of the world does not provide a safety net for a nation in the opposite corner and therefore there is need to look at this issue of child labor and child education from a different perspective as shown by the NGO.

The first thing that needs to be done is to formulate an education system that brings the vocation of the child into the curriculum rather than try to thrust the conventional curriculum covering physics, chemistry, botany, zoology, mathematics etc on the child. It is futile to expect every child to be trained to become a scientist or a literary figure! Thus, the children need to be given a path to progress in the non-conventional way and have a means to prosper. If this is to happen then the positions that are advertised must not be linked to an university degree but to the specialization that the position requires. Thus, the child has an option to choose the career path based on its interest rather than on the mandatory requirement of the need to have a graduation or post graduation degree from the university in a generic unrelated area. That is the condition of being a graduate with general specialization for all kinds of jobs must be discarded.

Therefore, we need an education system both at the lower (primary and secondary level) and higher (10+) level where the vocation is a part of the education making learning a meaningful exercise. This would allow the child/student to work part time in extreme condition to augment the earnings of the parents and still pursue his/her studies. Our educationists appear to have been lost in the equations and are glued to the idea of creating a society that has only scientists and no place for any body else. This will create a society that will not be able to support itself because of the kind of investments that are needed to create a high growth in the technology sectors. This high growth becomes necessary if we are to provide employment to the teeming scientists that would come out of our colleges. There is an urgent need for creating an alternate path in the non-formal education that is vocation based and not computer or information technology or bio-technology or management or marketing based.

This is more a chicken and egg problem. The management experts believe that the best thing to do is to allow the market forces to decide about which branches of science would survive. But what should not be lost sight of is the need to maintain certain basic standards in education and at the same time create other avenues of non-formal learning that would help in making a decent and respectable living. Therefore the need is to de-link the need to possess science degrees to get any job. That is, the need is to create more branches of specialization so that the student can choose from them depending upon one's interest. Also the criterion for job requirement must be changed in order to bring to an end the unnecessary rush to get hold of generic arts or science or engineering degrees to make a decent living.

Thus, WTO regime must be looked upon as a blessing in disguise so as to reform the education at all levels:

(a) Taking elementary schools to the children where by they can both earn and learn the basic reading, writing and arithmetic.

(b) This should be looked upon as a case of inculcating self reliance and enhancing self worth with in the family unit and not be looked upon as a case of child labour.

(c) This education at the primary level in India must not be equated to the western standards of education where the child does not have the burden of supporting the family.

(d) Give the children attending schools in their locality or place of work a wholesome mid day mean rather than allowing the food grains to rot.

Therefore, the first thing that needs to be done is to change the mind set of those who control WTO and make them understand the ground reality, see reason and not worry about the corporate quarterly reports. This will help in overcoming the mal-nourishment that is found in children and at the same time lessen the burden on the parents.

(a) Blend the learning process with the work environment so as to make the learning more meaningful and useful and relevant to the child. This requires the educationists to do more ground work.

(b) Remove the necessity to possess the degree in arts or science for all the general purpose jobs: non-engineering, non-commerce, non-scientific, non-medical etc.

(c) Introduce more job oriented courses both up to and after 10th standard catering to different vocational specialization so as to help the student

This helps in getting the students with the right attitude and aptitude for the right courses and specialization. This will enhance the quality of the students graduating from the colleges and would be more useful to the industry.

The change over in the education in the school to formal and non-formal education must take place from the beginning, 1st standard on wards. The aim is to attract the best talent to the right courses/specialization and ensure decent living for every one. The reason for choosing a course or specialization must not be financial benefits, even though this will always be one of the criteria for choosing a career path. The financial gains alone should not be the sole criterion. If financial gains alone become the sole criterion then the educationists would be helping in the creation of a neurotic generation. While this is unfolding, we would all the while be consoling our minds into believing that we are creating a great scientific society.

V

In the late 19th century and early 20th century, a few nations met and decided to divide Africa amongst themselves. This was the beginning of imperialism that also gave respectability to slave trade on the cotton farms of United States of America. The WTO tries to achieve this in a different manner. The WTO regime ostensibly aims at providing access to all the markets in all the countries to all the countries, often referred to as the regime of free markets. But a look at the levels of subsidies that are given either to their agriculture sector or the manufacturing sector by the developed countries clearly indicates that the developing countries have lost the battle even before it has started. A huge quantity of chicken legs is preserved in cold storage facilities in USA ready for export. The poultry industry in South Africa has been ruined due to the liberalization. There are food riots in Argentina, which is the latest victim of the free trade movement and market liberalization. Argentina is facing economic crisis and its economy has collapsed. One of the reasons for the economic crisis of Argentina is political expediency and fiscal mismanagement. However, the main reason is the inability of the local industry to come to terms with liberalized trade and its inability to compete with the imports that enjoy huge subsidy from the developed countries.

Thus, WTO regime is a case of imperialism with a difference. Here the geographic territories are not divided amongst the powerful countries. The control and owning of geographic territories create more problems. The basic assumption behind imperialism that initiated the process of controlling the geographical territories was not as much the love for the heritage and culture, but more for the raw materials and a market for the finished goods. The concept of imperialism put an added pressure on the western imperialist nations to ensure governance and upkeep of the occupied territory or the colony. In the case of WTO regime, the stress is on the access to the market with out the burden of the need to look after the colony. That is, there are no colonies even though the underlying philosophy is to create suitable markets in developing world for the finished products and services from the developed economies. The offer of quid pro quo is only on the paper as the subsidies that are provided by the developed countries is often invisible and the competition is in no position to counter such huge subsidies. Thus the WTO regime has put two un-equals to fight it out in the market place for a share of the market. There will be no prize for the correct guess.

Thus, in the future one would get to see many more economies in ruins and many more food riots. This would give the developed nations and the IMF an opportunity to provide humanitarian assistance and keep the other economies under check. We are committing the same mistakes all over again. The greatest mistake ever committed by man kind is to think that establishing dominance over others and other societies is the only way to live. Imperialism of the late 19th century is being recast into a different mold to establish a strangle hold on the weaker nations and societies in the name of free market economy. The age old Indian wisdom, "May every one by happy and may there be peace" is looked upon as an expression of weakness.

India presents a contrasting picture of inefficiency and inability to leverage the advantages of the abundant talent, massive food grains stocks and unfathomable stock of patience. India is a society that has been held a hostage by a few unscrupulous men, some of whom are in power and the remaining are close to the center of power. The governance mechanism is not able to use the enormous food stocks as a mechanism of implementing the rural development projects like rain water harnessing, building of roads, and grain, vegetable and poultry product storage and transportation facility etc. The enormous stock of food grains that are left to rot is an issue of mere statistics for government, either central or state. On the other hand, the food grains that are distributed to the people in exchange of work done is a matter of life giving elixir and therefore will be carefully preserved and looked after. This would also solve the problem of mal nourishment and help to build a reasonable safety net of food grain stock by the people themselves. This would also help the government to get some of the key rural development projects completed that would other wise have required enormous amount of money. Therefore the food grains including pulses, cooking oil and kerosene, and set of clothing must be transformed into a tenable currency in the same way as the plastic card has been transformed into a tenable currency in the urban India. This would in a way overcome the problem of burgeoning stock of food grains and the sick National Textile Mills.

India is in a strange dichotomous situation. One section of the urban population is slowly and surely getting accustomed to the use of the credit/debit cards. One section of the urban and the rural population is getting accustomed to the handling of hard cash, stashed in to their pockets and bags and suitcases. At the same time, the government of India is deeply concerned about the ways and means of increasing the buying power of the vast majority of the people in rural India who are literally living on the roots and carcasses. Why cannot the government use the inherent strength that has been created over the last fifty years and use it to the advantage of the rural population by creating infrastructure to sustain and improve the livelihood of the rural population?

In the fifties and sixties, during the time of drought and food shortage in India, the concept of land army was floated. This was the first attempt at resolving the food problem, absence of purchasing power in rural India and the high unemployment rate. Unfortunately, the absence of meaningful non-government organizations that had experience in rural reconstruction and the apathy of government machinery ensured the tardy implementation of this laudable scheme of land army. The present scenario is far different from what had prevailed in the fifties and sixties. There are a large number of active non-government organizations that are actively involved in the rural reconstruction. Further, the lofty ideals with which the concept of land army was floated are still valid today. Therefore, this is the time to resurrect the concept and involve the non-government organizations in the rural reconstruction process by giving food grains, pulses and clothes to be used as a mode of currency for the work done. These need to be village based. That is, the work to be carried out for village reconstruction under this program must be aimed at improving the

(a) Rain water harnessing by building ponds

(b) Preparation of usable roads

(c) Creation of cultivable lands

(d) Creation of storage shelters for food grain, fodder, etc.

(e) Distribution of the reclaimed lands amongst the villagers. No outsider must be allowed to come and occupy these lands.

(f) Creation of grass lands that shall belong to the community that provide grass for the cattle, sheep etc.

(g) Schools that are taken to the children and adults where knowledge about the environment, managing the grass lands, cattle, poultry are taught in addition to reading and writing. These schools must be accessible to both the children and the adults. The children and the adults who attend the school must be given a wholesome and nourishing mid day meal.

The details of these activities must be put on web sites so as to be accessible to any one and verifiable by any one. Therefore it should be made the collective responsibility of the entire nation so that the tax payer's money is properly and effectively utilized.

The Office of Vigilance Commissioner at the Center and the States also must be involved in the project monitoring by ensuring that all information related to the project are put on the website for easy access and reference by any one. This alone will avoid mis-appropriation of funds, food grains, clothes allocated for the implementation of the projects.

This is the only way to reconstruct the rural India as any other centralized process of planning and implementation of the planned projects will perpetuate corruption and the misery of the people.

vi

India is a nation of multi language, multi religion, multi culture, multi ethnic societies and therefore centralized solution and planning will not resolve any problem. Even if the problem is the same in different geographically located villages, the solutions to the problem cannot be the same. The process of finding the solution must be left to the local people and the mechanism of governance must work as a facilitator and not as a controller. Unfortunately the governments, both at the center and the state, function more as controllers rather than as facilitators resulting in creation of more problems. This process of controlling provides the power to the bureaucrats and politicians, and this also facilitates the process of manipulation. That is, the solution as proposed by the present mechanism of governance expects people to change their

(a) Mind set

(b) Ways of life

- This stems from the belief that the urban way of life, which is a poor imitation of the western way of life, is the best way of living.

(c) Value system

These changes in the ethos that are expected from the rural population makes the failure of the planned projects a fore gone conclusion. The people find that the process of economic emancipation is linked to their being forcibly pulled away from what ever they had valued over the centuries. Thus, even before the start of the project, a mental barrier that stops any meaningful interaction between the beneficiaries and the benefactors gets created. This gets compounded by the fact that the rural population have been given a raw deal by the government machinery and the local land lords. It is necessary that the land lords, who control every activity in the rural society, realize that the best security for them is the general well being of all the villagers. There cannot be an island of plenty or affluence surrounded by poverty and suffering. This is true about both the indigenous and global societies.

Therefore the role of the World Trade Organization becomes all the more important in diffusing the tensions between societies. There are two levels at which the tensions get created. The first level is the non-availability of the basic facilities or amenities like medicines and other basic necessities, fair access to the market and a fair distribution of wealth. The other level operates at the political level where the control of other societies for the purpose of exercising the pre-eminence of one society or section of a society over the others either through economic means or military means or terror means. This becomes the cause of tension. Thus, the assumption that the World Trade Organization regime would result in automatically making all avenues available to all societies for equitable and just development is misplaced. The issues that plague the local societies and the global societies are very similar. The issue of migration of large population of rural unemployed to the cities causing slums and the related problems finds a parallel in the attempted entry of people from one nation to the other by boat or other means just to be able to get a decent living. Therefore, the real solution to the ills of the society lies in improving the living conditions of the people at the lowest administrative unit of the society, the village. Mahatma Gandhi was far ahead of his times when he said that the well being of the village is the foundation for the well being of India.

William Fulbright has said, "International relations can be improved and the danger of wars significantly reduced by producing generations of leaders who have acquired some feeling of understanding for other people's culture, why they operate as they do, why they think as they do, and why they react as they do" This contrasts with Adlai Stevenson's statement, "Either you are with us or against us" Thus the battle is between the mind sets of different people, ethos of different societies and the value systems that they nurture. This is true about the problems faced by the villages in India or in any other developing society. This is also true about the problems concerning the various issues pertaining to the World Trade Organization Regime that exist between the developed and the developing societies.

If history is used as a frame of reference, the future of the World Trade Organization Regime will not be any better. Every effort will be made to use the new regime to ensure the economic domination over the developing society. This can be looked upon as the second phase of imperialism. The first phase that started in the later part of 19th century was primarily to use the military and economic strength for dividing the world as geographical entities amongst themselves. The second phase of imperialism that will begin with the World Trade Organization Regime will be with reference to the division of the world as market places amongst the militarily and economically powerful nations. Both the phases of imperialism were supposed to serve the interests of the indigenous people.

Thus depending upon the state of the mind, ethos and the value system of the decision makers, the World Trade Organization Regime could be converted into a blessing in disguise to build a new order. It would be possible to fulfill the dream of Mahatma Gandhi in this new world order and ensure to fulfill every one's needs and not every one's greed. But knowing the ability of the mind to rationalize the irrational, every attempt would be made to ensure that no level playing field is made available to the weak and the strong. Therefore, a farmer from a developing society will be expected to compete with another farmer from the developed society enjoying high subsidies. The same would be true with the manufactured goods. Therefore, the need of the day is to build a clause in the World Trade Organization Regime to factor the subsidy enjoyed by each product into the anti dumping duty that can be levied on the import of products. This is certainly an utopian idea that will never be accepted by the developed economies as this will go against their interests. A large stock of chicken legs lying in the deep freezers is waiting to be shipped from United States of America. So also a large stock of food grains, dairy products, fruits, pulses, sugar etc in different parts of the globe, all in developed economies who can afford to cut the prices, form a cartel and flood the market to destabilize the local production in the not so wealthy nations. This is good news for the farmers in the developed societies as this would help in creating a large permanent market for the food products. But if one keeps the history of man kind in view, dependence on outsiders for supply of food will set off instability resulting in damage to peace and stability of the recipient society. The assumption that the recipient nation benefits by getting the food products at competitive costs and therefore local food production is not of any importance is fallacious. The stability of a society is dependent on the self sufficiency of food and not on the dependency of food from an external source.

The onus for achieving this self sufficiency in food or for that matter of any thing solely rests with the local government. It is therefore necessary that United Nations must initiate the setting up of an organization to ensure that the necessary help and guidance is provided for the local administration to achieve localized self sufficiency in food, shelter and basic education. Therefore, in the same way as a joint declaration and action plan against terrorism, there is need to forge a joint action plan for the better governance of every member nation. This alone will usher in better living conditions for the vast majority of the people living in the developing societies. The better conditions refer to the

(a) Availability of food grains for and with each individual family, and not as a buffer stock in the warehouses of the Food Ministry

(b) Basic literacy so as to enable them to look after their interests by taking schools to the children. This literacy must be linked to their vocation and not the westernized concept of schooling. The solution is to take the schools to the children and knit their vocation with the learning process of reading and writing.

(c) Basic drinking water, health and sanitation facilities

(d) Basic shelter

This alone is the solution to the terror and the sloppy administrative machinery of the state that breeds such terrorists. Only then can the terror that has been unleashed with in the society and across international borders either in the name of ideology or God or perceived injustices be neutralized. It has become necessary to fight evil even if it is not in one's own society. Today, we are indulging in the blame game accusing others of committing injustices instead of looking at our own methods of governance and improving upon them. We have consoled our minds into believing that all our ills are due to others. This becomes the driving force for the terror attacks as was witnessed in September and December in United States of America & India respectively. In both these cases, freedom and the free society as enshrined as part of democratic society came in handy for the terrorists. Thus, instead of attacking societies that had no democracies that had curtailed freedom and brutalized women, children and ethnic minorities, the democracies became the target. The rulers of the Islamic societies are complaining about the injustices committed by every one else instead of taking steps to allow for the representation of the people in the process of governance. Often the Indian democracy is ridiculed without realizing that inspite of the drawbacks in the Indian system the party in power has invariably lost the election proving beyond doubt that there is no rigging of the elections on the scale that is often projected.

Therefore it has become necessary to fight dictators or despot rulers even if they are far away from one's own society. Thus international diplomatic pressure under the auspices of United Nations on erring rulers is the best security and not amassing of weapons. It is necessary that the two international financial institutions, World Bank and the International Monetary Fund, must play the role of a friend and a mentor to ensure that the governments provide the basic levels of comfort with reference to food, education, health and shelter to its people. The World Trade Organization must shed its fetish for imposing the western standards of human development on the developing societies. This will create more polarization than harmony. However, diplomatic and other efforts must be used to ensure that the standards of human welfare and development are enhanced on a continuous basis. If one takes a look at the governance of most of the developing countries, the societies are not as poor as they are made out to be. The problem is not of poverty but of mis-management of the tax payer's money. Thus, the problems of the developing societies will not be sorted out by infusing generous allocation of aid money at low rates of interest even though this would be the marketing pitch from the developing nations. The aid money from World Bank, International Monetary Fund or from donor nations will not solve the problems of any of the developing societies. There is a need to observe fiscal discipline and the administrative machinery must put in place accountability on every aspect of governance. The bane of the developing societies is corruption at all levels and improper formulation of projects and improper implementation of such projects.

In many of the developing societies the administrative machinery has failed to address the problems of the societies. Therefore, the time has come for the Non Government Organizations to step in and help formulate and implement development projects. This activity must be funded by the government machinery and monitored by making the entire process transparent. That is, the development project must be under the public gaze and not done as a favor to the society by the ruling party. Not only should the projects be under the public gaze but also the working on Non Government Organizations that implement development projects using the public money should come under public scrutiny. The key to successful usage of public funds is transparency of every activity, which alone can counter corruption. The World Trade Organization, United Nations Organization, World Bank and International Monetary Fund and the western societies must help the developing societies in achieving this process of using the government funds effectively and usefully. This alone would guarantee the effective usage of the funds. If the world bodies do not help in the setting up of institutions that can implement projects effectively, any amount of aid will only result in the increase of indebtedness of the recipient nation. The recipient nations would sooner than later get into the debt trap and would one day result in a melt down of the economy as witnessed in Argentina or Mexico. The effective use of funds will also ensure the well being of the developing societies that would help in preventing the need to migrate to developed societies, by legal or illegal means. This is an achievable state.

Thus the need of the hour is

(a) not to disburse aid

(b) to help in the publishing over the net the details of all development projects so as to create transparency in the implementation of projects and help in effective project implementation and improve governance

(c) to take schools to the children and integrate the learning with the work that the child will any have to do in order to augment the earnings of his parents due the exploitation of the rural landless by the middlemen

(d) to provide a nourishing mid day meal to the children in the school so that the child grows up to be a healthy citizen of the country instead of allowing food grains to rot

(e) to use the food stocks to start the food for work programs for building facilities like roads, rainwater harnessing, building tanks etc. Food stocks given to the poor people for the work they do will be preserved in a far better way than the food stocks stored in warehouses. Because, food stocks stored in warehouses is more a statistical information for the government and therefore can be allowed to rot as is happening in various parts of India.

(f) to improve the living conditions in the village and to make village as the basic unit of welfare state. This should help in the prevention of migration of people from village to city/metropolis/megalopolis in search of livelihood. This would

- prevent the formation of slums in the cities/metropolis/megalopolis, which in turn would result in drastic reduction in crime and underworld activities.

- result in drastic reduction in organized crime and therefore narcotics and arms trade, and therefore establishment of transnational links in the illegal trade of arms and narcotics would become very difficult.

- result in neutralizing the formation of terrorist groups as these groups need large amounts of money. The absence of meaningful, powerful and motivated terrorist groups ready to take arms and create strife any where, either in the name of Karl Marx or in the name of any God, make these groups unfit to become integral part of foreign policy of a nation!

These are achievable targets. Therefore the concept of village as a unit of the well being of the society needs to be accepted and pursued with all sincerity is as relevant today as it was about a hundred years ago.

The assumption that India is poor or for that matter any developing country is poor is a sham. None of the developing countries are poor. This does not mean that they can compete with the developed societies in terms of per capita consumption either of energy or calories, or in terms of natural wealth. There is definitely a vast difference between a developing country and a developed country with regards to these indicators of well being. But this does not mean that the developing nation is so starved of resources, as not to allow for fair governance and to ensure an equitable distribution of basic necessities of life like food, health and education. The term "basic necessities" has different connotations in different nations/societies. Therefore, keeping these differences in view, it is definitely possible to ensure an acceptable level of well being with in the framework of the society and without having to compare with any other society. The developing countries are intentionally mis-managed by the feudal lords who believe and behave as though the nation is their personal fiefdom.

Therefore the United Nations, as a world body, has a role to play in enforcing certain level of transparency in governance of the member nations. This is not to be construed as an act of interference in the internal affairs of a soverign nation. The basic needs that need to be enforced by the UN Body on its members are:

(a) There must be an independent institution to try all the cases related to corruption charges against men/women in public life.

(b) There must be a judicial mechanism to provide a quick hearing for all the cases that are filed without making the entire process of legal redressal a long drawn process.

(c) The governance must be sensitive to the basic needs like food, shelter, health and basic education of the people.

The UN body must decide the definitions of "quick hearing" and 'basic needs" keeping in view the inherent weak economic structure of a society. It should also keep in view the possibility of ensuring a decent level of living to all the people without any middle man or a feudal lord creating a condition that is going to disturb the peace both within and without the society. These two terms are extremely important for ensuring a peaceful development process in the basic unit of community living, the village. If we do not address the needs of the basic unit of community living, then we will be guilty of being responsible for

(a) migration of people from village to city/metropolis/megalopolis

(b) establishing slums in city/metropolis/megalopolis

(c) sowing the seeds for the nurturing of under world activity that would ultimately suck the narco and arms dealers into it leading to a parallel government that sees no boundary

Once this happens, then there are always nations and leaders who would be willing to use these parallel, uncontrolled structures of unaccountable influence as part of the governance mechanism

(a) to stay in power

(b) to serve the interests of the nation by using the under world for foisting unrest in other societies/nations in the name of religion or social up-liftment or freedom struggle

(c) to wage proxy wars against other societies in the name of religion or social up-liftment or freedom struggle

Therefore, the vision of Mahatma Gandhi on the necessity of improving the living conditions in a village and making it the building block of reconstruction of a society is valid even today.

Therefore, United Nations must ensure that the three issues

(a) food

(b) water

(c) God

do not become the fuel to feed the flames that can be started by the warped minds. Every society must become self sufficient to feed itself. Every society must harness rain water to provide sufficient drinking water and increase the level of ground water to help in the cultivation. Every society must make conscious efforts to teach the children that there is one God and one Cosmic Law, and there are many ways to realize God Consciousness. No religion can lay exclusive claim to the following prayer

Oh God, be with us at all times of misery, suffering, joy and happiness,

Oh, God, help us to remember that that what ever happens to us is due to Your Grace

Oh God, help us to remember that what ever happens to us can be handled by You and I together,

Oh God, give us the strength to face the difficulties in life,

Oh God, give us what You think is best for us,

Oh God, we thank you for every thing that you have given us.

The only hurdle in achieving the wonderful state of a happy international community, with village as the building block, is the strange ability of the human mind to rationalize the irrational, also called Consolation of Mind. This therefore raises the basic question, "Why does man Console the Mind?"

vii

It would be worthwhile to ponder over the reasons for the fall of Roman Empire, and the fall of Mauryan Empire and the Gupta Empire in India. All the three empires were powerful and affluent. The Roman Empire had a senate that debated issues and it was left to the King to take a decision with the views of the members of the senate as the background information. Similar was the state in the Mauryan Empire and the Gupta Empire in India, where the court was doing the role of senate. In addition there was a natural recourse to the Buddhist and Hindu scriptures on the way a society to be governed. Further, the first ever treatise on the governance, tax administration, etc was written during this period by Chanakya. Further, the first ever university called the Nalanda University was founded at Pataliputra, near the present day Patna. In spite of all this, the Mauryan and the Gupta Empires collapsed and so did the Roman Empire. It is necessary to recognize that all these three Empires were affluent and powerful. Yet, they could not survive for long indicating possibly that power and affluence of societies do not guarantee their survival. It appears that there are some factors that appear to have dominating and definitive influence on the well being of society and therefore the empire and unfortunately these are not recognized by the society.

In all these three cases, there was one common thing and that is these were "a few individual centric". That is the entire society worked for a few people who were powerful and rich. Therefore what mattered was the well being of these few rich and powerful ones. One cannot brush this away as a dynastic state that has no option but to fail and fall. The modern rational and demo-cratic societies are also best with the ills that the empires of the bygone era faced. Here also, the entire society hovers around a few rich, powerful and the beautiful ones who are loved and lionized by the media as they have a great commercial value. Thus, even in the modern age of rational and democratic thinking the society is "power and pomp centric". The ills of the Roman, Mauryan and Gupta empires are all there in the modern age too. The greed and self gratification of the few that caused the fall of the bygone empires are surely becoming the cause of the decadence and fall of the present day power-ful societies.

Today the quarterly financial reports of the multinationals decide the poli-cies of the governments. The opening up of the economies has created a con-flicting situation by putting the well being of the companies and the people on opposite sides. The well being or the profitability of the companies becomes more important than the well being of the society. Therefore, a strange state of dichotomy is created by having well heeled companies which indulge in busi-ness process outsourcing and therefore are cash rich. This would automatical-ly translate into a state where a fairly large number of the employees get the pink slip and therefore loose jobs. Does this state of dichotomy represented by affluent companies and jobless people help in the creation of stable society? The present scenario is no different from the scenario that existed during the times of the Roman, Mauryan and Gupta Empires. In both the scenarios the society as a whole was/is controlled by a few rich and influential families. The rest of the society was/is subservient to these powerful, influential and rich families. We have been the witness to the upheaval in Iran, disintegration of Soviet Union, terrorists who were nurtured by an empire strike the empire and the messy fallout of the attack on Iraq showing again, like in Chile, that the oil/mineral wealth is more important than any thing else. The case of Chile was worse as the empire plotted the killing of a democratically elected leader just because the government decided to nationalize the mining and other activities! Thus the well being and prosperity of the corporate offices of the empire serve as permanent interest. The other side of the coin that is making a gradual appearance is the unfortunate state of the people who are loosing their jobs due to business process outsourcing and also an unfortunate inci-dent of a person committing suicide in the Silicon Valley, which hopefully is an exception. Therefore, the inevitable question is, will the present empires also collapse economically in the same way as the other empires as recorded in the history books?

The empire, United States of America and United Kingdom, is in a state of dichotomy. The subjects, people, oppose war on Iraq and the policy makers plan meticulously every move to secure the oil wells. The irony is that the people in the western democracies and the free societies, the empires, screamed loud and clear against the war. The policy makers did not bother about these cries in the same way as Saddam Hussain did not bother about the voice of his people. What then is the difference between the democratic free societies and Iraqi dictatorship? The one and the only difference is that the free democratic societies provide the citizens with the freedom to protest, even though it may have no influence on the policy planning! The end result is that the oil wells are secured and the seven thousand year old heritage in the museum is ransacked and looted. Mission accomplished.

These events make it apparent that the developed societies have two faces, visible and the invisible. The visible face is compassionate and humane that believes in peaceful coexistence with other societies. But the invisible face is adept at making cold calculations and implementing ruthless decisions with the sole aim of furthering their own permanent interests. But some times, God in his efforts to create leveling effects in global society, wills otherwise. A similar situation has arisen in the entire episode of Iraq. The invisible policy makers in Washington and London had made meticulous plans of every action and reaction. This meticulous planning also included disinformation or wrong information given to the President of United States of America by the Central Intelligence Agency on the Iraqi plans on Weapons of Mass Destruction and Nuclear Weapons Program. But the one thing that they did not anticipate was the return of the exiled Khomeini, the exiled Shia leader of Iraq. But for some strange reasons the invisible policy makers in London and Washington do not seem to get along with the Shiite regimes as shown by the Iranian revolution that resulted in the violent removal of the regime of Shah of Iran, who was an American supporter. This portends a dangerous conflicting situation for the future. To put it in a nut shell, the amount of oil controlled by the Shiite clergy in Iraq and Iran is greater than or equal to the oil controlled by the rest of middle east. This will definitely spark off yet another conflict and war with some invisible moral ground as the basis. As of now, the American and British governments have not won either the war or the battle. The whole Iraqi issue is definitely a Greek Tragedy. The other Greek tragedy that is unfolding in Pakistan relates to the hunt for the Al Quaeda men who had been hiding in the mountains and for which the American government is paying the Pakistan government generous money for being part of the fight against terrorism! The American troops would face enormous difficulty in the Himalayan mountains in their search for these elusive men and Pakistan gets huge amount of money.

All through these strange policy planning and implementation, the American economy appears to be taking a beating. The economy is gradually and definitely being pushed into a state of high cost economy. This has resulted in a serious overdrive in the direction of outsourcing to contain the cost of conducting the business. At the same time the pay packets are becoming hefty, the population growth is slowing down and jobs are being lost. A strange dichotomy. The question that comes to one's mind is, "Will a society that has a few rich men and a large number of people with out jobs be a stable society?" Should profit making be the only motive of running business enterprises. Communism and socialism as two other alternatives of governance have failed. All nations appear to be moving towards free enterprise, with the World Trade Organization as the guiding light, believing it to be the only way of running and organizing of a society. Even though the philosophy behind the World Trade Organization of allowing access of every market to every nation and allowing for a seemingly flawless development opportunity for every nation is laudable, the ground reality is far from this. What happens when a developing society is not able to compete with the products, both from the point of view of quality and pricing, from the developed societies? Such a society becomes a market for the developed society. If this is so, then how would the developing society pay for the goods and services it receives from the developed society? This payment will have to be from

(a) the sale of raw materials or

(b) by allowing for the society to become a place where the developed society establishes manufacturing hub or a service hub which would require the availability of skilled manpower or

(c) through some other service, which might be in the form of allowing the developed societies to have military bases.

The above is identical to the conditions that prevailed during the days of imperialism when the continents were divided amongst the rich and the powerful for the supply of man power on the cotton fields, raw materials and market for the finished goods. The situation, in spite of the many stout defenses to the contrary has not changed. The guiding principle behind the WTO ethos is self preservation and not for the well being of global community in spite of the well orchestrated charade to the contrary. It is very clear and evident that the WTO ethos would create and fuel terrorism as the gap between the rich and the poor keeps widening.

The global society needs to decide on whether the issue of prime importance is the community well being or the well being of a few persons or organizations or a few powerful societies as was the case during the times of Roman empire. At this stage, it is worth while considering India as a case study.

"India is a multi cultural, multi religious, multi linguistic democratic society, which is facing great pressure to preserve its ethos. This is indeed a great battle as there are enough bigotry floating around that is willing to take a swipe at the society that is already under great pressure. It is worth while to understand the reasons for the cause and existence of such pressure.

About 2010 years ago there were only four religions in India, viz., Hindus, Buddhists, Jews and Jains. The southern part of India had maritime kingdoms who had a flourishing trade with the middle east countries. The tyranny of the Roman empire made a large number of Jews, Armenians and others flee their nation and take shelter in India. About 1940 years ago, India had the first Christians who came to be called the St. Thomas Christians. St. Thomas, one of the chief apostle of Jesus Christ came to India and spread Christianity. About 1300 years ago, the Zoroastrians from a place called Parsa, the place of Darius the Great, in the present day Iran fled their country unable to bear the tyranny of the invading Arab tribesmen and took shelter in India. They are called the Parsis. Till about 1100 AD, there was no communal strife in India even though there were times when Buddhism swept through India and later on around 7AD Hinduism replaced Buddhism. All this happened through the medium of discussion and debate, and without shedding even a single drop of blood. Around 1000AD the traders from the middle east came to southern part of India and settled down. With this, Islam came to coexist with the other religions as well."

During this period, India was a thriving and prosperous country, with stress on community well being. There was no hatred towards any other religion even during those cases where the king opted for a particular religion. Then came 1100/1200 AD which saw the first invasion of India from Afghanistan. This invasion left a permanent scar on the Indian psyche as the men on the horses who thought they had a revelation on their hands went about systematically destroying the Zoroastrian, Buddhist and Hindu heritage in the present day Iran, Afghanistan, Pakistan and India. The religious bigotry ruled the day and at all the holy places of the native religions/heritages, the invaders either destroyed the symbols of the native religions or constructed mosques adjacent to the existing places of worship to indicate the dominance of one over the other. These have become the constant source of altercation and the scar is never allowed to be healed. One finds this in Jerusalem, Bethlehem in Israel and in many holy cities in India. This started an era where God and religion became commodities to be spread and the followers to be looked upon as an index of the popularity of the God and the religion. Thus, spreading the message or the revelation assumed great significance with out realizing that all religions came from a single source. This one fatal disorientation of the middlemen caused religious hatred and set off crusades. The world was looked upon as a place where every thing is to be fought for and won, including a place in the God's kingdom and in as much the same way as fighting for a market share for a product. Higher the market share, the greater the dominance and therefore, larger the following for a God or religion, greater the supremacy. The stress was on the decimation of competition. When this was applied to all facets of life, the result was devastating leading to slavery and final solutions and ethnic cleansing through religious means as a foreign policy to imposing theocracy as represented by the views of God of one deranged man on the rest of the global society. The simple aim of all these acts was the desire to dominate others with in a society and also other societies that led to untold human suffering and misery.

Therefore, the issue before us is

"Should we continue to console our minds into believing that the best way to live to go on trying to dominate others irrespective of the suffering that would be caused to the other societies and members of he societies?

Or

"Should we stop consoling our mind and work towards the community well being and make each society self sustainable, which goes against the WTO ethos?"

The option before the man kind is

"Should one opt for a global society that has the ethos of the Roman empire with all the show of power and authority and no respect for the pluralism that the global society is made of?"

Or

"Should one opt for a society that existed in India up to about 1100 AD where all the religions like Hinduism, Buddhism, Jainism, Christianity, Zoroastrian, Judaism, Islam and many ethnic cultures including Armenian etc coexisted and there was no religious tension amongst the people?"

To put simply, "Is this not the time to stop consoling our mind and rationalize the irrational?"

9

Glossary

The translation of the Sanskrit words are taken from "The Students' Sanskrit—English Dictionary by Vaman Shivaram Apte, Pub.: Motilal Banarasidass, Delhi, 1968"

A

ashram:	hermitage
asura:	those with demonic haracteristics
adhyatmik:	pursuit of religious activities
aur:	and
adharma:	anti-dharma, unprincipled
asatya:	falsehood

B

bhakta:	devotee
brahmana:	A person belonging to the first of the four castes of Hindus

brahma danda:	The wooden support for a hand while performing penance.
brahma rishi:	A sanctified sage or ascetic who has realized the supreme spirit.
bhagwan:	God, God incarnate
bhai:	brother
bhai log:	brotherhood, normally referred to under world gangs
babu:	bureaucrat

C

chalta hai:	any thing is acceptable

D

daan:	alms given in charity		
dharma:	Religious or moral merit, virtue, righteousness, good works: regarded as one of the four ends of human existence.		
Dvapara yug:	Dwapara aeon		
daroga:	local police head during pre-British and British rule		
dhobi:	person doing the laundry job		
dhoti:	apparel used for covering the part of the body below the waste line		

F

faryad: request for help

fatwa: writ issued by Islamic clergy

G

guna: characteristic

goshala: cow/cattle shelter

guru: teacher

H

havan: sacrificial fire

J

janadesh: peoples mandate

jihad: fight against ignorance and evil within oneself; holy war

K

kshatriya: warrior, the second of the four castes of Hindus.

kulguru: advisor to the family/dynasty on religious matters

Kali yug: Kali aeon

kal chakra: wheel of time

kapada: clothing

khadi: hand spun cloth

Krit Yug: Krita Aeon or Sat aeon

M

mutt: seat of Hindu religious authority

mantra: religious chant

mulla: Islamic clergy

mai-baap: benefactor

makan: house

maha mantri: chief minister

mela: festivity, festive gathering

masjid: mosque

N

nawab: members of muslim royalty

neta babu raj: rule by the politician-bureaucrat clique

neta: leader (politician)

P

payasam: sweet porridge

panchama: fifth category that got created as part of the caste system; this later on became to be called untouchable; this had no place in the original formation of caste system that had only four categories: brahman (pursuing literary, religious, medicine and other intellect oriented activities), kashatriya (warrior, governance, administration), vaisya (business), shudra (labourers, workers)

patel: person involved in village administration during the pre-British and British rule

pundit:: persons belonging to Hindu brahmin community

panchayat: mechanism of village governance by a council of five (panch) head men/women

R

rishi(s): A sanctified saint(s) or ascetic(s)

rajo guna: The second of the three gunas or constituent qualities of all material substances. Rajas is supposed to be the cause of great activity seen in creatures. This predominates in men and women. Satva predominates in Gods and Tamas in demons.

rakshasa: man with demonic haracteristics/Tamas Guna

rakshasi: woman with demonic haracteristics/Tamas Guna

roti: bread

S

sadhana: practice

swarga: heaven

sati: wife; also refers to the medieval practice of burning of widow along with the dead body of her husband, which is now banned

sathvik guna: The quality that predominates piety/God

shastra: religious principles or tenets

sva-dharma: One's own duty in accordance with one's own guna/quality

shudra: labourers, the fourth of the four castes of the Hindus.

sutra: tenet

sthitha pragna: person with a detached and balanced out look

Sat yug: Sat aeon or Krita aeon

shishya: disciple

saksharata: literacy

sena(s): army(ies)

swadeshi: self reliance, self rule, home grown

sahibs: moneyed gentry

sarpanch: head of the five village elders who are to oversee the village governance

T

tapas: penance

thakur(s): feudal lord(s)

tamo guna: Ignorance, one of the three gunas or constituent of every thing in nature

tapovana: hermitage

Treta yug: Treta aeon

tarka: debate/logic

talukdar: person involved in the administration of taluk during the pre-British and British rule

taluk: an administrative unit comprising of a few villages

V

vaishya: business community, the third of the four castes of Hindus

vansh: family tree, dynasty

Y

Yug(as): an age of the world/aeon(s). There are four Yugas: Krit (Sat) Yug, Treta Yug, Dwapara Yug and Kali Yug. The duration of each is said to be respectively 1,728,000, 1,296,000, 864,000 and 432,000 man years. It is also sup[posed that the regularly descending length of the yugas represents a corresponding physical and moral deterioration in the people who live during each age. Krita or Sat Yug is called "Golden" and Kali Yug, the present age, is called "Iron"

Z

Zilla parishad: administrative unit comprising of a few villages and taluk

0-595-30874-0